The Lost Pharaohs

'Leonard Cottrell brings Egyptology to life.'—*Scotsman*.

'A vivid picture.'—*Times Literary Supplement*.

'A fascinating description . . . exceedingly well documented
and illustrated.'—*Good Housekeeping*.

D0774052

Previously published by
Leonard Cottrell in Pan Books

Leonard Cottrell

The
Lost Pharaohs

Pan Books London and Sydney

First published 1950 by Evans Bros Ltd
This edition published 1956 by Pan Books Ltd,
Cavaye Place, London SW10 9PG
8th printing 1977
All rights reserved
ISBN 0 330 02303 9
Printed in Great Britain by Richard Clay (The Chaucer Press), Ltd,
Bungay, Suffolk

CONTENTS

ILLUSTRATIONS IN PHOTOGRAVURE

LINE DRAWING

(*page 196*)

Carved relief from the tomb of Huya, superintendent of the treasury and household of Queen Tiyi

INTRODUCTION AND
ACKNOWLEDGMENTS

THIS is a book for the amateur by an amateur. It does not claim to be erudite, though factually it is as accurate as I can make it. My main object has been to interest the many thousands who would like to know more about Ancient Egypt, but are bewildered by the multitude of learned works, many of them on highly-specialised branches of Egyptology, which confront them in the reference libraries.

This is not said to forestall criticism. Fifteen years' experience in the writing of BBC documentary programmes has taught me that a 'popular' approach to a subject is no excuse for inaccuracy; so wide is the radio audience that the writer cannot hope that his smallest error will go undetected. On the other hand erudition is not always accompanied by imagination. One of the penalties of profound learning is that, sometimes, the Egyptologist becomes so absorbed in the *minutiae* of his subject that in time he may become insensible to the wonder and beauty which first drew him to it. To this occupational disease the amateur is, happily, immune. He shares with thousands of other ordinary folk the awe and delight which, during the recent war, drew thousands of Allied soldiers to the Egyptian Museum at Cairo.

Public interest in things Egyptological is far more widespread than most scholars are aware. I discovered this when I wrote and produced for the BBC a dramatic feature on the life of the Pharaoh Akhnaten, the 'Heretic King' of the Eighteenth Dynasty. For weeks afterwards letters arrived on my desk, not only from professional Egyptologists, but from men and women in many walks of life, all showing the keenest interest in and knowledge of the subject. One long and learned letter, politely correcting my chronology of the reign of Amenophis III, came from an eleven-year-old boy!

Similar reactions followed more recent programmes on Ancient Egypt, 'The Tomb Robbers of Thebes', 'The Lost Pharaohs', 'The Tomb of Tutankhamun', and 'Mother of Cheops', and it was this evidence of popular interest which encouraged me to embark upon this work; that, and the kindly promptings of my learned friends, Sir Alan Gardiner, D.Litt., and that wise and gentle scholar, the late Professor Newberry, OBE, MA, who died, alas, before this book was finished.

If further justification is needed for another book on Egyptology, it is this. Until fairly recent years, Egyptian archaeology was financed principally by men of wealth. Out of their pockets came the funds not only for excavation but for what was often equally expensive, the scientific publication of the findings. To-day, when both excavation and publication are far more costly than they were, scholars can no longer rely on wealthy patrons. There is, of course, the gallant Egypt Exploration Society, which has sponsored such splendid work in the past and which still, in spite of depleted funds and rising costs, manages to send expeditions to dig in the Sudan. It is obvious, however, that in the future archaeologists must depend increasingly on state subsidies. For instance, in 1948 the Egypt Exploration Society was successful in obtaining a modest Treasury grant to help finance its 'dig' at Amarah West. This is the first time such a grant has been made, a gesture which reflects great credit on the British Government. The French Government has for long subsidised the work of its scholars in Egypt, and if Great Britain is to maintain the traditions established by such great Egyptologists as Petrie, de Garis Davies, Carnarvon, Carter and many others, there must be an increasing measure of State support, backed by informed public opinion.

Egyptologists as a class are shy birds, hating publicity and rightly sensitive to anything which might vulgarise the science to which they have devoted their lives. Some of them may read this book. May I suggest to them that any book which honestly tries to present their work to a wider audience than that of the University lecture-room may be of some service to Egyptology?

In addition to the gentlemen I have mentioned above, I would like sincerely to thank Professor H. W. Fairman of Liverpool University, who read my chapters on the Amarna period, Professor Cerny of University College, London, and Sir Alan Gardiner, who read the book in manuscript. All these scholars gave me valuable corrections and suggestions, but I wish to make it clear that they are not responsible for my opinions or for any errors which may have crept into the book.

For the purposes of consistency the chronology I have used throughout is that suggested by Professor Glanville; and Sir Alan Gardiner has kindly given me the benefit of his vast philological knowledge in the rendering of Egyptian names. Here again, however, I have used my own discretion. In the main the orthography is his, but in some cases Egyptian names, though incorrectly rendered, have become so familiar through frequent usage that revised spelling would only confuse the lay reader. In such cases (*e.g.* the word Punt) I have stuck to the more familiar spelling. I am also grateful to Sir Alan for reading and commenting upon my two chapters on Tutankhamun's tomb, but I particularly desire to state that my account of the difficulties which Carter had to encounter were derived partly from Mr. Charles Breasted's book, and partly from the newspapers and journals which appeared at the time of the discovery; it formed no part of the information supplied to me by Professor Newberry or Sir Alan Gardiner.

Greetings and thanks also to Zakaria Goneim Bey, Chief Inspector of Antiquities for Upper Egypt, and to Raschid Nowere Effendi, Chief Inspector of Antiquities for Middle Egypt, for their help and companionship during my visits to their country. I am also indebted to the BBC who made it possible for me to visit Egypt, and who kindly gave permission to use some of the material originally broadcast in my feature programmes, of which they hold the copyright.

9

Finally, my grateful thanks to the authors and publishers of the books listed at the end of this volume, from some of which quotations have been made, with the hope that many readers of this book will be led to the original sources which inspired it.

L. C.

THE DYNASTIES OF ANCIENT EGYPT

1st and 2nd Dynasties . . . . . . *c.* 3200–2780 BC

In 3200 BC Menes combined in unity for the first time the Kingdoms of Upper and Lower Egypt.

OLD KINGDOM—2780–2100 BC

3rd Dynasty	2780–2720 BC
4th Dynasty	2720–2560 BC
5th Dynasty	2560–2420 BC
6th Dynasty	2420–2270 BC
7th to 10th Dynasties (The First Intermediate Period) .	2270–2100 BC

THE MIDDLE EMPIRE—2100–1700 BC

11th Dynasty	2100–2000 BC
12th Dynasty	2000–1790 BC
13th Dynasty	1790–1700 BC

HYKSOS PERIOD—*c.* 1700–1555 BC

14th to 16th Dynasties	*c.* 1700–1600 BC
17th Dynasty	1600–1555 BC

NEW EMPIRE—1555–712 BC

18th Dynasty	1555–1350 BC
19th Dynasty	1350–1200 BC
20th Dynasty	1200–1090 BC
21st Dynasty (Tanites)	1090– 945 BC
22nd Dynasty	945– 745 BC
23rd Dynasty	745– 718 BC
24th Dynasty	718– 712 BC

LATE EGYPTIAN PERIOD—712–525 BC

25th Dynasty	712–663 BC
26th Dynasty	663–525 BC

PERSIAN DOMINATION—525–332 BC

27th Dynasty	525–338 BC
28th Dynasty	404–399 BC
29th Dynasty	398–379 BC
30th Dynasty	378–332 BC

GRAECO-ROMAN PERIOD—332 BC–AD 638

(i) Alexander the Great and Ptolemies . . .	332–30 BC
(ii) Roman Period	30 BC–AD 395
(iii) Byzantine Period	AD 395–638

CHAPTER I

THE LAND AND ITS HISTORY

"THE land of Egypt is six hundred miles long and is bounded by two ranges of naked limestone hills which sometimes approach and sometimes retire from each other, leaving between them an average breadth of seven miles. On the North they widen and disappear, giving place to a marshy meadow plain which extends to the Mediterranean coast. On the South they are no longer of limestone, but of granite; they narrow to a point; they close in until they almost touch: and through the narrow gate thus formed the River Nile leaps with a roar into the valley, and runs north towards the sea.

"In the winter and spring it rolls a languid stream through a dry and dusty plain. But in the summer an extraordinary thing happens. The river grows troubled and swift; it turns red as blood, and then green: it rises, it swells, till at length, overflowing its banks, it covers the adjoining land to the base of the hills on either side. The whole valley becomes a lake from which the villages rise like islands, for they are built on artificial mounds."

So Winwood Reade began his great work *The Martyrdom of Man* and there could be no better introduction to a book on Egypt. For the Nile *is* Egypt. We remember when crossing the river on our way to Tell-el-Amarna, the Arab boatman turned to us and said, "Egypt is the gift of the Nile, and the Nile is the gift of the good God. Therefore we are all the children of God."

Why did the earliest civilisation on earth grow up beside this great river? Because civilisation can only flourish where communities can live together in one spot over long periods of time. Ten thousand years ago, before man had learned to control his environment, there were few places on earth which were favourable to permanent settlement. Man was a nomad, always moving from place to place in search of fresh hunting- or grazing-grounds. Sometimes he would plant a snatch crop, reap it and move on again, but he never stayed long in one place.

Although it is not generally agreed, it seems probable that the earliest inhabitants of the Nile Valley came from the south, passing up the coast of the Red Sea and entering Egypt through the Wadi Hamamat. The Ancient Egyptians themselves believed that their ancestors came from the land of Punt, which is now called Somaliland. These nomadic peoples, of Hamitic stock, found a valley of papyrus and reed-marshes, inhabited by hippopotami and other beasts which have since been driven south. They also found the most fertile soil in the world, brought down for them annually from the mountains of Abyssinia. For the marvellous fertility of Egypt is due to a unique geographical circumstance. The great lakes, Victoria and Albert, like cisterns fed by the equatorial rains, provide the impetus which drives the mighty river through 1000 miles of parched desert which otherwise would swallow it; but the annual flooding is due to another cause. Once a year the high mountains of Abyssinia intercept the rain clouds of the Indian Ocean as they move north. The falling rain fills the dried-up beds of the Atbara and the Blue Nile, tributaries of the White Nile.

The torrential outflow of these two rivers swells the White Nile, until, when released from the imprisoning cliffs which wall it in on its course through Nubia, it overflows its banks and spreads over the low-lying land to the north, carrying the Abyssinian mud which is the source of Egypt's fertility. Thus, when the flood receded, all the prehistoric inhabitants of the Valley had to do was to cast their seed, which, in good season, would give them a year's crop in return for a few weeks' work; the perpetual sunshine did the rest. No wonder the wanderers elected to stay in the Valley.

However, it was not the 'gift of the Nile' which made them

14

into a civilised community, but the fact that sometimes the gift was withheld. In some years there would be a 'bad Nile'. The tropical rains would be insufficient to provide enough soil, or they would be so heavy that the floods would rise too high, sweeping away houses and villages and drowning men and cattle. When this happened the people starved. In Professor Glanville's words:

> The Nile's annual flood is the key to success or failure of agriculture. Most that is significant in Ancient Egyptian civilisation derives from this fact—from the central control of Government to the conservative temper of the peasant.

Gradually, over scores of centuries, the primitive Egyptians learned to control the river. The more intelligent among them noticed that the rising of the water coincided with certain aspects of the stars. This led to astronomical observation and the invention of the calendar. They learned to keep records of the level of the river at different seasons over a number of years, and from these they could predict with some accuracy the extent of the annual flooding. The necessity of keeping records led naturally to the invention of writing, first as a few primitive symbols which later developed into a written language of considerable flexibility. They also mastered the science of hydraulics, digging dykes, irrigation canals and reservoirs in which the surplus water could be stored against a bad season. Again, the annual obliteration of landmarks made it necessary to devise a precise system of surveying, so that the land could be accurately re-parcelled, and this led to the development of geometry which was applied later to the planning of buildings. It is therefore true to say that the Great Pyramid and all the other architectural marvels of Ancient Egypt owe their origin to the Nile.

This struggle to master the Nile threw up an intellectual élite, the mathematicians, astronomers, and engineers; and since, among primitive races, science is closely linked with religion, these men were also priests. Simultaneously there arose another class of rulers, the military class. The prosperous inhabitants of the Valley must have excited the envy of the nomadic desert tribes; and in the subsequent fighting, the bravest and cleverest soldiers rose to the top, becoming the natural leaders and founding an hereditary aristocracy.

All these developments took place long before Egypt became a united nation. Along the 600-mile length of the river, hemmed in on the east and west by the enclosing deserts, lived scores of tribes, each with its local chief and ruling caste, its local priests serving a local god. Of these gods, some were deified chieftains, the 'great father' of the tribe or community. Some were birds, animals or reptiles. Some were totems, such as trees, rocks or pillars. For instance there was Sobk, the crocodile god; Ape(t), the hippopotamus-goddess; Bes, the god of music, singing and dancing; Ubaste, the cat-goddess of Bubastis; and Sakhme(t), the lioness-goddess of Memphis. Over 2000 of these primitive gods have been recorded. It is important to remember this when trying to understand the complexities of Egyptian religion. To most of the Ancient Egyptians it must have been as bewildering as it is to us. Even when Egypt became a unified state there was never a unified, universal state religion. The simple peasant continued to worship his local god, even though that deity might owe a temporary allegiance to the god of the ruling dynasty. But we will deal more fully with Egyptian religion in later chapters.

Throughout this archaic period of primitive civilisation the independent tribes fought among each other. Sometimes an ambitious chieftain would conquer several of his neighbours and form a powerful federation against which his rivals would also have to combine. Thus, gradually the units of government grew larger, until towards the end of this pre-Dynastic period, as it is called, Egypt was divided into two kingdoms, the North and the South. The Southern King controlled the river valley down to the Delta. The Northern King ruled the Delta itself.

This archaic division persisted in theory long after the whole country had been united. One of the Pharaoh's titles was always 'King of Upper Egypt and Lower Egypt', and to keep up the fiction there was a double palace, a double granary, and so forth. However, this period of division actually came to an end in about 3200 BC when Menes, who was also called Narmer, conquered the whole country and for the first time brought Egypt under a single ruler. It was with Menes that the dynasties began, and with them the beginning of recorded history.

A word concerning these dynasties. Throughout this book frequent mention is made of the Fourth Dynasty, the Sixth Dynasty, the Eighteenth Dynasty and others. On page 11 the reader is given a table of dynasties subdivided into the principal periods, such as the Old, the Middle and the New Kingdoms. These classifications are useful as a guide but it should be remembered that they are to some extent arbitrary and artificial. They were first drawn up by an Egyptian historian named Manetho (about 305–285 BC), who wrote a history of his country in Greek. He divided the names of the Pharaohs which had come down to him into thirty royal houses, or dynasties. His list is not accurate; not all his divisions are correct and he missed out a number of dynasties, but the list has been in use for so long by historians that they continue to use it for the sake of convenience.

As each chapter of this book describes some notable monument or archaeological discovery, readers who are not familiar with Egyptian history may like to have a general outline to which they can relate the various subjects. The rest of this chapter will therefore be a brief survey of the historical period, particularly the Old, Middle and the New Kingdoms, with a note of the principal features of Egyptian religion. Any reader who is allergic to dates has our warm sympathy, and if he should decide to skim through or even skip this introductory chapter, he will still be able to enjoy what follows. But though the fascination of Ancient Egypt does not lie in its records of war and conquest, but in details of everyday life, these details cannot be *fully* appreciated without some knowledge of the main structure.

When, thirty centuries before Christ, Menes founded the First Dynasty, most of the characteristic features of Egyptian civilisation were already present. It is believed that hieroglyphic writing arose very rapidly just before the First Dynasty, and during the time of Menes we can almost see it developing before our eyes. It might be thought that few objects could have survived dating from these pioneers of Egypt's past, but when the distinguished English archaeologist, Petrie, excavated the tombs of the First Dynasty kings at Abydos he found articles of palace furniture in ivory and alabaster revealing fine artistry and craftsmanship, beautifully fashioned jewellery, including a gold ornament inscribed with the name of Menes, which may have been worn by the King himself.

Those to whom the tomb of Tutankhamun represents remote antiquity might reflect on the fact that to Tutankhamun Menes was as ancient as Nero is to us. Although Menes chose to be buried near his native This, in Upper Egypt, he established his capital at Memphis, near what is now Cairo. Memphis became the Royal City and centre of government for the next thousand years.

Students call the period of the first two dynasties (3200–2780 BC) the *Archaic Period*. It was a time of consolidation and development following the conquest of the Northern by the Southern kingdom, and there are records of frequent rebellions by the kings' northern subjects. It was also an age of economic development.

> The kings were constantly laying out new estates and building new palaces, temples and strongholds. Public works, like the opening of irrigation canals or the wall of Menes above Memphis, show their solicitude for the economic resources of the kingdom, as well as a skill in engineering and a high conception of government . . . (Breasted: *A History of Egypt*).

Next comes a succession of four dynasties, from the Third to the Sixth, which together constitute the *Old Kingdom* (2780–2270 BC). This was a period of vigorous growth, when the kings wielded supreme and absolute authority. Centralised power was essential to the prosperity of the land, for only in this way could the economy of the whole country be co-ordinated. Under the Pharaohs of the Old Kingdom this condition was achieved. Egyptians of later centuries looked back upon these kings as a race of Titans and their period as a golden age. Through their unchallenged control of man-power they were able to carry out public works and to raise monuments which still inspire awe even in the 20th century. These were the pyramid-builders: Djoser, whose step-pyramid is the first large structure in stone known in history; Snofru, who built the first true pyramid; and, greatest of all, Cheops, builder of the Great Pyramid at Giza, a monument which, down to the beginning of the 19th century, remained the highest building in the world.

The rule of these monarchs was authoritarian in the extreme. The king was a god, descended from the sun-god Re himself, and round him gathered his courtiers and high officials through whom he controlled every department of administration. In these early days the chief officers were usually of the royal family. Sometimes the vizier or prime minister of the land would be the king's eldest son. Upper and Lower Egypt were divided into provinces or *nomes* as they were called later, each with its own governor, with his own land office, treasury, court of justice and militia, together with the multitude of the scribes who served these departments. In the beginning of the Old Kingdom these provincial governors, who were often of royal blood, lived at court with the king, who could then keep a tight hold on the administration of the entire country.

> In the thirtieth century before Christ it (the Old Kingdom) had reached an elaborate development of state functions under local officials such as was not found in Europe until far down in the history of the Roman Empire (Breasted).

The chief deity was the sun-god Re, who was served by a powerful priesthood at On (later called Heliopolis). Gradually this priesthood assumed greater influence over the court, until in the Fifth Dynasty (2560–2420 BC) the name of the reigning king always included the name of the god—*e.g.* Sahure, Neferirkere, Shepseskere, Nuserre. These kings built, near modern Abusir, elaborate sun-temples of the god, the central feature of each being an obelisk, symbol of Re, enclosed by a large courtyard. A thousand years later one of the chief titles of the Pharaoh was still 'Son of Re'.

The nobles lived in large, spacious villas of wood and mud-brick lightly constructed to suit the climate. Even the palace of the king was similarly built. This is why most of the domestic buildings of Ancient Egypt have disappeared save for a few foundations, whereas the tombs and temples, being built of enduring stone, have survived. The poor of the town lived in squalid mud hovels huddled close together, though on the large country estates their lot was easier. The armies of workmen who laboured on the Pharaoh's great works lived in huge barracks, a multitude of tiny rooms with connecting galleries under one roof. In art the freedom of the craftsman was constrained by a rigid religious convention, but within the limits set by this convention, perhaps because of them, the Old Kingdom sculptors produced work of an austere beauty and majesty; work which, in the writer's opinion, was never equalled by Egyptian craftsmen of later centuries. The wonderful diorite statue of Chephren, in the Cairo Museum, epitomises this art in all its dignity and power.

The Sixth Dynasty, which lasted about 150 years, saw a gradual weakening of the royal authority. The nobles who under previous monarchs had lived at court now settled in their nomes and increased their personal power, just as in England's feudal age the provincial barons eventually became powerful enough to challenge the authority of the king. And when the Sixth Dynasty ended in 2270 BC it was followed by an age of confusion. Historians call this, the period of the Seventh to the Tenth Dynasties, the First Intermediate Period. We need not linger over it.

With the Eleventh Dynasty began the second of the main periods into which, for convenience, we divide Egyptian history; the *Middle Empire* (2100–1700 BC). After 100 years of anarchy in which Egypt seems to have suffered an Asiatic invasion, power passed to a family of nomarchs, *i.e.* provincial nobles, whose seat was at Hermonthis, in Upper Egypt. Nearby was a small provincial town, later called Thebes by the Greeks, which became the leading city of the south under its nomarch, Intef. His son, another Intef, assumed royal honours and became the first king of the Eleventh Dynasty. This was the beginning of the rise of Thebes, an obscure town which was to become the capital of Egypt and subsequently of an empire which included most of the known world. This transfer of power to the south did not take place immediately. Amenemhet I founded his capital at a place which he named Itjtowe, from which he was in a better position to control the northern nomarchs. The kings of the Eleventh and Twelfth Dynasties made war on these powerful lords who now ruled their territories like little Pharaohs. One of the greatest of these kings was Amenemhet, founder of the Twelfth Dynasty (2000 BC). An inscription states:

> . . . he restored that which he found ruined; that which a city had taken from its neighbour; while he caused city to know its boundary with city, establishing their landmarks like the heavens, distinguishing their waters according to what was in the writings, investigating according to that which was of old, because he so greatly loved justice (Breasted's translation).

The Middle Kingdom has been called Egypt's Feudal Age. The Pharaohs of this period, men such as Amenemhet, Sesostris II, Sesostris III, though they eventually secured control of the country, never wielded the absolute power commanded by the Memphite kings. The king had to rule through the nomarchs, keeping constant watch lest any of them should become too powerful. He now employed professional soldiers called 'followers of His Majesty', though he was able to call on his feudatories to supply men and arms for foreign expeditions. Of these there were many. The Pharaohs of the Middle Kingdom pushed the frontier southward into Nubia.

Sesostris I, Amenemhet's successor, carried the war above the Second Cataract. Amenemhet II reopened the gold mines of Sinai in the north-east, and Sesostris III caused his engineers to cut a channel 260 feet long and 34 feet wide through the granite of the First Cataract to enable his war-galleys to sail farther up the river. He also invaded Syria for the first time. This was a period of foreign conquest and trade expansion.

In religion Re, the sun-god, remained supreme, and other priesthoods began to identify their local gods with him. Amun, the god of Thebes, was pronounced to be a manifestation of Re; his name was changed to Amun-Re, an important development, as we shall see when we study the rise of Thebes. But the most interesting religious development of the Middle Kingdom was the rise of the Osiris-cult. To understand this we must take a brief backward glance at Egypt's pre-history. Like most primitive peoples the ancestors of the Ancient Egyptians had their folk-myths which explained the origin of the world. They believed that in the beginning only the ocean existed, and on this ocean appeared an egg (in some versions a flower) from which was born the sun-god. He had four children, Geb and Shu, Tefnut and Nut. Planting their feet on Geb, Shu and Tefnut raised their sister Nut to the heavens. Thus Geb became the earth, Shu and Tefnut the atmosphere, and Nut the sky. Geb and Nut had four children, Osiris and Isis, Nephthys and Seth. Osiris succeeded to the throne of his father and governed the world wisely and justly, aided by his sister Isis, whom he married. Seth, jealous of his brother's power, plotted to destroy him and eventually succeeded, afterwards cutting the body of Osiris into pieces which he buried in several parts of Egypt. The head he buried at Abydos. The faithful Isis recovered the scattered fragments of her husband's corpse and with the aid of the jackal-god Anubis, who subsequently became the god of embalmment, re-animated it. Though unable to return to his life on earth, Osiris passed to the Underworld, where he became the god of the dead and later the judge of souls. Isis bore a son,

Horus, who took revenge on his uncle, Seth, defeating the usurper in battle and winning back his father's throne.

This legend became the most popular of all Egyptian folk-myths. It never lost its hold on the people, because of its human appeal, Isis becoming the type of loyal wife and mother, Horus the ideal son. In the Middle Kingdom, which we are now considering, it developed into the leading cult, and Abydos, supposed burial-place of the head of Osiris, became a place of pilgrimage. Every year thousands flocked to Abydos to watch a dramatic re-enactment of scenes in the life of Osiris, and to follow the procession of the god's body to his supposed tomb. Abydos thus became one of the most sacred places in Egypt. Noble families sought burial there, and humbler folk, who could not afford a tomb, erected memorial tablets in the hope that the God of the Dead would remember their names. It was during the Middle Kingdom that the conception of Osiris as a *judge of souls* became predominant, and for the first time the idea of accountability in the after-life for sins committed on earth began to take hold of the human mind.

Like that of the Old Kingdom, the latter end of the Middle Kingdom was chaos following a succession of weak rulers. Then came a period of about 150 years when Egypt was invaded and occupied by the *Hyksos* or Shepherd Kings from Asia. Of this period from the Fourteenth to the Seventeenth Dynasties very little is known, except that it was an age of bitter internal struggle. Finally the Hyksos were driven out by a succession of rulers of whom the most famous were named Seknerre. The son of the last of these, Kamose, pursued the Asiatics into Syria, and became undisputed King of Egypt with his capital at Thebes, the home of his family. Thus began the Eighteenth Dynasty, and the commencement of Egypt's greatest imperial expansion, an epoch known to historians as the *New Empire* (1555–712 BC). Each of Kamose's successors extended his conquests, until Tuthmosis III, greatest of warrior kings, raised the military glory of Egypt to its highest point. In campaign after campaign he subdued the Asiatics of the north and east, the Nubians of the south, and the Libyans of the Western Desert—even the islands of the eastern Mediterranean. Again and again he returned to his imperial capital Thebes, bearing the spoils of the world to lay before the Theban god Amun.

> I have come, giving thee to smite the princes of Djahi,
> I have hurled them beneath thy feet among their highlands,
> I have made them see thy majesty as Lord of Radiance,
> So that thou hast shone in their faces like my image.

So Amun is made to address the Pharaoh in a famous hymn of victory. Thebes, in Upper Egypt, was now the greatest city of the world, adorned with splendid temples, palaces and monuments, its quays crowded with ships. The kings hollowed out great rock-cut tombs for themselves in the Theban hills. Six hundred miles down river, the monarchs of the Old Kingdom slept forgotten in their Pyramids, already 1000 years old, while around them lay the neglected temples of their god, who had now to share his divine authority with the ram-headed god of Thebes.

In time the Amun priesthood grew so rich and powerful that Tuthmosis IV, grandson of the great Tuthmosis, again began to favour the priests of Re, whose centre of worship was at Heliopolis. His son, the luxury-loving Amenophis III, carried this movement a stage further. In his reign arose a small cult of the Aten, which seems to have been the solar disc. This movement was partly political, as the King now ruled a large empire which included peoples to whom the Egyptian gods were unfamiliar. By encouraging the worship of the sun-god, with whom he identified himself, the astute Amenophis may have been seeking to establish a universal religion which all his subjects, Egyptian and foreign, could accept. The successor of Amenophis III was that fascinating enigma, Akhnaten, which name he adopted after breaking completely with Amun-worship and establishing a new capital at Tell-el-Amarna, roughly mid-way between Thebes and modern Cairo. Here, with his Queen, the lovely Nefretiti of the world-famed portrait-bust, and surrounded by his courtiers, he devoted himself to the worship of the Aten, whose symbol was the sun's disc with descending rays. Meanwhile, one by one, his overseas possessions slipped from his grasp.

Akhnaten has had more written about him than any other Pharaoh, some writers seeing in him a religious revolutionary and the first monotheist, others a hedonistic weakling who almost lost an empire. His reign was also associated with a freer, more naturalistic, if somewhat decadent art, which is seen at its best in the palace furniture of one of his successors, Tutankhamun. During the reign of the latter king, the priests of Amun regained their supremacy, the court returned to Thebes, and the name of the hated 'Heretic King' was hacked out of his monuments. The triumph of Amun was complete, and down to the end of the Theban period he reigned as chief god (Plate 3). With the short reign of Ay, who had been one of Akhnaten's ministers, the Eighteenth Dynasty came to an end with most of Tuthmosis III's Asiatic dominions lost to Egypt.

Some of them were re-conquered by the founder of the Nineteenth Dynasty, Sethi I. Both Sethi and Ramesses II, who followed him, waged war in S.W. Asia and succeeded in regaining control of Palestine, though Syria remained part of the Hittite Empire. Ramesses is the name most closely associated with the Nineteenth and Twentieth Dynasties. Ramesses II, of the Nineteenth Dynasty, was a mighty builder and a devotee of Amun, to whom he built many temples, the walls of which are carved with vivid reliefs representing the King's conquests and victories. In fact one becomes a little tired of Ramesses, particularly his oft-depicted Battle of Kadesh, which he almost lost through his inept generalship, though (according to the inscriptions) his personal valour saved the day.

A later Ramesses, the Third, was a much more able general. He had to contend with repeated attacks by the Libyans of the Western Desert. These he decisively defeated, but his greatest victory was gained over the 'sea-peoples' moving down upon Egypt from Syria. Not only did he crush these invaders on land but in a great sea-battle, the first of which there is any historical record. Like his predecessor he had these triumphs depicted on the walls of his temple at Thebes. His reign represented a peak in Egypt's military history. The eight Ramesses who followed had little in common with the conqueror but his name, and when the last died in 1090 BC the Twentieth Dynasty was at an end and nothing remained of the Egyptian Empire but Nubia—'the land of Kush'.

After the aesthetic changes introduced by Akhnaten, the art of Egypt regained its former grandeur and dignity, though some of the delicate grace of the Amarna period remained. On the other hand much of the sculpture of this time, particularly the temple reliefs, tends to be mechanical and repetitive. It seems as if art was now firmly fixed in a conventional mould which it was impossible to break. The kings continued to be buried in the great Necropolis in the Theban Hills, and their deep rock-cut tombs, hewn out of the mountain, are perhaps the most striking memorial of Egypt's Imperial Age.

In religion, the priesthood managed to combine the principal cults of Amun, Re, and Ptah into a complex and rather bewildering theological system, in which the hundred and one minor gods also had to be fitted. The paintings on the walls of the royal tombs at Thebes depict the journey of the deceased through the caverns of the Duat, or underworld, in the sun-god's boat. Near the end of this perilous journey, during which he was questioned by a multitude of gods and demons, the dead king entered the Judgment Hall of Osiris, where, with Isis, Nephthys, and other deities, the God of the Dead decided whether or not he was fit to be deified, and become himself an Osiris (Plate 2).

At the end of the Twentieth Dynasty power passed to the High Priest of Amun, Hrihor, although the nominal king, Ramesses XI, still maintained the fiction of Pharaonic authority. At the same time the unity of Egypt came to an end. While Hrihor ruled in Thebes an independent prince,

Nesubenebded, commanded the Delta. Manetho calls him the first king of the Twenty-first Dynasty but in actual fact Thebes was now independent, though for a brief time Paynudjem, Hrihor's second successor, gained control of the whole country.

During this time of decadence, Thebes steadily declined in importance. This was the period of the great tomb-robberies described in a later chapter. Abroad, conditions were no better, and during the Twenty-first Dynasty the Israelites, overcoming the Philistines, gained increasing control of Palestine.

Most of the monuments and archaeological discoveries described in the following chapters belong to the period already covered, so we will summarise the remainder of Egyptian history very briefly. From the beginning of the Twenty-first Dynasty (1090 BC) to the end of the Twenty-fourth Dynasty (712 BC) Egypt was ruled by Libyan and then Nubian kings. Among the Libyans, Shoshenk, the first Pharaoh of the Twenty-second Dynasty (745–724 BC), has a certain interest. He fought several campaigns in Palestine and is certainly the 'Shishak, King of Egypt' mentioned in the Old Testament. One of his predecessors married his daughter to King Solomon.

> And Solomon made affinity with Pharaoh king of Egypt, and took Pharaoh's daughter, and brought her into the city of David . . .

Later, when Solomon quarrelled with Jeroboam, 'the mighty man of valour', the latter sought the protection of the Pharaoh:

> And Jeroboam arose, and fled into Egypt, unto Shishak, king of Egypt, and was in Egypt until the death of Solomon.

In the fifth year of the reign of Solomon's successor, Rehoboam, Shishak invaded Palestine and Judea in considerable force, encouraged no doubt by the exiled Jeroboam. According to the Book of Kings:

> . . . it came to pass in the fifth year of King Rehoboam, that Shishak King of Egypt came up against Jerusalem. And he took away the

treasures of the house of the Lord, and the treasures of the king's house: he even took away all: and he took away all the shields of gold which Solomon had made . . .

As always, the Hebrew priest-chroniclers ascribed the disaster to the Israelites' neglect of Jehovah; there are the usual charges of sodomy, and that they did

evil in the sight of the Lord, and they provoked him to jealousy with their sins which they had committed

—but it seems clear that Shoshenk was merely using Jeroboam's quarrel to reassert his ancestral right to his Palestinian provinces, whose petty armies would be no match for Shoshenk's powerful force of Libyan mercenaries.

This was the first time a Pharaoh had penetrated Asia for nearly 300 years, and for a time it must have seemed that the great days of the Empire were returning. The prosperity of the kingdom at this time is shown in the vast temple donations, and in the buildings erected at Thebes, and Bubastis, the Delta town which was now the royal seat. However, under succeeding kings this prosperity waned: there was civil war and revolt and in about 745 BC a new dynasty arose founded by another Bubastite family. Once again a deficiency of power at the centre led to the rise of many independent city-states which were frequently at war with each other, and after thirty-three turbulent years a Nubian lord, taking advantage of the unsettled state of Egypt, led his armies down the Nile Valley and in a brilliant campaign captured town after town and finally brought Egypt under his rule. His name was Piankhi, and there is something in his chronicle which makes him stand out as a human being, unlike most of the Pharaohs who have left formal records of their conquests.

There is a story about him which is often told but is worth repeating. When, after a bitter siege, he captured the town of Hermopolis, Namelot, its defeated King, showed him the palace stables. Then, says the chronicle:

His Majesty proceeded to the stable of the horses and the quarters of the foals. When he saw that they had suffered hunger he said, "I say as Re loves me . . . it is more grievous in my heart that my horses have suffered hunger than any evil deed thou hast done in the prosecution of thy desire" (Breasted's translation).

Somehow one rather likes Piankhi.

There must have been great suffering among the common people of Egypt during this period. Deprived of a strong central government they were at the mercy of any local tyrant who managed to seize power. There were revolts against extortionate taxation, followed by bloody repression. Worse was to follow when, after Piankhi's successors, Shabaka, Shabataka and Taharka had ruled for half a century Egypt was invaded by the armies of the great Assyrian King, Ashurbanipal. Even Thebes itself was plundered and burned by the savage Assyrian troops. The prophet Nahum, foretelling the coming destruction of Nineveh, wrote:

> Art thou better than populous No (Thebes) that was situate among the rivers, that had the waters round about her; whose rampart was the sea, and her wall was of the sea? Ethiopia and Egypt were her strength and it was infinite. . . . Yet she was carried away, she went into captivity . . . they cast lots for her honourable men, and all her great men were bound in chains . . .

Nineveh fell, the Assyrians withdrew their garrison and once again a native dynasty arose, the Twenty-sixth, whose founder was Psammetichus, from the Delta town of Sais. Egyptologists writing of the 'Saitic Period' (663–525 BC) are referring to this phase of Egyptian history. This was the time of the so-called 'Renaissance', a misleading term in the writer's opinion because it was not a time of vigorous rebirth but of revived archaism. Surveying their contracted dominions from their capital in the Delta the rulers and priests of the Twenty-sixth Dynasty looked back nostalgically to the giants of the Old Kingdom, the pyramid-builders, who were as remote from them as Psammetichus is from us. They studied and reproduced the ancient religious texts, revived the ritual and tried to imitate the art of that far-off age. To the modern observer there is much that is pleasing in the art of the Twenty-sixth Dynasty, but it should be remembered that unlike the European Renaissance the Saitic Period was not a starting point from which new ideas could spring, but a last backward glance at the glories which would never return.

The new ideas were to come from the other side of the Mediterranean. Already the Greeks were on the move, founding colonies, spreading their culture to many parts of the Mediterranean coast. Soon they had discovered Egypt; the Pharaohs allowed them to settle in their dominions and even enlisted Greek mercenaries in their armies. Once again the Egyptian kings tried, with the aid of these foreign troops, to re-conquer their former possessions in Asia, but final defeat came when the Babylonian King Nebuchadnezor crushed the Egyptian armies at Carchemish.

In 525 BC Egypt was again conquered, this time by the Persians under Cambyses, and remained a Persian province until 332 BC, when Alexander the Great added it to his empire. He founded the Ptolemaic line which ruled from Alexandria for 300 years, but so tenacious were Egyptian religion and culture that the Macedonian conquerors became in some way more Egyptian than the Egyptians themselves. Finally in 30 BC Egypt became a Roman province, and with the rise of Christianity and the subsequent Arab conquest the old religion died out. The secret of the ancient writing was lost and the history of Ancient Egypt was known only through the works of the Greek and Roman historians, and by the mighty monuments of stone at which each succeeding generation marvelled. It was not until the 19th century, with the decipherment of the hieroglyphs and the arrival of the modern Egyptologist, that men were able at last to draw the veil from the oldest of civilisations.

CHAPTER II

ARRIVAL OF THE EGYPTOLOGIST

FAR more material relics of Egyptian civilisation have survived than those of Greece, Rome, or even medieval Europe
—due partly to the climate and physical characteristics of the
land, and partly to the Ancient Egyptians' preoccupation
with preserving their bodies and preparing for a life after
death. This has led many writers into the mistaken belief
that the Egyptians were morbidly obsessed by death itself.
In the early 19th century Napoleon's conquest of Egypt
awakened a new interest in its ancient inhabitants, and the
subject inspired imaginative flights by romantic authors.
Théophile Gautier, in a short story, makes Cleopatra say:

> Charmion, I tell you, I have a thought that terrifies me; in other
> countries of the earth they bury their dead, and the ashes are soon
> mingled with the ground. Here one might say that the living have no
> other occupation than that of preserving the dead: powerful balms
> snatch them from destruction: all of them keep their form and
> appearance . . . under this people are twenty peoples: each city has its
> feet on twenty layers of tombs: each generation that goes leaves a
> population of mummies in a city of darkness . . .

Powerful, spine-chilling stuff, but hardly fair to the
Ancient Egyptians, who, like their modern descendants,
seem to have been a happy, somewhat materialistic race, lov-
ing life and hating to leave it. It was because they enjoyed
their earthly existence so much that they desired nothing
better than to continue it in the world to come. There the
country gentleman would still have the satisfaction of surveying his flocks and herds as they were driven past him by
his servants: the court official would still hold his high office,
served by his faithful scribes; the general would have his
army, the admiral his fleet; the nobleman would entertain his
friends at gorgeous banquets where minstrels played and

slaves served the guests with delicious food and wine; or he would take his sport in the reed marshes beside the heavenly Nile, bringing down the wild geese with a throwing-stick, or spearing fish with a two-pronged harpoon while his slim young wife held his legs to prevent him falling out of his papyrus-boat. All these scenes, painted and sculptured on the walls of the tomb, were intended, not to remind the living of the dead man's position on earth, but to assure him in the next life all the amenities of this one. The only exception was the Pharaoh, who, being a god himself, would, if justified before Osiris, enjoy the privilege of accompanying Re in his daily journey across the sky. Looking at the happy domestic scenes painted in the tombs of lesser men, one feels that they probably didn't envy him.

The Egyptians were able to make these tombs and monuments because, throughout the length of Egypt, the limestone cliffs which bordered the Nile provided an abundant supply of easily-worked stone. They have survived partly because of their massive strength and partly because the hot, dry climate has prevented the weathering of the stone. Even to-day inscriptions cut in the time of Ramesses II look as if they were carved yesterday. The dry climate has also preserved scores of thousands of lesser antiquities which have lain buried in the dry sand between the cliffs and the cultivable land.

Archaeologists still find, buried on the desert's fringes, the bodies of pre-dynastic Egyptians who died long before the invention of embalming. They lie in shallow graves usually accompanied by jars of food, toilet articles and weapons, and quite often the bodies still retain their skin and hair. There is one in the British Museum. It is easy to see how the mind of the ancient Egyptian, observing this phenomenon, would be led to believe in the necessity of preserving the material body for its owner's use in the life to come. Thus came the development of embalming, which was known before the Pyramid Age, and continued to be practised to the very end of Dynastic history. This belief in the necessity for *material* preservation is at the very heart of Egyptian religion; and since the body had to continue, then so, they argued, must its material needs—for food, clothing, and other earthly necessities. So they provided them, and in so doing left to later generations what Professor Glanville calls "a unique national park of ancient life".

They were essentially a practical people; everything they produced, their mathematical system, their engineering achievements, even their art, had a utilitarian purpose. They were not given to abstract philosophy, and have left us no mystical literature. Their imagination was bounded by the arid deserts which hemmed them in on each side, and by the twin sources of their existence: the life-giving river in its fertile valley, and the white-hot sun which they saw every day sweeping across a harsh, cloudless sky. Theirs was a clearly-defined world of hard white sunlight and black shadow; probably they would have been amused by the reputation for mystery with which later generations have endowed them.

Part of the mystery lay in the *hieroglyphs*, as the Greeks called them, meaning sacred signs. Temples, tombs, *stelae* throughout Egypt and her former empire were inscribed with this strange picture-writing, the secret of which had been lost. Besides the hieroglyphs carved in stone there was a modified, cursive form known as *hieratic* and sometimes rolls of papyri were found covered with this equally unintelligible script. The history of Ancient Egypt was known through Greek and Roman historians such as Herodotus, Pliny and Diodorus Siculus, who had talked to Egyptian priests of the Ptolemaic and Roman periods, but the information they gave, though valuable and sometimes picturesque, was scanty. With the decipherment of the hieroglyphic and hieratic script by Young and Champollion in the early 19th century modern Egyptology begins, but long before this time European travellers visited Egypt and have left fascinating records.

In the Middle Ages, for instance, physicians believed that portions of an Egyptian mummy, crushed to powder, was a

33

valuable medicine. "The mummy", wrote a doctor, "must first be ground to a powder, then mixed with vegetable oil till it has attained the consistency of an unguent or salve. It is then ready for use and will prove efficacious in treating breaks or sprains, inflammation, pleurisy and pneumonia." Not any mummy would do however. The French physician Savary wrote:

Il faut choisir la momie la moins luisante, bien noire, et d'une bonne odeur . . .

Apothecaries paid a high price for this macabre medicine and European merchants travelled to Egypt to buy the new material. In the 16th century the trade was in full swing. The fellahin rose to the demand, and during the inundation, when they could not dig the fields, they went to the desert and dug for mummies. When the supply seemed in danger of running out the Jews of Alexandria turned to making faked mummies. Corpses of slaves were bought, stuffed with bitumen, and sold as the real thing. But for centuries the chief source of supply of genuine mummies was at Sakkara, near Cairo.

The Earl of Sandwich, an 18th-century traveller, visited Sakkara in 1739. He wrote:

. . . the greatest part of the plain of Sakkara is hollowed into sub-terraneous cavities, all cut out of the solid rock. . . . The entrances are many in number, and are in form a square of three feet, and about twenty feet deep. We descended one of these passages with the assistance of a rope ladder, after which—finding the horizontal entrance almost filled up with sand—we were obliged to creep upon our bellies for a considerable space, till we entered into a vault about seven feet high. We immediately discovered several embalmed bodies, scattered in confusion about the vault, and many of them broken in pieces. These had all of them been taken out of their clefts or coffins, and after having been ransacked in search of any idol of value, which are frequently found within the bodies, thrown aside by persons who would not be at the trouble of carrying them away . . .

Richard Pococke, another English traveller, went to Sakkara in 1753. He wrote:

Another day I went to see the Catacombs. The usual method of
letting people down by rope is very painful, but I brought with me a
ladder made of ropes, by which I descended more conveniently,
though not without being discommoded by the sand which falls
down from the top. I saw several of the swathes lying about, and
some remaining almost entire, only the bodies taken out of the middle
for the sake of the mummy, and to search if they could find anything
in them. . . . I also saw many skulls there, as well as on the plain
beyond: many of which had probably been rifled of the bitumen or
balsam that was in them, when that sort of medicine was more in use
than it is at present . . .

Pococke was a painstaking student of Egypt and his two
weighty folios bring home vividly the difficulties and dangers which travellers of his time had to face. He sailed up-
river to Luxor and visited the Theban Necropolis, including
the famous Biban-el-Maluk which even then had been a
show-place for centuries.

Having viewed these extraordinary sepulchres of the Kings of
Thebes with the utmost pleasure [he writes], by the help of wax-lights
we bought, and being much fatigued, we thought to sit down and
take some refreshments we bought . . . [a phrase which will win the
sympathy of any modern traveller who has 'done' the tombs with an
Arab dragoman] . . . but unfortunately we had forgot to bring water;
the Sheikh also was in haste to go, being afraid, as I imagined, lest the
people should have opportunity to gather together if we stayed too
long. From Gournou to this place there is a very difficult foot-way
over the mountains, by which the people of Gournou might have
paid us a very unwelcome visit . . . the people had come rudely to the
boat when I was absent, and said they would see whether this stranger
would dare come out another day, having taken great umbrage at my
copying the inscriptions; and they dropped some expressions as if they
would assault the boat by night if I stayed . . . for they seemed
strongly desirous that I should leave the place, being possessed of a
notion of a power the Europeans have of finding treasures, and
conveying them away by magic art . . .

Pococke's description of the Theban tombs is surprisingly
accurate in the main, and his engravings are delightful. Try
as he will, the 18th-century draughtsman cannot make the
statues and monuments look even remotely Egyptian; they
remain obstinately 'classical'. Readers with a taste for the

curiosities of 18th-century literature should try Richard Pococke's *Travels in Egypt*.

While Pococke and other travellers of his time laboriously copied the inscriptions, they could make nothing of them. The hieroglyphs remained a tantalising mystery for another sixty years. The story of how, eventually, the key was found is a commonplace to Egyptologists, but as this book is addressed principally to the general reader we propose to tell it once again. At the time of Napoleon Buonaparte's short-lived conquest of Egypt in 1799 the Emperor took with him a number of distinguished French *savants* to make a survey of the country. In August of that year a detachment of French soldiers was working on the fortifications at Rosetta in the Nile Delta when a man named Boussard or Bouchard found an irregular-shaped stone (Plate 5), of ancient origin, built into the wall of an Arab fort which was being demolished. The stone was inscribed in what appeared to be three languages, one of which was Greek, the other two being the hieroglyphic and demotic forms of the Ancient Egyptian language. (*Demotic* is a modified shorthand form of the hieratic.) In actual fact, therefore, the inscription was bilingual.

The stone was despatched to the Institut National in Cairo and eagerly examined by the *savants*. Napoleon himself was deeply interested in it and ordered ink copies to be made and distributed among the scholars of Europe. In 1801, under the Treaty of Capitulation, important Egyptian antiquities had to be handed over to the British as spoils of war, and among these was the Rosetta stone. Its removal was attended with some embarrassment as, in the meantime, the stone had been sent to the home of General Menou, who claimed it as his private property. Eventually, it was taken from the French General's house by a Major-General Taylor with the aid of a detachment of British artillerymen and an artillery-engine, "but with some difficulty", wrote Taylor, "amid the sarcasm of numbers of French officers and men; being ably assisted by an intelligent sergeant of artillery, who commanded the party, all of whom enjoyed great satisfaction in their employment." So the Rosetta stone was acquired (or if you prefer it, 'won' or 'liberated') by the British Army and came to rest in the British Museum, where it still is.

Several translations of the Greek text were made, and it was found that the inscription on the stone was "a copy of a decree passed by the General Council of Egyptian priests assembled at Memphis to celebrate the first commemoration of Ptolemy V, Epiphanes, King of all Egypt". The original decree had been in demotic: the hieroglyphic and Greek texts were translations of it. Once the Greek version had been translated the next problem was to decipher the hieroglyphs. If once that could be achieved, scholars might have at their command a portion of the Ancient Egyptian alphabet, and as every de-coding expert knows, once one has a part of the code it is usually possible to arrive at the missing portions. Credit for unravelling the secret of the Rosetta stone and ultimately of the Ancient Egyptian language is shared chiefly by two men, an Englishman, Dr. Robert Young, and a Frenchman, J. F. Champollion. Young proved by demonstration what other scholars had suspected for some time:

(a) that there were *alphabetic hieroglyphs*, and
(b) that whenever an oval or *cartouche* appeared on an inscription, it always contained a proper or royal name.

He also realised that there was a phonetic principle underlying the hieroglyphs, and applied it. To take a single example; when he found that the oval cartouche signified a royal name it was obvious that the cartouche on the Rosetta stone contained the name Ptolemy. As Ptolemy is a Greek name and its pronunciation known, the hieroglyphs within the cartouche must represent the sounds P, T, L, M and so on. This text was then applied to other cartouches; the name Cleopatra was found in Greek on an obelisk at Philae, together with a hieroglyphic inscription containing the royal cartouche. Since Cleopatra also contains the sounds P, L, and T it was now possible to test the accuracy of Young's interpretation of the Ptolemaic cartouche. Sure enough the same symbols were present, and in the positions they should occupy relative to the other parts of the name. Whereas the hieroglyphic equivalent of P was the *first* sign in the Ptolemaic cartouche, it was the *fifth* sign in the Cleopatra cartouche. Therefore the sign immediately preceding the L sign in Cleopatra must be K. In this way Young and his followers gradually worked out the phonetic equivalents of other hieroglyphs until gradually an alphabet began to form. Now this was all very well as far as it went. It enabled scholars to read Ancient Egyptian names but not to translate the language. To do that they had to learn the grammar and vocabulary. The key to this lay in the ancient Coptic tongue.

When Christianity came to Egypt, Egyptian Christians translated the Greek scriptures into their native language. These Christianised Egyptians became known as Copts, which is simply the old name for Egyptian, and they have continued to use their ancient language in their religious rituals down to the present day. It was the French scholar Champollion, following up Young's discoveries, who made use of this fact. While still a young man he studied Coptic and became an authority on the language.

"In his studies of the inscriptions on the Rosetta stone", says Budge (*The Rosetta Stone*), "his knowledge of Coptic enabled him to deduce the phonetic values of many syllabic signs, and to assign correct readings to many pictorial characters, the meaning of which were made known to him by the Greek text on the stone."

This also answers the question which Egyptologists are often asked: how can you know the pronunciation of Ancient Egyptian words? The key to the pronunciation exists in the still living Coptic language.

But the work of Young and Champollion was only the beginning. Decades were to pass before even the simplest inscriptions could be read accurately from one end to the other. Egyptian philology—the study of the Ancient Egyptian language—is a highly specialised branch of Egyptology to which certain scholars have devoted their lives, and it was the 19th-century philologists, notably Chabas, Brugsch and Goodwin, who, starting from the foundations laid by Champollion, built up bit by bit the complex grammatical structure of the ancient tongue. The results of their researches were codified by Erman, the founder of modern Egyptian philology. An interesting point is that some of the finest work was done by men to whom Egyptology was a spare-time occupation, a labour of love. Chabas, for instance, was a French wine merchant, Goodwin an English barrister. Thus the hieroglyphs which had baffled generations of students at last gave up their secret, and the road was open by which men could travel back 5000 years to rediscover the world of Ancient Egypt.

Almost contemporary with this discovery was another one, which was in some ways even more dramatic. This was the decipherment of the *cuneiform* writing first used by the early Babylonians, and later by the Persians and Hittites, all of whom played an important part in Egyptian history. Unlike the Egyptians, who used stone or papyrus, these peoples wrote in wedge-shaped characters on tablets of baked clay (Plate 4). The most interesting examples were found at Tell-el-Amarna, the temporary capital of Egypt at the end of the Eighteenth Dynasty, in the ruins of what had evidently been the King's Foreign Office. Here were hundreds of letters written by the governors of Akhnaten's Assyrian, Phoenician and Babylonian dominions, a discovery which revealed to Egyptologists the extent of the Ancient Egyptian Empire at the height of its power. Like the hieroglyphs, the cuneiform script had been known for centuries, but it remained a secret until 1810, when a German scholar named Grotefend deciphered it. His feat was even more astonishing than that of Young and Champollion, because, unlike them, he had not the advantage of a bilingual inscription. He noticed that on a certain cuneiform tablet the same set of symbols occurred repeatedly in successive lines. It occurred to him that this might be a chronological list of the Persian kings and that the

recurrent symbols might represent the words 'the son of',
thus, part of the inscription might read:

> (A) the son of
> (B) the son of
> (C) the son of
> (D) etc. (A, B, C, D representing the kings).

Naturally Grotefend was familiar with the chronology of
the Archemenid kings, so he tried putting their names to the
symbols A, B, C and D. He knew that one of the kings
should be Xerxes, which was a great help, as the King had
two X sounds in his name which should be represented by
the same cuneiform symbol. To his delight he found that the
lines (B) and (D) *did* contain two similar symbols in the position where they should occur if the name were indeed
Xerxes. Now there were two kings named Xerxes in the
Archemenid Dynasty. Therefore if (B) and (D) each represented Xerxes, (A) must represent Darius, son of Xerxes II,
(C) must be Artaxerxes I, father of Xerxes II, and (E) must
signify Darius I, father of the first Xerxes. Thus the inscription might read:

> (A) Darius II the son of
> (B) Xerxes II the son of
> (C) Artaxerxes I the son of
> (D) Xerxes I the son of
> (E) Darius I

In each case Grotefend found that the cuneiform signs
were identical where the same names should have occurred,
and so, bit by bit, he was able to establish the phonetic
equivalents of a number of cuneiform signs. This, of course,
was only the beginning of the discovery, and readers who
wish to follow the whole fascinating story should go to
Grotefend's own work, or to Professor Sayce's *Primer of
Assyriology*. There they can read how an inspired guess followed by years of laborious research enabled a great philologist to unlock another door into the ancient world. Incidentally, just before the First World War there was discovered at Boghaz Keui a cuneiform tablet recording a treaty

between Ramesses II and the Hittite King Khattusil. There is a duplicate of this treaty in hieroglyphs, in the Temple of Karnak in Upper Egypt, by means of which Egyptologists were able to confirm the accuracy of Grotefend's decipherment.

Following these discoveries a new interest in Egypt spread throughout Europe and America. Much of it was mere curiosity and it is sad to reflect on the amount of valuable archaeological evidence which must have been destroyed by those who ransacked Egypt in search of objects for national museums and private collections. Hundreds of statues were shipped to Europe; huge granite obelisks were uprooted from their ancient sites and re-erected beside the Thames or the Hudson; inscriptions were hacked out of the walls of tombs and valuable papyri smuggled out of the country. Mr. E. M. Forster, writing of this period, asks:

> What had happened? Partly an increase in science and taste, but also the arrival of a purchaser, wealthier than cardinals and quite as unscrupulous—the modern European nation. After the Treaty of Vienna every progressive government felt it a duty to amass old objects, and to exhibit a fraction of them in a museum, which was occasionally open free. "National possessions" they were now called, and it was important that they should outnumber the objects possessed by other nations, and should be genuine old objects, and not imitations, which looked the same, but were said to be discreditable.

Even to-day a surprisingly large number of people still believe that the object of archaeology is to dig up 'old objects', preferably valuable ones, for collections; whereas to the modern scientific excavator the place where an object was found, and the exact position relative to the site and other objects found there, may be more important than the thing itself. The excavator is in search of *facts*, and a dated scrap of potsherd found in an ancient mud wall, though worthless in itself, may establish a vital date and cause the re-writing of a whole chapter of history. On the other hand the museums and collections of the world are cluttered up with objects which, though charming in themselves, would be infinitely more valuable to science if the exact place and circumstance of their discovery were known. Usually, however, they were found by a 'treasure-seeker', sold to a dealer and passed from hand to hand until by the time they reached the museum their origin was lost and as historical documents they were value-less. As Sir Leonard Woolley has said:

Treasure hunting is as old as Man, scientific archaeology is a modern development, but in its short life of about seventy years it has done marvels. . . . The old historians, relying principally on written documents, were largely confined to those events which at every age writers thought most fit to record—wars, political happenings. . . . The digger may produce more written records,—but he also brings to light a mass of objects illustrating the arts and handicrafts of the past, the temples in which men worshipped, the houses in which they lived, the setting in which their lives were spent . . .

To the men of this later period of scientific excavation and painstaking research we owe most of our knowledge of Ancient Egypt. They include men of many nations, British, American, French, Belgian, German and others. Their learned works, products of a life-time's study, are in daily use throughout the libraries of the world, but to the general public most of them are unknown. To recall all their achievements would fill many books larger than this, but we can at least salute them before we pass on to enjoy the wonders they have uncovered. Here are some whose names should be remembered: the great Mariette, discoverer of the Serapeum and founder of the Egyptian Museum at Cairo; Burton, Rosellini, Wilkinson and Lepsius, those pioneers of Egyptology; Sir Flinders Petrie, who excavated the tombs of the First Dynasty kings at Abydos, threw new light on the pyramid builders, and whose excavation of Akhnaten's city revealed the glories of the Amarna Age; Borchardt, the German archaeologist who excavated the sun-temples at Abusir; Sir Gaston Maspero, perhaps the most distinguished of the many French scholars who have directed the Egyptian Government's Antiquities Service; Adolf Erman, who helped to unravel the complexities of Egyptian religion;

Professor J. H. Breasted, the great American Egyptologist whose *History of Egypt* combines exact scholarship with rare imagination and literary skill; the late Professor P. E. Newberry, one of the most able and least assuming of English Egyptologists, and Sir Alan Gardiner, the philologist; Howard Carter and Lord Carnarvon, best known of all for their discovery of the tomb of Tutankhamun; Leemans, the Dutch scholar who published the whole Museum of Leiden; Dr. G. A. Reisner and his staff of the Harvard–Boston Expedition, who discovered the only intact royal tomb of the Old Kingdom; and coming to more recent years, the late Professor T. Eric Peet, whose translations and studies of papyri relating to the Ramesside tomb robberies have made this ancient drama live again; C. M. Firth, J. E. Quibell and J. P. Lauer, who under M. Etienne Drioton, Director-General of the Department of Antiquities, are bringing to light the marvellous complex of buildings surrounding Djoser's step-pyramid at Sakkara; Professor W. B. Emery; J. D. S. Pendlebury, who, with H. W. Fairman, carried on Petrie's work at Tell-el-Amarna and who died heroically in Crete during the Second World War.

These are the names of some representative Egyptologists, chosen because, in the main, their discoveries form the subject-matter of subsequent chapters. But they do not exhaust the list. Many other names equally deserving of honour will be found in "Books Consulted" at the end of this book.

CHAPTER III

RETREAT OF THE FRONTIER

THE frontier is Time, and this chapter is the story of the men who pushed it back several thousand years; first M. J. de Morgan, followed by Sir William Matthew Flinders Petrie (1853–1942), one of the greatest Egyptologists of all time.

Petrie published many books on Egypt, including a famous *History* which is one of the standard works on the subject. In the edition published in 1894, Chapter II, on the first three dynasties, contains the following observations:

> The first three dynasties are a blank, so far as monuments are concerned. They are as purely on a literary basis as the kings of Rome or the primeval kings of Ireland. . . . We cannot regard the first three dynasties as anything but a series of statements made by a state chronographer, about three thousand years after date, concerning a period of which he had no contemporary material . . .

When Petrie wrote that, he was making use of the latest material available to him at the time. For him, as for earlier generations of Egyptologists, the time frontier stopped at the reign of Snofru, last king of the Third Dynasty (*circa* 2740 BC). As far back as his reign, historians were on firm ground. History could be traced not only from the written chronicle of Manetho and others, but through the physical existence of tombs, monuments, inscriptions, works of art and antiquities of many kinds. But the period before Snofru was, as Petrie wrote, a blank. There was a handful of earlier monarchs, including the great Menes, founder of the First Dynasty, but of their tombs, their art, their monuments, hardly a thing was known. In fact it was by no means certain that they had ever existed outside the imagination of later Egyptian chroniclers.

In the 1894 edition of his *History*, Petrie could cover the whole of Egyptian pre-history and early dynastic history in eleven pages. Yet *only eight years later* the 1902 edition contained concrete historical information on most of the eighteen kings who ruled before Snofru, with an account of their tombs, inscriptions, furniture and art! In subsequent editions this section was expanded to forty-four pages, while as for the prehistoric period, so much new knowledge had been gained that Petrie had to issue a complete volume on Egyptian pre-history alone! Imagine the 3000-year span of recorded Egyptian history as a tunnel, brightly lit in places where our knowledge is greatest, dimmer in other sections, but on the whole sufficiently well illuminated to allow us to travel all the way back to the builders of the first pyramids. After that the light fades into utter darkness. Then suddenly the darkness recedes, light floods our path, and we are able to move on for another thousand years and more. This dramatic retreat of the chronological frontiers, which occurred at the turn of the century, is one of the greatest events in the history of Egyptology. It was brought about by three discoveries, all made between the years 1894 and 1900.

The first was the finding by Petrie and J. E. Quibell of 3000 graves of a people who were quite different from the Egyptians of the dynastic ages. Petrie had long suspected that the race which eventually conquered Egypt, the founders of the First Dynasty, invaded the country from the Red Sea, crossing the desert via the Wadi Hamamat and entering Upper Egypt at Koptos. In the earliest sculptures he had traced five different races older than the dynastic people, and a sixth quite separate from these, a race with "a straight bridge to the nose and a very vigorous and capable kind of face". Excavating the temple at Koptos in 1893 he found parts of three great statues of the anthropomorphic god Min, covered with surface carving belonging to "far earlier art than anything hitherto found in Egypt". Two of these statues now stand in the Ashmolean Museum at Oxford. Near the statues he found pottery, also of an unfamiliar pattern. In the following year, 1894, Petrie and Quibell decided to dig on the west bank of the river opposite Koptos, between Nagadeh and Ballas. Quibell worked the northern part near Ballas, Petrie the southern section near the ancient town of Ombos. At first they found and unearthed a number of Old Kingdom and Middle Kingdom tombs of a familiar type. Then one day Quibell found one of the local Arabs digging up a piece of slate shaped like a fish, together with a number of earthenware pots.

Almost at the same time Petrie, digging two miles to the south, came upon slight depressions in the soil. He dug one of these and found a shallow grave containing a skeleton, a peculiar-shaped slate, and some pottery. The most remarkable feature was the position of the body. The Egyptians of the dynastic ages were always buried stretched out on their backs. This skeleton lay on its side, arms and legs drawn to the body in the embryonic position. Petrie turned to the other depressions and found more graves, each with a skeleton in the same position, on its left side, the head to the south, the face to the west. Grave after grave was unearthed, nearly all containing contracted skeletons, usually with a slate at the breast or before the face, and accompanied by pottery of a completely new type. No inscriptions were found, but on some of the clay jars there were marks: a cross, a crescent, a palm tree, a mark like a gallows, and a scorpion. The excavator had come upon a lost cemetery of a completely unknown people quite different from the dynastic Egyptians. Three thousand graves were found, excavated and recorded.

In some of the larger graves other objects were found: a game, with pieces consisting of four lions and a rabbit of limestone, little ivory rods and spherical flints like playing marbles; ivory combs and bracelets, stone maces, a lamp with a floating wick, small statuettes of painted clay and, in a few graves, objects of copper. Most of the pottery was unlike any found in dynastic graves, ranging from red and black pots, polished and unpolished, to painted and decorated vases which had originally contained food or in some cases cosmetic oils. Some of these objects bore a faint resemblance to Old Kingdom work. The slates which were carved to represent fish, antelopes, tortoises and birds' heads were evidently used for grinding green malachite used for face-paint.

One peculiar feature of these graves puzzled the excavators considerably. In some of them the skull and certain of the limbs were missing. At first it was thought that this was the work of ancient plunderers who had broken up the bodies in search of valuables. In many cases the graves had undoubtedly been robbed in antiquity, but there were others in which the objects had never been disturbed, yet the body had been dismembered. Furthermore in certain graves the skull had been carefully placed on a brick or pile of flints apart from the rest of the body. In others, where hands or feet were missing, small objects had been put in their place. In one grave the spine was perfect, but all the ribs lay in the recess of the grave at the back, as if the ribs had been cut off the spine. Obviously robbers could not have done this, and Petrie concluded that in some cases the bodies must have been mutilated *before* burial; but why? The findings in yet another grave led the excavators to a sinister conclusion. "Here a mass of bones, broken and split," Petrie writes, "lay together on the floor in a heap. . . . Not only were the ends broken off but in some bones the cellular structure had been scooped out forcibly . . . and beside this were grooves left by the gnawing of the bones . . ." Animals could not be responsible, as the bones had been carefully placed in the grave in what was evidently an artificial arrangement, ornaments being buried with the skulls. Petrie's deduction was that before burial the bones were—with all respect—cut up and partly eaten. An odd fact is that as late as the Greek period, historians stated that Osiris reclaimed the Egyptians from cannibalism. Since the discovery Petrie's theory has been seriously challenged, some scholars affirming that the bodies may have been broken up by robbers and that subsequently the fragments were re-buried by their relatives. Perhaps the truth will never be known.

The chief problem which faced Petrie was to identify the strange people. At first he thought he had discovered a new race of foreigners who invaded Egypt at some unknown date, keeping themselves apart from the indigenous inhabitants and so preserving their own primitive customs. These were certainly unlike any Egyptians whose graves had been discovered up to that time. He and his helpers were tempted to allot them to a pre-dynastic age, but Petrie was always a cautious and careful archaeologist, who never made wild guesses unsupported by evidence. Most of the objects found in the tombs were of a hitherto unknown type, but in some of the larger and probably later graves there were a few articles remotely resembling Old Kingdom work. The presence of these persuaded him to assign the unknown people, at least temporarily, to the period of the Sixth and Seventh Dynasties (*circa* 2400 BC), this being the only period about which little was known and into which, therefore, they might be fitted. As it turned out he was quite wrong.

The second great discovery was made three years later by M. J. de Morgan, then Director of the Antiquities Service of the Egyptian Government. He found near Nagada a royal tomb containing objects bearing the name Menes, founder of the First Dynasty (3200 BC). At first it was thought that this tomb was that of Menes himself but it has since been decided that this king was buried at Abydos and that the Nagada tomb is probably that of a queen. However, it was undoubtedly a tomb of the First Dynasty, and inside it were found *objects of the 'New Race' style discovered by Petrie*. It now seemed pretty certain that these unknown people lived at a time *previous* to Menes. Final confirmation came when, in 1897–8, Petrie himself dug through cemeteries at Dendereh ranging from the Sixth to the Seventh Dynasties. As no objects of the New Race were found there and as all the other dynasties had been accounted for, the so-called New Race must have been anterior to the First Dynasty. Petrie had discovered the primitive ancestors of the Ancient Egyptians. The pottery found in some of their graves which appeared to be of the Old Kingdom type must have belonged to the intermediate period between the pre-dynastic and dynastic ages.

However, there was still a great gap to be filled, that of the first two dynasties, down to the time of Snofru. De Morgan had found the tomb of Menes, or at least a tomb of Menes' time, but Manetho and other chroniclers gave the names of nine kings before Menes, and twenty-four who reigned between his time and that of Snofru. Where were they? Perhaps, after all, they were not, in Petrie's phrase, "as purely on a literary basis as the kings of Rome or the primeval kings of Ireland"? The answer came in 1898, when another French Egyptologist, Etienne Amélineau, announced that he had found, at Abydos, the tombs of the kings of the First and Second Dynasties.

Abydos, in Upper Egypt, is one of the places which every conscientious tourist has to see. He arrives by train or river-steamer at the little town of El-Balyana, and from there a car takes him up the rough, dusty road through the cotton-fields until suddenly the black soil gives place to sand, and the barren cliffs of the Western Desert close the horizon. That is Abydos, "wild and silent": as Petrie writes, ". . . close around it the hills rise high on two sides, a ravine running up into the corner where the lines meet. Far away, and below us, stretches the long green valley of the Nile, beyond which, for dozens of miles, the eastern cliffs recede into the dim distance."

Most visitors make for the two great temples of Sethi I and Ramesses II, built during the Nineteenth Dynasty (1350–1200 BC), and having seen them, return satisfied. Yet it is not these buildings, magnificent though they are, which make Abydos historically the most important site in Egypt, but a dark mound of broken potsherds lying near the mouth of the ravine. For under that mound Amélineau discovered the tombs of the kings and queens of the First and Second Dynasties (*circa* 3200–2780 BC), the founders of the Egyptian state.

As we mentioned in the first chapter, these rulers came from a nearby city called This, and though after their conquest of the Northern Kingdom they established their capital at Memphis, they continued to be buried in what was probably the family burial-place at Abydos. Even after the kings had ceased to be buried there, Abydos was held in reverence for centuries as the ancient royal sepulchre. But a time came when only a royal tradition survived, and by the Eighteenth Dynasty (1555–1350 BC) the exact site of the tombs was no longer known. In the intervening centuries Abydos had acquired a newer distinction as the burial-place of the god Osiris. It had become the chief centre of religious pilgrimage at which, every year, the Osirian 'passion play' was enacted. The royal tombs, most of them ransacked long ago, lay hidden under drift-sand, but one of them, that of King Djer, had been rediscovered and pronounced to be the tomb of Osiris himself. So from the Eighteenth Dynasty onwards this tomb became one of the holiest shrines, and more than fifty generations of Egyptians journeyed there to make their offerings. The fragments of the countless pottery jars which contained these offerings have formed a great mound over the site, so that to-day the place is known to the Arabs as *Um-el-Qu'-ab*— 'the Mother of Pots'. With the coming of Christianity the fanatical Copts, who had a monastery nearby, wrecked the tomb, smashing every object of beauty they could find in their determination to end the worship of Osiris. Once again sand drifted over the ruins and the site was almost forgotten.

In the 19th century the treasure-seekers and antiquity hunters turned their attention to Abydos, and the site was plundered by men who were ignorant of its historical importance. Then in 1897 came the *Mission Amélineau*, which discovered the tombs, but excavated them in a manner which was severely criticised by Egyptologists who followed them. The operation appears to have been carried out with more dash than devotion, and the excavators seem to have been more anxious to secure specimens for sale than to make a serious contribution to archaeological science. Petrie was bitterly disappointed. On four occasions he had sought permission to dig at Abydos, but his concession was only granted when the *Mission Amélineau* had finished with the site. How they left it is best described in Petrie's own words. "In the royal tombs," he wrote in the report of his first season's work, "there had been not only the plundering of precious metals and the larger valuables by the wreckers of earlier ages; there was after that the systematic destruction ... by the vile fanaticism of the Copts ... and worst of all, for history, came the active search in the last four years for everything that would have value in the eyes of purchasers ... a search in which whatever was not removed was deliberately and avowedly destroyed in order to enhance the intended profits of European speculators ..."

Unlike the discoverers of the tomb of Tutankhamun and other intact sepulchres, Petrie and his helpers had nothing to work on but a mass of ransacked ruins left by plunderers and speculators, and it is this which makes their achievement so memorable. For season after season they worked there, removing the debris, patiently and systematically excavating and drawing the tombs, identifying their owners from the inscribed fragments of pottery which was practically all that the previous excavation had left behind. Even the stone jars, broken in ancient times by the Copts, were, by Amélineau's own admission, deliberately smashed to bits by his men. Yet from this confused mass of evidence Petrie was able to trace the development of these protodynastic tombs from the single brick-lined pit graves of the dynasty before Menes, to the large elaborate tombs of the Second Dynasty kings with their surrounding chambers and galleries.

Whereas Amélineau left only a confusion of names without historical connection, Petrie established the chronology of nineteen kings in their correct sequence, from Ka, who belonged to a dynasty before Menes, through the First Dynasty down to Khasekhemui, the ninth king of the Second Dynasty. Also, by means of the fragments of pottery, ebony and ivory tablets (Plate 6), and other articles found among the rubbish, he was able to trace the fluctuations and development of art throughout the whole of this archaic period, and so fill a 400-year gap in Egyptian history.

At the risk of boring the reader we would like to add a few notes on the actual construction of these tombs, since they were the prototypes of the *mastaba* tombs of the Third Dynasty, from which in turn the pyramids were to develop. The oldest was a simple rectangular grave dug in the sand, 23 feet long, 16 feet wide and 10 feet deep. The walls were of brick and originally there was a wooden ceiling supported by props, with a mound of sand on top. The tomb of King Djer, largest of the earlier royal sepulchres, had a wooden chamber 28 feet square, surrounded by offering-chambers covering an area of about 48 by 38 feet. Around it were seven rooms of 338 graves belonging to the household, including those of women, probably of the royal harem. Among the fragments left behind by Amélineau were ivory cups, two ivory lions for a game, and finely-wrought jewellery.

Densemti, fifth king of the First Dynasty, had an even larger tomb paved with granite, the first instance of stone being used as a building material.

By the time of Khasekhemui, ninth king of the Second Dynasty, the tomb had developed into a huge structure, 223 feet long and 54 feet wide with fifty-eight separate rooms built round a central chamber of stone—*the oldest stone building known*. No doubt the King had been buried in the stone chamber; of the others some were for offerings, and some to contain the burials of his family.

"Only a belief in the survival of the body", writes Budge, "can explain the presence of furniture and provisions. The king, being the successor of Horus and Osiris and their living image on earth, had to be treated after death like those gods themselves." A primitive form of embalment was practised even at this early period of Egyptian history and the religious beliefs and burial customs of later ages were already strongly developed. Osiris, Isis and other familiar gods are shown in inscriptions, and the kings were known as the 'Sons of Horus'.

These, then, were the kings who ruled Egypt at the dawn of her recorded history. They lived in regal state; some of the inscribed tablets show them going in procession with their chamberlains and high officials to celebrate a victory over their enemies (Plate 7). They made war; an inscribed mace states that Narmer had captured 120,000 men, 400,000 oxen and 1,422,000 goats. Their art was highly developed; the tombs contained fragments of finely-wrought palace furniture, jewellery, and alabaster and diorite bowls ground to a translucent thinness. Ebony labels of Menes' time show the earliest known examples of hieroglyphs for continuous writing. Even at this period they not only possessed phonetic signs, representing a whole syllable, but also alphabetic signs

—over 2000 years before any other race used them. Had they been less conservative they could have abandoned phonetic symbols entirely and used an alphabet of twenty-four letters 5000 years ago; but, being Egyptian, they did not.

This was some of the information which Petrie gleaned from an archaeological junk-heap, but of precious objects he found few. It is pleasant to record therefore that he did have one piece of luck. When excavating the tomb of Djer, which had also been the shrine of Osiris, one of his workmen found a hole in the mud-brick wall near the entrance stairway. He put in his hand and found a mummified arm. Being an unusually honest workman he brought it to Petrie, who unwrapped it and found, still clasping the dried bones, three beautiful jewelled bracelets of gold, cornelian and lapis-lazuli. The workman had found the arm of Djer's queen.

Thousands of years ago one of his ancestors helped to rob the tomb, tearing the royal body to pieces in search of valuables. Perhaps disturbed at his work, or because he was over-burdened with loot, the robber had thrust the arm into a hole in the wall, no doubt intending to collect it later. For some reason he never returned. From the Eighteenth Dynasty onwards, when the tomb became the shrine of Osiris, thousands of human beings passed up and down the entrance stairway within a few feet of the arm, but they did not see it. Neither did the Copts. Neither did the treasure-seekers. Nobody saw it until that moment. "Not even," adds Petrie, drily, "the *Mission Amélineau*."

CHAPTER IV

ORIGIN OF THE PYRAMIDS

BEGINNING a chapter on the pyramids is like being asked to describe dawn or sunset, or the arrival of spring. Behind stretch the unnumbered generations who have seen and described them, and ahead are the unborn millions who will also feel and respond to the same eternal stimuli. Beside the visitor to the Great Pyramid are the shades of writers, travellers and historians stretching back to the time of Herodotus and beyond. In such company he must avoid on the one hand the banal and the obvious, and on the other the oh-so-superior attitude of the seasoned traveller who knows it all.

However, let the writer say at the outset that he is on the side of the naïve and marvelling visitor. In four separate visits to Cairo he has never failed to make his way to the Giza plateau and will do so again whenever he gets the chance. For the Giza pyramids are beyond doubt the supreme expression of Pharaonic majesty and power, whether one sees them far across the valley, lifting their golden tips above the morning haze, or from close by at glaring mid-day when their huge limestone sides lean against the sky like a flight of heavenly stairs. Framed as they are against the Western Desert, it is not their size which impresses at first but their colour, a warm shining gold, stippled with black shadows thrown by the rectangular blocks of which they are built. Each of these blocks, built in courses rising stepwise from base to peak, weighs about two and a half tons; in the Great Pyramid, built by King Cheops in about 2720 BC, there are 2,300,000 of them. Partly because, monumentally, they are the finest, but chiefly because of their accessibility to Cairo, the Giza pyramids are by far the best known; in fact many people are unaware that any other pyramids exist. It should be realised, however, that this group is only one of several. Groups of pyramids stretch from Abu

Roash in the north to as far south as Merôe in the Sudan; and some of these are older than the Giza group. To understand the significance of Cheops' Great Pyramid one must know something of its predecessors; this chapter therefore will be devoted to examining the origin of the pyramid, and to showing how it may have developed from earlier forms.

First, what was the purpose of these buildings? The answer is quite simple; they were the tombs of kings. All of them, from the largest to the smallest, contain, or have contained, sarcophagi, and most bear the names of the kings whose sepulchres they were. Some people, bemused by the splendour of the Great Pyramids, have rejected this explanation as being too prosaic. They have devised elaborate theories seeking to prove that Cheops' pyramid was an astronomical observatory-cum-table of measurement, the dimensions of which can be interpreted as a chronological guide to the principal events of past and future history. These beliefs were more prevalent in the last century, until Petrie scientifically demolished them in his great work *The Pyramids and Temples of Gizeh*. To-day, though the theorists still have their adherents, we believe that most people will find more wonder in the archaeologists' revelations of how these mighty structures were planned and built in an age which possessed no more elaborate mechanical aids than the lever, the roller and the inclined plane.

Another question needing an answer is why did the Old Kingdom Pharaohs adopt a pyramidal shape for their tombs? Until quite recently most Egyptologists accepted the theory advanced by the great German archaeologist Borchardt, that the shape evolved through a logical process of development from earlier and simpler types of tomb. Recent discoveries at Sakkara, however, have thrown doubts on this explanation, and a new and interesting theory has been advanced, notably by Mr. I. E. S. Edwards, to whom we are indebted for much of the material in this chapter. Mr. Edwards' theory, which is fully expounded in his book *The Pyramids of Egypt*, is summarised at the end of Chapter V.

As we have seen, the kings of the First and Second Dynasties were buried in brick or stone-lined pits divided into chambers and covered by rectangular structures of sun-dried brick, also divided into compartments containing food, weapons, furniture and other objects needed in the after-life. These structures, which had inward-sloping sides, are known as *mastabas*, an Arabic word meaning a bench. They are so called because when buried in drift sand the upper projecting portion looks like one of the stone seats found outside Arab houses. Thousands have been excavated, and some of the finest of the archaic mastabas have been found by Professor Walter Emery at Sakkara, near the ancient capital of Memphis in Lower Egypt.[1] One found in 1937 was 46 yards long and 17 yards wide; it covers five subterranean rooms originally roofed with wooden beams and planks (as at Abydos). An interesting point is that the walls of these chambers had been hung with reed mats, portions of which still remained; probably the walls of the king's palace were decorated in this way.

Clay sealings of food and wine-jars found in this tomb bear the name *Aha*, whom some Egyptologists identify with Menes, the first king of the First Dynasty. Probably, therefore the tomb at Abydos which Petrie ascribed to this king is not his, as it is smaller and less elaborate than the Sakkara tomb; or he may have possessed two tombs, one at Abydos near This, the home of his family, and another near his new capital. Incidentally each king of Egypt bore several names, which sometimes makes identification difficult. The owner of this tomb had been buried in the central underground chamber. The mud-brick superstructure was subdivided into twenty-seven compartments or magazines provided with false doors. Little remained in them beyond fragments of furniture left by the ancient tomb-robbers. The exterior walls were built in the form of panelled recesses such as are usually found in the mastaba tombs of the Archaic Period.

[1] The most recent discovery was made at Sakkara in 1954, also by Professor Emery.

Probably they were intended to represent the walls of the king's palace; in fact the whole tomb may have represented a house with its various rooms. Evidently at this time the after-life was believed to be spent in and around the tomb, which therefore had to resemble the dwelling which the owner inhabited in his earthly life. Real doors between the chambers would be unnecessary, false doors being sufficient to allow the spirit of the dead man to pass from room to room. We shall see more of these false doors later.

During the Third and Fourth Dynasties, when large numbers of mastabas were built for the nobles, the general structure underwent a considerable change. The body was buried in a small subterranean chamber at the foot of a deep shaft hollowed out of the rock. The mud-brick superstructure, instead of being hollowed into numerous cavities, became almost solid, except for a small offering-chamber on the west side. In time mud-brick gave place to stone, until later mastabas were a solid mass of masonry, apart from the offering-chamber, where relatives and friends of the dead man could place food and wine for the sustenance of his *bai* or spirit. This *bai* seems to have been the spiritual element in man which separated from the physical after death, but was still dependent on the presence of the earthly body, which had therefore to be preserved. There was also another spirit entity called the *ka*, whose exact nature is still in dispute, some authorities believing it to be the dead man's double, others a kind of protecting presence, while another school of thought affirms that the *ka* was the embodiment of certain abstract qualities which were necessary for the continuance of life. Those who wish to go more deeply into the matter should read Adolf Erman's *Religion of the Egyptians*. The chief point to remember is that these spiritual entities could survive only *if the physical body was preserved and supplied with the means of life*. Unless these conditions were fulfilled survival was impossible.

Burying the body at the foot of a deep rock-cut shaft overcame some problems, but created others. The body was now much safer from attack by robbers but it was also further from the offering-chamber. How could the relatives of the dead man be sure that his spirit would receive the food they brought for it? The Egyptians overcame this difficulty in their usual practical way. Into the masonry of the mastaba they built a chamber to contain a life-sized statue of the deceased, fashioned to represent him exactly as he appeared in life. These beautiful statues were never intended to be seen by the living. Each was walled up in its dark chamber, known to the Arabs as the *serdab* (cellar), only a narrow slit at the eye-level of the statue enabling it to 'see' into the offering-chamber beyond. Thus the spirit of the dead man, recognising his likeness in the statue, could inhabit it and so partake of the offerings. Most of the masterpieces of Old Kingdom sculpture which adorn the museums of the world came from these mastaba tombs. Magnificent though they are as works of art, they were designed for a purely practical purpose. The exquisitely carved bas-reliefs on the walls of later mastabas served a similar purpose to the statues. Fearing that later generations might neglect the necessary offerings at his tomb, the Egyptian noble had himself represented on the walls in the act of receiving his due tribute. To the Egyptian mind the carved representation of the offering was enough to ensure that the *ka* would never perish through want of sustenance.

On the east (inner) wall of the offering-chamber a false door would be carved to enable the spirit to enter the chamber. In some mastabas these doors were also carved on the outer west wall so that the spirit of the dead man could leave the tomb and, gazing across the valley to its former home on the east bank, enjoy the sweet air of evening as it had done in life.

This is not merely a pleasant fancy. The following inscription, though of later date, is typical of many found in Egyptian tombs:

> May I inhale the sweet air of the North Wind
> Which is fragrant with the incense of my God.

The Egyptians believed that the west was the home of the dead, who were known as 'the Westerners', Osiris being 'the first of the Westerners'. In the west the sun-god's boat, having crossed the sky by day, entered upon its nightly journey through the Underworld. Consequently nearly all burials were made on the west bank, on the edge of the Western Desert, while the east bank was the home of the living.

The most ancient pyramid surviving in Egypt was built by King Djoser, founder of the Third Dynasty (2780–2720 BC), at Sakkara, several miles up the river from Memphis. This is the famous Step Pyramid, so called because it is built in a series of terraces; it is the oldest large stone building in the world (Plate 10). Here one sees the very beginning of architecture, the first attempt by man to build monumentally in stone. Even to-day, after generations of plunderers have stripped its finely-masoned limestone casing and blurred the clean sharp edges of its steps, Djoser's great monument still stirs the heart; not only the pyramid itself but the marvellous complex of courts and buildings which once surrounded it, and which have recently been unearthed and partially restored by C. M. Firth, J. E. Quibell and J. P. Lauer working for the Egyptian Government's *Service des Antiquités*.

To appreciate its full significance one should remember that even as late as the end of the Second Dynasty, King Khasekhemui, Djoser's predecessor, built his mastaba of sun-dried brick, using stone only to line the burial-chamber. Djoser himself built at Bet Khallâf, near Abydos, a massive brick mastaba which he seems never to have used. Then apparently without precedent, arose this enormous structure of stone, surrounded by an elaborate complex of stone buildings covering an area of 180,000 square yards and exhibiting amazing artistry in design and craftsmanship in execution. The genius who planned this work was the King's chief architect, Imhotep, who was revered by later generations of Egyptians as the traditional wise man. He was also regarded as a philosopher and magician, and scribes were in the habit of pouring out a libation to him before commencing their work. His sayings are remembered to this day and small statuettes of him exist in their thousands. Eventually he was deified and the Greeks identified him with Aesculapius, their god of medicine.

From the air the Step Pyramid appears as a dark square mass in the centre of a large rectangle within which are lines and geometrical shapes indicating walls and buildings. The entire site and the desert surrounding it are criss-crossed with tracks and pitted with holes made by centuries of digging and plundering. Even so, Imhotep's grand conception is still clear. From the ground it is easy to see why he chose this site for the tomb of his royal master. It stands on the edge of the Libyan plateau overlooking the ancient capital of Memphis. Below, to the south-east, the eye follows the green valley of the Nile until it merges into the Delta. The rectangle we saw from the air is revealed as a great enclosing wall which originally stood 33 feet high. Djoser's former subjects, looking up from their valley towards the plateau, would see only this wall of shining white limestone, and, rising majestically above it, the pyramid which was the eternal home of their deified king. Such a monument could only have been raised by a monarch who controlled the economic wealth of a united country. Consolidation of the two kingdoms was now complete.

The clearing of the enclosure wall and its inner buildings by Firth, Quibell and Lauer is one of the most important Egyptological works undertaken in the past twenty years. It has thrown new light on the origin of the pyramids and enabled us for the first time to trace their development from the simple brick mastabas of the Thinite kings to the monumental structures of the Fourth Dynasty.

In earlier times the burial-places of the kings were usually surrounded by a wall, within which the relatives of the dead monarch, or priests appointed by them, could regularly place offerings. Djoser's architect went much further than this. Against the northern side of the pyramid he built a temple where the funerary rites and subsequent offering ceremonies could be performed. Also, within the enclosing wall, he erected a number of buildings which have no parallel anywhere in Egypt. They seem to have formed a kind of stage-set within which the spirit of the dead king could perform, in the after-life, the same important religious rites in which he had taken part on earth. Chief of these was the *heb-sed* ceremony, which was of very ancient origin. In prehistoric times the king was probably killed when he had reached an age at which he was judged to be too old to rule. In later periods this custom was dropped but the king had to go through a ceremony in which he renewed his youth and vigour. Part of this consisted in offering at the altars of the gods of the Northern and Southern Kingdoms, after which the king was ceremonially re-crowned. He also had to run a fixed course, presumably to test his vitality, and one of the most beautiful carved reliefs in Djoser's pyramid appears to show him performing this ritual sprint.

Imhotep erected his buildings around several courtyards, one of which, called the *heb-sed* court, was designed for this ceremony. Here numbers of dummy chapels were found, each with an open door carved in stone. The façades of these chapels were adorned with tall fluted columns which may have been designed in imitation of a plant with a fluted stem. Professor P. E. Newberry believes that this plant was the *Herculanem gigentum* and showed the writer a specimen which he had grown in his Surrey garden and which resembled these columns quite remarkably, even to the pendant leaves, which are exactly like the capitals. These fluted columns, slightly resembling the Doric type but taller and without bases, are a prominent feature of Imhotep's buildings. The closer these 5000-year-old remains are studied, the clearer it becomes that one is looking at Man's earliest attempt at large-scale building in stone, *before he learned to develop architectural forms suitable to the material.* Here he is still feeling his way, imitating in stone the forms he had previously made in wood or some other substance. For instance the entrance colonnade, in the words of J. P. Lauer, "supported a heavy stone roof made of slabs placed perpendicularly and *curved at their lowest edges to represent palm logs*". (My italics.) Again, the columns "seem to have been a reproduction of wooden columns whose form in turn is based on a support made from the stem of reeds bound in bundles". Another example is to be seen in one of the subterranean galleries beneath the pyramid. We mentioned that the central chamber of the First Dynasty tomb of Aha, discovered by Emery, had been hung with reed-matting. In the east gallery of the Step Pyramid this reed-matting is exactly imitated in small blue-glazed tiles. No doubt such mats hung on the walls of Djoser's palace.

East of the entrance to the Mortuary Temple was the *serdab*, and in this walled-in chamber was found a life-sized statue of Djoser (Plate 8), a regal figure in a chair, wearing a long wig falling below his shoulders, and a robe reaching from shoulders to feet. This statue is now in the Cairo Museum but a plaster replica has been replaced in the serdab. Within the Mortuary Temple on the north side of the pyramid a steep flight of steps leads to a sloping tunnel which descends through the rock under the pyramid. It bends westwards, then joins another tunnel and finally debouches at a point half-way down a vertical shaft which plunges 92 feet below ground level. Above this shaft stands the pyramid, and at its base is a tomb chamber of black granite. From galleries surrounding the chamber a maze of corridors extends in all directions. One of these corridors contained sculptured reliefs of Djoser performing religious rites, and in others were found alabaster coffins, one containing human remains. Alabaster pedestals for coffins showed where others had stood, but these had been broken up and robbed in antiquity. From the east side of the pyramid eleven other tunnels are driven into the rock beneath the building; these were probably intended for the burials of the king's family.

To the Egyptologist the most significant fact concerning the Step Pyramid is that it began not as a pyramid but as a simple stone mastaba. A close study of the structure reveals that there were five distinct stages in its development before it acquired its present form. Djoser first built a mastaba like the one at Bet Khallâf; but it was of stone, not brick, and square instead of oblong. As his reign continued he extended it on all four sides, but the exterior was two feet lower than the original structure so that a step was formed. He altered it again, making it oblong. Still unsatisfied, he adopted a new plan. He enlarged the mastaba a fourth time and superimposed on top of it a series of three mastabas, each smaller than the one below, thus forming a miniature step pyramid. This seems to have appealed to him, so he extended the base still further until it measured 411 feet by 358 feet. On this he built his final step pyramid with six terraces and cased the whole structure with fine Tura limestone. That, minus the limestone casing, is substantially the building which remains to-day (Plate 10).

Credit for discovering the secret of this pyramid's evolution belongs mainly to Ludwig Borchardt, but it had been excavated several times during the past century, by General Von Minutoli (1821), by the Englishmen Colonel Vyse and Howard Perring in 1837, by Lepsius in 1843, and by C. M. Firth from 1924 to 1931. To each of these in turn it yielded a few more of its secrets, but when the most recent excavators explored the deeper underground galleries they discovered objects which their predecessors had missed. These included two alabaster sarcophagi, one containing the body of a child, and 30,000 stone vases which took three seasons' work to remove. The body of Djoser was never found. Like most tombs, the pyramid had been robbed in ancient times, though a mummified foot found in 1934 may be all that remains of the great king.

Djoser was not the only Third Dynasty king to plan a pyramid. At Zawiyet-el-Aryan, near Giza, are the traces of two buildings which may have been planned as pyramidal tombs but were never finished. One of these, called the 'Unfinished Pyramid', has a deep vertical shaft cut in the rock with a long sloping corridor adjoining it down which the builders lowered the granite slabs for the tomb-chamber.

This corridor is similar to those found in later pyramids: it has a flight of stone steps with raised ramps running along the centre and on each side down which the blocks of masonry were slid. Dr. Reisner found on certain of the blocks the name Nebka, a king of the Third Dynasty, of whom nothing is known but his name. He may have intended to build a monument like that of Djoser but he never got beyond the foundations. Of the other unfinished specimen, the 'Layer Pyramid', hardly anything has survived. At the end of the Third Dynasty, King Snofru, the last of his line, carried the development of the pyramid a stage further. At Dashur, several miles north of Sakkara, he raised one of the most interesting buildings in Egypt, the so-called 'Bent' or 'Blunted' Pyramid, which is not stepped but straight-sided except for a curious change of angle in the middle. It is 320 feet high and measures 620 feet along the base.

Until recently this building had been ascribed to a Third Dynasty king named Huni, but in the spring of 1947 Abdessalam Hussein Effendi,[1] Director of Pyramid Studies for the Egyptian Government, reopened the inner chambers of the pyramid for the first time in 100 years. On one of the casing-blocks was found the cartouche of King Snofru and the building is now considered to be his. At the same time the excavators discovered on one of the blocks of the small adjoining pyramid the name of Snofru's queen, Hetephras. It happened that the writer was in Egypt at the time of this discovery and had the privilege of being among the first Englishmen to enter the Upper Chamber of the pyramid since Perring saw it in 1837.

To reach Dashur we travelled about 20 miles up-river from Cairo. We rode over the desert along a shallow wadi, until the rhomboidal pyramid rose grandly before us, standing on its high rocky plateau and distinguished from its neighbours by its unusual shape, for its sides do not follow a straight line from base to peak but are bent in the middle, the upper angle being shallower than the lower. This was probably done to

[1] Since deceased.

reduce the superincumbent weight above the central chamber, or maybe, as Perring suggests, the builders were in a hurry to finish.

Half-way along its northern face a few pieces of scaffolding clung to the rock outside the entrance. The scaffolding supported a capstan by which the excavators working in the pyramid could be lowered down the steep 300-foot entrance gallery on a small trolley. Accompanied by Abdessalam Hussein we made the descent, lying flat on our backs on the trolley, as the passage is only about three feet square.

Down, down we went, watching the receding square of sunlight getting smaller and smaller until we reached bottom. We found ourselves standing on the floor of a lofty hall about 20 feet square and soaring upwards to a height of 80 feet. The roof was lost among the shadows thrown by our hurricane lamps. It was like being inside the spire of a church. We were so far beneath the earth that the top of this shaft was approximately at ground level and above it lay the solid mass of the pyramid itself, over 300 feet high. Up the centre of this chamber the excavators had fixed a series of vertical ladders lashed to flimsy scaffolding. Up there we climbed until we reached the top and our lamp shone on hundreds of bats which hung from the corbelled roof of the shaft. At this point, 80 feet above the floor, Abdessalam pointed to a hole cut in the wall. This was the entrance to a horizontal gallery about two feet square. Along this we wriggled on our stomachs, noting at one point the words 'discovered 1837' left by the British archaeologist Perring 100 years ago.

At last we could stand upright. It was very hot in the heart of the pyramid. As we paused to recover breath we saw that we were standing below the entrance to another pyramid chamber, but this one was not so high. With the help of the Arab workers we were hauled up an almost vertical wall and arrived, very hot and dusty, on the floor of the Upper Chamber. At a sign from the Director the Arabs held up their lamps and we could see that the ceiling of this room, unlike that of the Lower Chamber, was rough and broken.

Great lumps of stone had fallen from it, no doubt due to the tremendous pressure of the masonry above, and some of the remaining blocks looked as if they might fall at any moment. Abdessalam told us that when Perring discovered this chamber he was so alarmed by the state of the ceiling that he decided it was unsafe to work there. Whether this or the Lower Chamber contained the King's body is not known.

From the Upper Chamber another gallery passes through the masonry of the pyramid to emerge at a point near the middle of the west face. This passage has never been used since the pyramid was built, as its entrance is still sealed with the outer casing of the pyramid, and at its lower end is a portcullis-stone plastered on both sides. It must therefore have been closed at the time when the narrow horizontal passage was open, or the workmen could have been trapped inside the pyramid. Perring himself points this out in his book and we could not, therefore, agree with Abdessalam, who believed that the roughly-hewn horizontal gallery by which we had entered was the later work of thieves. Neither of these two chambers contained a sarcophagus or the remains of a burial, though Abdessalam found, in a shaft adjoining the Lower Chamber, remains of incense. He also discovered at the top of this shaft two false doors cut in stone. These have a particular interest because the Pyramid Texts, the most ancient religious documents known in Egypt, contain the words 'Opened are the doors of the sky to the ascending King'.

Here for the first time were found, inside a pyramid, the actual representation of these doors. As no body had been found and no sign of a sarcophagus, Abdessalam suggested that the ancient robbers never found the body, which might still be lying hidden in a secret chamber, possibly in the masonry between the floor of the Upper Chamber and the roof of the shaft with the false doors. This is an attractive and romantic theory, but, up to the time of writing, no burial has been discovered. Possibly Snofru was never buried in this pyramid. He built another at Meidûm, some miles to the south, though when Maspero excavated it in 1881 he found no trace of a sarcophagus.

Alas for the hopes of these monarchs of the Old Kingdom. Their mighty monuments still stand, ravaged by time and the plundering hands of centuries; but of the frail human bodies they were designed to protect nothing remains.

"To be but pyramidally extant," wrote Sir Thomas Browne, "is a fallacy in duration . . ."

CHAPTER V

HOW AND WHY THEY WERE BUILT

THE oldest *true* pyramid surviving in Egypt is the Southern Pyramid at Dashur, a short distance from Snofru's 'Bent' Pyramid. Although earlier in date than the Great Pyramid it is not greatly inferior in size. The base measures 720 feet and it is 325 feet high. Its builder is not known; for many years it was ascribed to Snofru, but as his name has been discovered on a foundation stone of the Bent Pyramid its neighbour must presumably have been built by another Third Dynasty king, possibly Huni, who came before Snofru. Snofru built another pyramid at Meidûm which seems originally to have been stepped, but subsequently the steps were filled in, making it straight-sided. Later generations stripped the outer courses of masonry, leaving the curious structure which survives to-day, a mound of sand and rubble surmounted by a tall tower which is actually the core of the pyramid. Many pyramids suffered in this way. They formed a convenient quarry for later Pharaohs who were not at all loth to destroy their ancestors' monuments.

Snofru's son and successor was Cheops. Determined to outdo any of his predecessors, he selected a commanding site at Giza and built the mightiest pyramid of all, the Great Pyramid, 755 feet along the base and 481 feet in height. It bears the name 'The-Horizon-of-Cheops'. Even to-day, when its dimensions have been reduced to 746 feet by 450 feet, it is still monarch of all pyramids; none of Cheops' successors equalled his achievement. Chephren, next but one in succession, came near to it. His pyramid, which adjoins that of Cheops, originally stood to a height of 471 feet and was 707 feet square, but he cheated, building his pyramid on higher ground so that it actually appears taller than its predecessor. But Mycerinus fell far behind, building a pyramid which covers only half the area of Cheops' monument. This gradual decrease in size is an indication of the diminishing power of successive kings. The Great Pyramid could only have been built by a monarch who exercised complete control over the economic resources of the country. All were his to use, material, unlimited manpower and the skill of the finest craftsmen in the kingdom. Evidently Cheops reached the high-water mark of power; after his reign the tide receded.

As a group the Giza pyramids are without parallel. Approaching them from Cairo along the smooth tarmac of the Giza road, one passes the smart villas of the wealthier Cairenes, set in their palm-shaded gardens, backed by the lush green fields where the sun glints on the irrigation canals. The road rises and swings left to climb the plateau, and suddenly the Great Pyramid rises ahead, 450 feet of sun-baked limestone; behind it is the Second Pyramid of Chephren and behind that the Third Pyramid of Mycerinus. Beyond lie street after street of mastabas, the tombs of the nobles, viziers, chiefs of the treasury, officers of the royal household, attending the kings in death as they did in life. Around these broken, plundered tombs the desert has been churned up by centuries of excavation and the ground is littered with broken potsherds, but beyond them the turbulent sea of sand quietens to a smooth golden waste, stretching endlessly to the west, as sterile and empty as it was in the days of the Pharaohs.

That is the first unforgettable impression. The second is not so pleasant. The pyramids, so accessible from Cairo, have paid the penalty of all great monuments which have become show-places. Thousands of visitors crawling around like pigmies are no hindrance to one's enjoyment. The pyramids are vast and the desert is vaster. But there are also the Arab dragomans. These gentlemen descend on the visitor in swarms and will not be shaken off. Armed with a little picturesque and highly-inaccurate information they demand, nay insist on showing him round, after a fierce initial struggle over the body of their victim ("I saw him first"). Quite often they are charming and amusing guides and will sometimes produce a tattered piece of notepaper which they claim is a personal testimonial from some celebrity. Lord Lloyd and Lord Kitchener are favourites, though we met one man who proudly claimed to have escorted Noel Coward. Of course, one should not blame the dragomans. They have their living to earn and Egypt is their country. But sometimes one envies the explorers and archaeologists of the past who knew these buildings before they became the targets of commercial 'tourism'.

One of the earliest European visitors was Herodotus, the Greek historian who came to Egypt in about 450 BC. He got most of his information from the priests, who told him that Cheops, the builder of the Great Pyramid,

... closed the temples, and forbade the Egyptians to offer sacrifice, compelling them instead to labour, one and all, in his service. Some were required to drag blocks of stone down to the Nile from quarries in the Arabian range of hills. Others received the blocks after they had been conveyed in boats across the river, and drew them to the range of hills called Libyan. A hundred thousand men laboured constantly and were relieved every three months by a fresh lot. It took ten years' oppression of the people to make the causeway for the conveyance of the stones, a work not much inferior, in my judgment, to the pyramid itself.

... The Pyramid itself was twenty years in building. It is a square, eight hundred feet each way and the height the same, built entirely of polished stone, fitted together with the utmost care. ... The Pyramid was built in steps, battlement-wise, or as some say, altar-wise. After laying the stones for the base, they raised the remaining stones to their place by means of machines formed of short wooden planks

69

... the upper portion of the pyramid was finished first, then the middle, and then the part which was lowest and nearest the ground.

There is an inscription in Egyptian characters on the pyramid which records the quantity of radishes, onions and garlic consumed by the labourers who constructed it; and I perfectly well remember the interpreter who read the writing to me said that the money expended in this way was 1,600 talents of silver ...

Archaeological evidence gathered by Petrie and others confirms the accuracy of most of these statements, though the dimensions are wrong, and the item concerning the 'radishes, onions and garlic', etc., suggests that Herodotus had been talking to a dragoman. He also relates a hoary old scandal concerning Cheops' daughter, who was said to have built a pyramid out of her immoral earnings.[1] This story, too, sounds as if it came from the same source.

There are, however, two facts mentioned by Herodotus which should be remembered. First, that when the pyramid was completed it was covered from top to bottom with a smooth polished casing of fine limestone and capped by an apex or a *pyramidon* of granite, gilded to catch the first rays of the sun. On the Great Pyramid nothing remains to-day of this limestone casing. It has been completely stripped, so that instead of a smooth gleaming surface we see a series of steps. We do not see the pyramid as its builders, or even Herodotus, saw it.

The second fact is that originally each pyramid was joined to the river bank by a causeway, which served two purposes: as a road along which the quarried stone could be dragged to the pyramid plateau, and later as a ceremonial way along which the funeral and subsequent processions could pass. At the foot of each causeway near the river was a valley Building, where certain rituals concerned with embalmment were performed, and at the top, under the shadow of the pyramid itself, was a mortuary temple. In its finished state each causeway was roofed, so that it presented a long enclosed corridor, its walls covered with sculptured reliefs. The roofs and walls of the causeways have gone, and apart

[1] One stone from each man.

from Chephren's valley building, little remains of the temples, but in the days of the Old Kingdom these buildings were an essential part of whole pyramid complex. To consider the pyramids in isolation, as they are to-day, is to get quite a false idea of their original appearance.

Herodotus does not say whether he entered the Great Pyramid; probably not, or such an eager observer would certainly have mentioned it. If he had entered he would have found an empty tomb, for Cheops' sepulchre and those of his successors had been robbed 2000 years before, in the troubled times of the Seventh to the Tenth Dynasties. No doubt in time the entrances would be re-sealed and their position forgotten, as there are records of re-discoveries and forced entries in later centuries. It was open in Roman times, as Strabo describes how the entrance was opened and closed. But later it was sealed again. Eight centuries later the Arab Khalif Ma'mun thought the building contained treasure and hacked out of the west face a tunnel which is still called Ma'mun's Hole. The attackers chose the wrong spot and would probably never have found the entrance gallery had their battering not dislodged the granite plug-block which sealed the entrance to the Ascending Passage. It must have been a dramatic moment when Mamun's men heard the great stone fall in the depths of the pyramid. Guided by the sound they started tunnelling west and finally broke through into the original entrance passage. Eagerly they stormed up the great gallery and into the King's Chamber in the heart of the pyramid, but too late; thirty centuries too late. There was only an empty sarcophagus.

Interest in the pyramids began to grow during the 18th century. The indefatigable Richard Pococke saw them, of course, and the publication of his *Travels* attracted more European visitors. But the 19th century was the heyday of pyramid investigation. They were scrutinised, measured, drawn and theorised over by a succession of Egyptologists, Caviglia, Belzoni, Vyse and Perring, Lepsius, Borchardt, Petrie and others.

Among the early visitors, Giovanni Belzoni is interesting. An Italian engineer domiciled in Britain, he went to Egypt in 1815 to try to sell to the Sultan Mahomet Ali a new hydraulic machine he had invented. In this he failed, but finding himself in Egypt with a little ready money, Belzoni decided to tour the country in search of antiquities. Altogether he spent five years in Egypt and the Sudan, and subsequently wrote a naïve and charming account of his adventures under the title *Narrative of the Operations and Recent Discoveries within the Pyramids, Temples, Tombs and Excavations in Egypt and Nubia*. Modern Egyptologists look askance at his methods, but his delightful book reveals a true love of Ancient Egypt, and he worked under dangers and difficulties which would turn most 20th-century travellers grey.

Belzoni was the first to enter the Second Pyramid in modern times, and his account of this feat is worth quoting:

> My undertaking was of no small importance; it consisted of an attempt to penetrate into one of the great pyramids of Egypt, one of the wonders of the world. I was confident that a failure in such an attempt would have drawn on me the laughter of all the world for my presumption in such a task: but at the same time I considered that I might be excused, since without attempting we should never accomplish anything.

First Belzoni studied the south side of the Second Pyramid.

> I examined every part, and almost every stone. I continued to do so on the west—at last I came round to the north. Here the appearance of things became to my eye somewhat different from that at any of the other sides. The constant observations I made on the approach to the tombs at Thebes perhaps enabled me to see what other travellers had not; indeed, I think this ought to be considered as a standing proof that in many cases practice goes further than theory.

Now Giovanni mounts his favourite hobby-horse, the narrowness of the academic mind:

> I certainly must beg leave to say, that I often observed travellers who, confident of their own knowledge, let slip opportunities of ascertaining whether they were correct in their notions: and if an observation is made to them by any one, who had not the good fortune of having received a classical education, they scorned to listen

to it, or replied with a smile, if not a laugh of disapprobation. . . . I often had the satisfaction of seeing such travellers mortified by the proof of being wrong in their conjecture.

Belzoni had little money, but he managed to enroll a gang of Arabs and set them to work clearing the accumulated sand from the north side of Chephren's pyramid. After much labour they found the entrance to a 'forced passage' probably made at the same time as the forcing of the Great Pyramid by Ma'mun. The condition of this passage was dangerous.

I set a few men to work, but was soon convinced of the impossibility of advancing any further in that excavation. In the passage below, one of the men narrowly escaped being crushed to pieces. A large block of stone, no less than six feet long and four wide, fell from the top, while the man was digging under it . . . the man was so incarcerated that we had some difficulty in getting him out . . . the falling of this stone had moved many others in this passage: indeed we were so situated that I thought it prudent to retreat out of the pyramid . . . the danger was not only from what might fall upon us, but also what might fall in our way, close up the passage and thus bury us alive . . .

Undaunted by this setback, Belzoni examined the Second Pyramid again, and compared it with the Great Pyramid. He calculated that the entrance to Cheops' building was not in the centre of the north face, as it ran in a straight line from the east side of the King's Chamber:

The entrance consequently must be as far from the middle of the face as the distance from the centre of the chamber to the east side of it. . . . Having made this clear and simple observation, I found that if there were any chamber at all in the Second Pyramid, the entrance could not be on the spot where I had excavated, which was in the centre, but calculated by the passage in the First Pyramid, the entrance to the second would be near thirty feet to the east. Satisfied with this calculation I repaired to the second pyramid to examine the mass of rubbish. There I was not a little astonished when I perceived the same marks, which I had seen on the other spot in the centre, about thirty feet distant from where I stood. This gave me no little delight, and hope returned to my pyramidical brains . . .

Again the excavator summoned his Arabs, who set to work murmuring *"magnoon"* (madman) . . .

The entry proved to be as hard as that of the first excavation, with this addition, that we found larger blocks of stone in our way, which had belonged to the pyramid, beside the falling of the coating.

But hopes rose on the 1st of March, when Belzoni discovered three large blocks of granite, two on each side, and on the following day:

we came at last to the right entrance into the pyramid. . . . Having cleared the front of the three stones, the entrance proved to be a passage four feet high, three feet six inches wide, formed of large blocks of granite, which descended towards the centre for a hundred and four feet five inches at an angle of twenty-six degrees.

At the bottom a portcullis block of granite 1 foot 3 inches thick barred their path.

The raising of it was a work of no small consideration. The passage is only four feet high, and three feet six inches wide. When two men are abreast of each other they cannot move, and it required several men to raise a piece of granite not less than six feet high . . . the levers could not be very long, otherwise there was not space to work with them; and if they were too short I could not employ men enough to raise the portcullis. The only method . . . was to raise it a little at a time. . . . I continued to raise the portcullis, and at last made the entrance large enough to squeeze myself in; and after thirty days' exertion had the pleasure of finding myself in the way to the central chamber of one of the two great pyramids of Egypt, which have long been the admiration of beholders.

After describing the entrance passage Belzoni found himself in a horizontal one, cut out of the solid rock, which led to a large chamber:

My torch, formed of a few wax candles, gave but a faint light. I could, however, clearly distinguish the principal objects. I naturally turned my eyes to the west end of the chamber, looking for the sarcophagus, which I strongly expected to see in the same situation as that in the first pyramid; but I was disappointed when I saw nothing there. . . . On my advancing towards the west end, however, I was agreeably surprised to find that there was a sarcophagus buried on a level with the floor. The sarcophagus contained nothing but rubbish and a few bones. On the walls of the chamber was an inscription in Arabic roughly scrawled in charcoal. Translated, it read:

"*The Master Mohammad Ahmed, lapicide, has opened them: and the Master Othman attended this (opening) and the King Ali Mohammad at first (from the beginning) to the closing up.*"

74

Belzoni found the tomb empty, as no doubt had the Arabs who preceded him centuries before, but his excavation, measurement and description of the remaining passages were of no small value to Egyptology. As for the fragments of bone in the sarcophagus, Belzoni thought at first that they belonged to a human skeleton, but he adds, "Having been sent to London, they proved to be the bones of a bull. Some consequential persons, however, who would not sacrifice a point in history, rather than lose a *bon mot*, thought themselves mighty clever in baptising the said bones those of a cow, merely to raise a joke. So much for their taste for antiquity."

There, cocking a final snook at his old enemies, we leave Signor Belzoni, though we shall meet him again in the Valley of the Tombs of the Kings at Thebes.

After him came Colonel Vyse and Howard Perring, an energetic pair who investigated, measured and drew many of the pyramids, then the German scholar Lepsius, who formed the 'accretion theory', the basis of which was that each king added a certain amount to his pyramid during every year of his reign; *ergo*, the larger pyramids were built by the kings with the longest reigns and *vice versa*. This theory, which has since been disproved, was reasonable compared with the fantastic notions put forward by cranks who were now attracted to the Giza pyramids; the buildings were alleged to be observatories, temples, granaries, standard tables of measurement—anything but mere tombs. The man who blew all this nonsense sky-high and at the same time revealed the real wonder of the pyramids was Sir Flinders Petrie; and he did this, not by divination and esoteric reasoning, but by scientific measurement and precise mathematical calculation.

He spent three seasons at Giza, from 1880 to 1882, studying every inch of the site, carefully checking the orientation of the pyramids and measuring every dimension, inside and out, with the most modern surveying instruments available to him at the time. The results are published in his *Pyramids and Temples of Gizeh*, which is now one of the standard works on the subject, though even more accurate surveys have been made since. The orientation of the Great Pyramid is phenomenally accurate. The four sides, each over 700 feet long, are aligned almost exactly on true north, south, east and west. In fact their orientation is so incredibly precise that compass errors can be checked against them. In 1925 Mr. S. H. Cole of the Survey Department of the Egyptian Government, using more accurate instruments than Petrie, estimated the errors on each side as follows:

North side	0°	2′	28″	south of west.
East side	0°	5′	30″	west of north.
South side	0°	1′	57″	north of west.
West side	0°	2′	30″	west of north.

The maximum error was therefore only 5′ 30″, or a little over *one twelfth of a degree*. On the south side the error was only *one thirtieth of a degree*. Who, one wonders, was the master engineer who planned and laid out this great structure with such precision? And how was it done? The magnetic compass was unknown to the Ancient Egyptians. They could of course have determined east and west approximately by sighting on the rising and setting sun on the equinoctial days, but in the words of Mr. I. E. S. Edwards (*The Pyramids of Egypt*) "the resultant error . . . would have been greater than the amount revealed by at least two of the main pyramids of Giza . . ."

Edwards believes the pyramid-builders may have determined by "sighting on a star in the northern heavens and bisecting the angle formed by its rising position, the position from which the observation was made and its setting position". For example, imagine a vertical rod driven into the ground and surrounded at some distance by a low circular wall the top of which is perfectly horizontal. By the rod stands a man, and near the wall, on the inside, is another man. A certain prominent star in the northern heavens has been selected for observation. When the man near the wall sees this star rising he warns the man standing by the rod. As soon as the star rises above the rim of the wall the first man, sighting across the rod, takes a bearing on the star, and the second man marks its position on the wall. The star arches across the sky, and as it sets twelve hours later the same process is repeated and a second mark is made. This procedure would be repeated several times to check the accuracy of the observation. Then lines would be drawn joining the rod to the two points on the ground immediately below the marks (accuracy being ensured by the use of a plumb-line). By bisecting the angle thus formed the observers would have a line running due north and south. The other two cardinal points would, of course, be at right-angles to it. This is a simplified explanation, but it will serve to show how the pyramids may have been orientated.

Petrie carefully examined some of the outer casing-stones, which originally covered the whole pyramid. There are still a few in position near the base. The fineness of their workmanship was almost beyond belief. He wrote:

> ... the mean thickness of the eastern joint of the northern casing stones is ·020″ [1/50th of an inch], therefore the mean variation of the cutting of the stone from a straight line is but ·01″ [1/100th part of an inch] of 75 inches up the face ... these joints, with an area of 35 square feet each, were not only worked as finely as this, but cemented throughout. Though the stones were brought as close as 1/500th of an inch, or, in fact, into contact, and the mean opening of the joint was 1/50th of an inch, yet the builders managed to fill the joint with cement, despite the great area of it, and the weight of the stone, some 16 tons ...

The Egyptian workmen used bronze tools. The jewelled cutting joints may have been of beryl, topaz, chrysoberyl, sapphire, or hard uncrystallised corundum. For cutting the stones they employed great bronze saws with jewelled cutting points. In some places, e.g. the granite sarcophagus of Cheops, the marks made by these saws can be clearly seen. By curving the saw-blades into a circle drills were formed which could cut out a circular hole by rotation. For smaller objects the cutting edge was held stationary while the work was revolved; "the lathe", says Petrie, "appears to have been as familiar an instrument in the Fourth Dynasty as in our modern workshops". Some of the superb diorite bowls must have been turned. They are too accurate to have been made by hand. Though chisels have been found, no examples of jewelled saws and drills have been discovered, but this is not surprising as owing to their value they would be carefully looked after, and when worn the jewels would be removed and replaced in new tools.

Most of the limestone of which the pyramids are built was quarried from the Mokkatam Hills, on the opposite bank of the river, and floated across in barges at flood-time. The granite for the galleries, burial chambers, portcullis blocks, etc., came from Assuan in Upper Egypt. The description by Herodotus of how the blocks were raised into position was confirmed by Petrie's investigations. As each course, or layer of blocks, was laid, a long ramp of stones and earth would be built up to it, along which the blocks for the next course would be dragged. When the course was laid the earth ramp would be raised, ready for the next course, the angle of slope always remaining the same, so that the ramp would get longer and longer as the work proceeded.

The heavy blocks, each weighing several tons, would be manoeuvred into their final positions by levers—the "machines formed of short wooden planks", mentioned by Herodotus. There is no evidence in tomb-paintings or elsewhere that the Egyptians possessed any machinery more elaborate than the lever, the roller and the inclined plane. Even the largest blocks in the Great Pyramid, the 56 roofing beams in the King's Chamber, could have been raised by leverage, though each weighed 54 tons. Petrie described the method which was probably used, that of resting the block on two piles of wooden baulks, then rocking it alternately from one side to the other with crowbars and heightening each pile in turn. In this way the block would gradually be raised to the height required. "No other system", he says, ". . . would enable men to raise such a mass with only the aid of crowbars . . ." Ten men, he calculated, could raise one roofing stone by such means, and six gangs could have raised all the blocks in one year. Plates of sheet iron, fragments of which were found in the pyramid, were used to prevent the crowbars biting into the stone.

Herodotus describes Cheops as a sacrilegious tyrant who exhausted the manpower of the kingdom in building his colossal monument, but, as Petrie points out, this is a little unfair. During three months of the year, during the inundation season, the men were unable to work in the fields and would therefore be idle anyway. It was during these three months that 100,000 labourers were employed to float the quarried stone across the Nile. Manoeuvring the heavily-laden barges across the fast-flowing river must have required considerable skill. Then the blocks had to be hauled on sledges up the causeway to the pyramid plateau. Probably not more than 4000 men were regularly employed throughout the year. These would be the skilled workers, masons and others and Petrie identified their barracks, foundations of which still exist. He also found, on the north side of the plateau, a huge dump of mason's chippings which had been thrown over the cliffs. Among this rubbish he found "specimens of workmen's water jars and food vessels, mixed with chips of wood and charcoal, and even a piece of string, probably used in pulling a rubbish basket".

One wonders what they were like, these unknown thousands who laboured for twenty years to raise the greatest stone monument in the world? Did they feel themselves to be slaves, the tools of a megalomaniac tyrant? Or did they, perhaps, identify themselves with the power of the King made manifest in stone, as the subjects of modern dictatorships are conditioned to worship the state?

Like Djoser's Step Pyramid, Cheops' building reveals several changes of plan. At first it was intended to carve the burial chambers out of the rock beneath the pyramid, and these still exist in an unfinished state. When the lower parts of the pyramid had been built, however, it was decided to build these chambers in the heart of the pyramid itself.

Accordingly a new Ascending Corridor was driven upward through the masonry at a steep angle, and this leads to the Grand Gallery, 153 feet long and 28 feet high with a corbelled roof, one of the finest surviving architectural works of the Old Kingdom. After climbing its steeply sloping staircase we enter the King's Chamber, in the heart of the pyramid; 19 feet high, 34 feet 4 inches long, 17 feet 2 inches wide, and built of granite. Its roof has been computed to weigh 400 tons, and above are a series of three so-called 'relieving chambers', designed to prevent the roof collapsing under the weight of the pyramid above it. At one end of the chamber is a lidless granite sarcophagus which once contained the body of Cheops. Compared with other parts of the pyramid it is crudely made, with saw-marks and drill-holes still visible. There are also some curious flaws in the chamber itself. The masonry is superb but the levels are all wrong. Petrie's survey showed that the whole chamber was tilted over at one corner, so that the courses are $2\frac{1}{4}$ inches higher on the north-east than the south-west. These and other errors seem to indicate hurried building; perhaps the master engineer who laid out the foundations with such precision did not live to superintend the building of the King's Chamber.

Below the King's Chamber is a second, smaller, chamber reached by a horizontal passage leading off the Ascending Corridor just where it joins the Grand Gallery. Though this has been misnamed by the Arabs the 'Queen's Chamber' it appears to have been intended originally as the resting-place of Cheops. Then there was a second change of plan and the Grand Gallery was built with the King's Chamber at the top of it. On the other hand the so-called Queen's Chamber may have been the *serdab* of the pyramid. There is a niche in one wall which may have contained a statue of the king.

There is no space, in a general work on Egyptology, to deal fully with the other buildings on the Giza plateau, the Second and Third Pyramids, the smaller pyramids of the Queens, the Valley Temple of Chephren, and, of course—the Sphinx, which appears to have been a portrait of Chephren, represented as the sun-god guarding the Necropolis. For these the reader is referred to the more specialised works given in the Bibliography at the end of this book. Before we close this chapter, however, there is another interesting question to be considered.

Why did the Old Kingdom Pharaohs choose the pyramidal shape for their tombs? Borchardt and others, as we have seen, believed that the shape was arrived at by a process of development from mastaba to step pyramid, from step pyramid to true pyramid. This is still the generally accepted belief, but the flaws in this theory have been pointed out by Mr. I. E. S. Edwards, who suggests that the reasons for choosing this shape may have been religious rather than practical. His theory might be summarised as follows:

The mastaba tombs of the First and Second Dynasty kings were conceived as eternal homes for their owners. The after-life was to be lived in and around the tomb. Then, at an undetermined period, possibly between the Second and Third Dynasties, a different conception gained ground, of an after-life lived with the sun-god. The Pyramid Texts, the earliest religious documents known in Egypt, contain the text, "A staircase to heaven is laid for him so that he may climb to heaven thereby". It is tempting to believe that the step pyramid represented this heavenly staircase. Djoser, as we have seen, built a tomb of each type, a mastaba at Bet Khallâf and a step pyramid at Sakkara; there was also a second mastaba in the enclosure wall of the Step Pyramid. At this time the two rival religious systems may have been fighting for supremacy; perhaps Djoser was trying to make the best of both (other) worlds.

If Borchardt's evolutionary theory is correct, then after the first true pyramid had been built all succeeding pyramids would be of this type. There would be no reversion to an earlier pattern. Yet Snofru, who built the Bent Pyramid at Dashur, which was almost certainly begun as a true, straight-sided pyramid, built another at Meidûm, 28 miles away. This Meidûm building, which archaeologists now believe was built *after* or perhaps at the same time as the Bent Pyramid, *was originally a step pyramid*. Here again there may have been a change in development of religious thought. Professor Breasted stated that the true pyramid was nothing more than a large-scale reproduction of the sacred symbol of the sun-god which was kept in the 'holy of holies' at Heliopolis. This symbol was a *pyramidon*, or miniature pyramid, called the *ben-ben*. "Why", asks Edwards, "was it chosen?" By way of answer he describes the appearance of the sun's rays as they shine down through a gap in the clouds. "When standing on the road to Sakkara and gazing westwards . . ." he writes, ". . . it is possible to see the sun's rays striking downward . . . at about the same angle as the slope of the Great Pyramid." Now we turn again to the Pyramid Texts. Here is No. 523:

> Heaven hath strengthened for thee the rays of the sun in order that thou mayest lift thyself to heaven as the eye of Re . . .

Was this, then, the purpose of the true pyramid, to be a material representation of the sun's rays? Edwards also cites philological evidence to support his theory. For instance the Egyptian name for pyramid was *M(e)r*. If it could be proved that this word was a compound word consisting of the prefix *M* which conveys the meaning 'place' and a known root composed of the consonant *r* which means 'to ascend', *M(e)r* would then mean 'Place of Ascension'. But there is no positive proof of this derivation.

If there had been two rival cults, that of the step pyramid and the true pyramid, this would explain why Snofru first built one of each. Then when the latter cult triumphed he changed his Meidûm building from a step pyramid to a straight-sided building—after which all his successors seem to have built true pyramids, with the possible exception of Dedefre, successor to Cheops. Instead of building at Giza, where there was plenty of room, Dedefre constructed at Abu Roash, a now-ruined building which *may* have been a step pyramid. Was he, perhaps, the last diehard adherent to the old faith? We have presented Mr. Edwards' theory very sketchily and readers should study it in full in his book (see "Books Consulted", p. 219). He has propounded a fascinating question which, as yet, admits of no certain answer.

CHAPTER VI

MOTHER OF CHEOPS

THE Giza pyramids and their hundreds of attendant mastabas have been known for nearly 5000 years. Unlike later sepulchres there was no attempt at concealment; the brick and stone superstructure revealed plainly where the burials were. For the better part of fifty centuries they have been open to the attacks of robbers and it would seem impossible that any tomb, above all a royal tomb, could remain undetected until the 20th century. Yet this did happen once, and the story of how the tomb was discovered, excavated and its splendid furniture reconstructed from a mass of decayed wood and fragmented metal is one of the great romances of Egyptology. We propose to describe this discovery in the manner of a detective story, so that the reader can, if he wishes, piece together for himself the evidence provided by the successive clues which the excavation found. Afterwards he can compare his reading with the dramatic story which the archaeologists themselves were able to reconstruct from these same clues.

Historically there are only two personalities who need be borne in mind. The first is Cheops, who built the Great Pyramid at Giza. The second is Cheops' father, Snofru, builder of the Bent Pyramid at Dashur and the half-destroyed pyramid at Meidûm.

The story opens in 1902, when the Harvard–Boston Expedition took over the excavation of a commission granted by the Egyptian Government at Giza. Then followed

83

twenty-three years of excavation covering two-thirds of the cemetery west of Cheops' pyramid, the area of the smaller pyramids and east of the Great Pyramid as far as the Sphinx. Street after street of mastaba tombs were carefully cleared and excavated, but every one of the royal tombs, *i.e.* those of the royal families, had been plundered, most of them in ancient times. Still the expedition carried on with the work, year after year, digging, clearing, photographing and record-ing the wall-paintings, sculptured reliefs, statues and hiero-glyphic inscriptions.

During 1924–5 the expedition, directed by Dr. Reisner, began to excavate the mastabas to the east of Cheops' pyramid, where they found the cemetery of the royal family of Cheops, including three small pyramids built for his queens. Here also, between the cemetery and the pyramid itself, were the foundations of Cheops' Mortuary Temple, with its pavement of black basalt. Running through the cemetery was a large avenue which the excavators named Queen Street because on its western side stood the three small pyramids of the queens. Opposite was a field of very large mastabas which were identified as belonging to the sons and daughters of Cheops, including Prince Kawaat (the eldest son), Hardjedef, Khnumbraf, Princess Meresankh, who was married to King Chephren, and Princess Hetephras and two other sons called Khufukhaf and Menkhaf. All these tombs had been ransacked by thieves.

On November 1st, 1924, Reisner's staff commenced work on the south-western corner of the cemetery. It was a labori-ous task, first clearing away the sand, stone and rubbish down to the first floor-level, then through this to a deeper floor, and finally down to the rock itself. Every square yard of the site had to be cleared in this way, and the rubbish care-fully sifted. Only by such methodical excavation could Reisner be sure that nothing was missed.

Not far from the row of queens' pyramids the excavator found a cutting in the rock which ran under a pile of masons' debris. On clearing the site it proved to be the base of an unfinished pyramid. The descending stairway had been begun, and some of the lower courses of masonry laid and subsequently removed; the mortar still remained to show where the stones had been. The type and dimensions of this unfinished tomb were similar to those of the easternmost of the queens' pyramids. North of this unfinished pyramid the ground rose to a low ridge and nearby was an ancient quarry from which stone had been cut in the time of Cheops, but the quarry had not been exhausted. All this was found beneath a floor dating from the Fourth Dynasty.

On February 9th the staff photographer was about to photograph this quarry when he noticed some white plaster on the slope leading to the ridge. Ahmed Said, Reisner's head *reis*, cleared the debris and disclosed an elongated oval patch of plaster which on analysis turned out to be sulphate of lime. When this was removed the excavators found to their astonishment a rectangular cutting in the rock, packed with limestone blocks. When these were removed the cutting, which sloped downwards at an angle, was found to open into a vertical shaft, also filled with stone blocks. The shaft had evidently been sunk through the rock above, so Reisner's men examined the ground and found that the entrance to the shaft had been sealed with irregular blocks of stone, cunningly placed to look like the natural surface of the rock. There was no trace of a superstructure ever having existed.

At the time of the discovery Dr. Reisner was in America on short leave, and the work of clearing the vertical shaft was carried out by his assistants, Alan Rowe and T. D. R. Greenlees, with the aid of Ahmed Said. On February 23rd work on the clearing began. Down to the level of the entrance tunnel the packing was of well-cut limestone blocks but below that it deteriorated. At 30 feet down the excavators expected to be nearing the burial chamber, as under most mastaba tombs the shafts are between 30 and 50 feet. All they found at this level, however, was a small chamber cut out of the side of the shaft and blocked by masonry. When this was removed a niche was revealed containing a sacrificial offering of a skull and three legs of an ox, two beer jars, some charcoal and a few fragments of black basalt.

Below, the shaft still went on down. At 40 feet down there were fragments of red pottery and the shaft descended through hard seams in the rock. There were dangerous fissures in the walls. At 55 feet the diggers found fragments of copper but still no signs of a burial chamber. Said Ahmed and four of his picked men worked in the pit day after day, two breaking up the stone and the others operating a basket-hoist. All were excited, for the deeper the shaft the greater likelihood there seemed of finding an intact burial. When they got down to a depth of 60 feet the east wall of the shaft sloped westward, forming a shelf, and a few feet farther down they reached a firmer stratum of rock and the walls were cut with more regularity. Seventy feet; fragments of red pottery bowls, but still no burial chamber. Eighty feet; rock still sound and the shaft growing narrower. Eighty-five feet; and in the south wall of the shaft the excavators uncovered the topmost course of a wall of masonry.

It was late afternoon on March 7th, thirteen days after the excavation had begun. Alan Rowe removed one of the blocks. Beyond was black emptiness. He called for a candle and thrusting it through the hole looked into the chamber which had not been seen by human eyes for 5000 years. The candlelight flickered on a white alabaster sarcophagus and the glitter of gold. Then he replaced the block to keep out the dust, and the excavators returned to their camp, but one imagines there was little sleep for any of them that night.

On the following morning they returned and removed more of the masonry. With the aid of reflected sunlight thrown by mirrors they were able to recognise some of the objects in the chamber. Near one wall stood the sarcophagus, sealed with its lid, on which lay a number of gold-encased rods which were recognised as supports for a collapsible canopy. More rods and gold-encased beams lay between the sarcophagus and the wall. Practically every inch of the remainder of the floor was occupied by a confused mass of objects. There were bits of gold inlays which had once covered the surface of wooden furniture, the wood having decayed. There were sheets of gold inlaid with faience, lion-legs, palm capitals, decorated arms, all of gold, but practically everything had disintegrated. Beyond, mixed up with the fragments, were vessels of alabaster, pottery and copper. To the laymen such a sight would have been fascinating but also disappointing. After all, one would think, what had the excavators found after all their labours? The ruins of what had once, no doubt, been splendid furniture, now reduced to a heap of rubbish. The archaeologists knew better. They realised that their work had only begun, that with care and patience it would be possible to reconstruct this furniture. But that lay in the future and belongs to the second part of our story.

The immediate problem was to identify the owner of the tomb. The chamber was so crowded with fragile objects that it was not possible to take a step inside it without cracking something. However, using a pair of field glasses Mr. Battiscombe Gunn examined the inlaid gold sheets with ease, and discovered that one of them formed an inscription with the words:

Lord-of-the-two-Crowns, Snofru; the Horus, Nebmaat

On hearing of this inscription a newspaper correspondent jumped to the conclusion that this was the tomb of King Snofru himself. Of course the inscription proved no such thing. It merely indicated that the owner of the tomb had lived in the time of Snofru.

Rowe and Greenlees noticed that the chamber was unfinished. The walls were roughly hewn, and cuttings in the east and west walls had been begun, then sealed up with masonry and plastered over, the plaster still bearing the finger-prints of the mason. In one corner of the chamber was a pit filled with masons' rubbish. Everywhere there was evidence of haste: in the sinking of the shaft and the unfinished state of the burial chamber. When Dr. Reisner himself came out to Egypt in July and examined the tomb, he decided that the confused and jumbled state of the objects was not due merely to decay. The furniture had probably been intended for a larger tomb but had been removed here and hurriedly piled up without regard for order. The sarcophagus could only have been admitted to the small chamber by lowering it down the deep shaft lengthways, an operation which could not be carried out with the body inside it. The mummy also would have had to be lowered in the same way. Reisner decided that this was a *reburial*, that the sarcophagus and furniture had originally been buried in another, possibly larger tomb and that for some reason, presumably violation of the original sepulchre, the contents had been removed to this one.

By a process of deduction he was able to place the date of the tomb within a year of the reign of Cheops himself. All the clues which led him to this decision are in the foregoing paragraphs. First the fragments of black basalt found in the sacrificial niche proved that when the tomb was being made Cheops' Mortuary Temple was built, or in process of building. (The basalt chips came from its pavement.) Second, the fact that the tomb was found *under* a Fourth Dynasty floor proves that it was earlier in date than the four pyramids which Cheops built for his queens. Third, that when work on the unfinished pyramid was stopped and the site shifted 90 feet to the east, this tomb was already in existence. Work on the quarry was probably abandoned for fear of disclosing the entrance to the tomb, and the fact that no superstructure existed and that the entrance had been deliberately concealed, strongly suggested a *secret* burial.

As to the tomb's owner, all that could be decided at this stage was that he or she had lived in the time of Snofru, Cheops' father. Reisner believed that the tomb did not contain the burial of a king, but that it must have been of some important member of the royal family, since burial on such an important site could only have been done with the royal permission.

The final clearing of the shaft was completed at the beginning of February 1926, and then began the clearing of the chamber. Of this work Reisner wrote:

> The duty rested on the Expedition of recovering every scrap of archaeological evidence, whatever it might be. We had practically nothing from contemporary tombs to guide us and could not even be sure that further inscriptions would reveal the name of the owner . . . the wood had shrivelled or disintegrated . . . much had been reduced to grey ash by fungus; cloth, matting, basket work . . . was preserved only in fragments or traces which could never be moved . . .

The floor was cleared area by area. Every tiny fragment was registered and photographed *in situ* before removal. Each item was entered in a register which eventually grew to 1600 sheets of foolscap paper. On these pages the expedition kept a day-to-day account of the work as it progressed: observations, theories, drawings, and photographs. Gradually, piece by piece, the excavators were able to recognise the objects from which the fragments came. There were the gold-cased beams and poles which had supported a tent-like canopy which was erected over the royal bed. There was the bed itself, also encrusted in gold with golden legs shaped like lions' feet. There were two gold-covered armchairs, one of which had arms supported by curved struts made to represent three entwined papyrus-flowers. This was a valuable piece of evidence proving that the owner of the tomb was not a king. If this had been the case, the design would have shown the flower of Upper Egypt in conjunction with the papyrus of Lower Egypt. Also there were remains of a gold inlaid box which had probably contained bed curtains. The contents of this and other boxes had been carelessly packed, and included fragments of plaster and masons' rubbish which had presumably been swept up from the original tomb when the burial was removed. The excavators found another wooden box containing eight beautiful alabaster jars and "a long slender copper dipper". The lid of each jar was inscribed with the name of the oil or cosmetic it had contained, *e.g.* *sti-hab* (festival perfume), *wadj* (green eye-paint) and *hatet-tjehnu* (prime Libyan oil).

On February 28th an area was reached covered with fragmented gold inlays. Altogether there were eight layers and their recording and removal took four months. One of the Expedition staff, Dunham, lay on a mattress supported by a beam projecting over the floor and carefully picked up the tiny fragments with pincers and placed them on a tray without disturbing the rest of the deposit. One day in February he came upon a row of gold hieroglyphs on a bar of decayed wood. In March they were carefully removed on a tray and eagerly examined by the Expedition. They read:

> . . . *Mother of the King of Upper and Lower Egypt, follower of Horus, guide of the Ruler—*

The owner of the tomb was, therefore, a queen, possibly the mother of Cheops or perhaps his grandmother. Then, on April 14th Dunham found another row of gold hieroglyphs. Dr. Reisner was summoned. He read the name 'Hetephras'. At last the owner of the tomb was known. She was Queen Hetephras, the mother of Cheops, who built the Great Pyramid. The full inscription read:

> *Mother of the King of Upper and Lower Egypt, follower of Horus, guide of the ruler, favourite lady whose every word is done for her, daughter of the god of his body, Hetephras . . .*

The box of alabaster jars was her make-up box. The name Snofru on the bed-canopy seemed to point to her being the wife of King Snofru.

Near the sarcophagus lay a heap of gold sheets, among which were silver objects which turned out to be rings, inlaid with dragon-flies in light green malachite relieved with lapis lazuli. Nearby was an inlaid panel with the inscription:

> *Mother of the King of Upper and Lower Egypt. Box containing deben-rings*

Reisner decided that they were a set of anklets, graduated in sizes to fit the leg from the ankle to the middle of the calf. Originally they had been contained in a gold-covered box fitted with a peg to hold them. The Queen had been well provided with her personal possessions and domestic articles. Besides her two armchairs there was a gold-cased carrying-chair on which she could be borne on the shoulders of her bearers. She also had an ample supply of food vessels, some of which had evidently been used in the royal household. There was a gold drinking-cup and two gold dishes, a copper ewer and basin, a set of tiny copper and gold razors, and a manicure instrument pointed at one end for cleaning the nails, and rounded at the other for pushing back the cuticle.

More boxes had contained clothes and linen, but in one of these Reisner found tiny fragments of alabaster. This discovery came as a considerable shock, because the alabaster chippings came from the sarcophagus. The fact that they were found *inside the box* suggested that the sarcophagus had been attacked and possibly forced open by the thieves who had robbed the Queen's original tomb. Later, when that tomb was cleared, the tiny fragments had been swept into one of the boxes with the linen. The lid of the sarcophagus showed signs of an attempt to force it. Nevertheless, Reisner was fairly certain that it would prove to contain the Queen's mummy, as there would have been no point in removing the sarcophagus and funerary furniture from one tomb to another unless the body, the most important point of the burial, were present. Now the investigators were able to remove the beams for the canopy which lay behind the sarcophagus. On one of these was the inscription:

The Horus, Nebmaat, great god, endowed with life, endurance and prosperity. The King of Upper and Lower Egypt, Lord of the Two Crowns, Nebmaat, the Horus lord of Nubt, Snofru, lord of 'hepet', the golden Horus, foremost in the places of the god forever.

The canopy was therefore, in all probability, a gift from King Snofru to his wife.

Perhaps the most interesting item of furniture found in the tomb was this big collapsible canopy which had probably been erected in the original tomb, then dismantled for removal to the smaller sepulchre at Giza. When assembled it is just over 10 feet long, 8 feet wide and 7 feet high. It is a tent-like framework supported at each corner by beams and joined at top and bottom by cross-beams with narrower vertical rods spaced at equal distances along each of three sides. Other horizontal rods join the top cross-beams. Thus the general appearance is that of a room with one side open. The beams and posts are of wood, encased in gold, and originally curtains would cover the roof and hang down each side, with a set of draw-curtains across the front. Inside these was space for the Queen's bed and chairs, and when the curtains were drawn she would be enclosed in a kind of tent. The whole structure was ingeniously made with copper-sheathed mortise-and-tenon joints for rapid dismantling and re-erection. Probably the Queen took the canopy with her when she travelled from palace to palace.

As they completed the clearance of the burial chamber the excavators found objects which seemed to have no place in a royal tomb, such as copper chisels and stone crushers which seem to have been left by the workmen who built the tomb—more evidence of haste. By December 16th, 1926, the chamber was clear at last, and nothing remained but the white alabaster sarcophagus, standing within four bare walls. It had taken 326 days to clear the tomb. On March 3rd, 1927, the excavators and a small party of high officials gathered in the burial chamber for the opening of the sarcophagus. Everyone felt the excitement of the occasion. Everyone believed that there would be found, lying within her coffin, the body of a great queen who had died 5000 years ago.

With infinite care the lid was prised loose, a sling was attached and as the lid swung upwards the guests peered forward to look inside the sarcophagus. It was empty.

The disappointment of Dr. Reisner and his devoted staff can be imagined. "It had seemed to me inconceivable," he said, "that Cheops should have ordered the remains of his mother's burial to be transferred to Giza and hidden under 100 feet of masonry unless the body . . . had been brought along with the coffin." All that Reisner was able to find of Hetephras was her canopic chest concealed in a niche and sealed up with masonry. This chest, which is found in nearly all Egyptian burials of royal and noble families, contained the vital organs of the deceased removed from the body during the process of embalming.

Why was the body missing? We have now reached the point in our detective story when all the clues have been given. This is how Reisner interpreted them.

When Queen Hetephras died she was buried near her husband's pyramid at Dashur. There is a small pyramid near the Bent Pyramid which may have been her tomb. But at this time her son, Cheops, had begun his Great Pyramid at a new site at Giza, 12 miles away, and it is likely that the Dashur necropolis was not as well guarded as it should have been. Not long after, the burial thieves broke into the Dashur tomb, perhaps aided by the necropolis guards, or they may have been some of the masons who worked on the tomb. They had to do the job at night, and were desperately short of time. When they had tunnelled through the masonry filling and broken into the burial chamber they saw the great gold canopy with its curtains covering the sarcophagus. Probably they tore down the curtains and flung aside the gold furniture, which they had no time to strip or remove. Even small portable articles like the gold drinking-cup were overlooked. They went straight to the sarcophagus, knowing that the most precious objects would be on the royal body. With hammers and chisels they forced open the lid, dragged out the body and carried it out of the tomb to a hiding-place where their torches would be concealed. Then they tore the mummy apart, wrenching off gold necklaces and armlets and jewelled rings. Perhaps the inner coffin itself was of gold. Hurriedly sharing the loot, they dispersed, leaving what remained to the jackals, or they may have set fire to the wrappings in the superstitious belief that by so doing they would escape the vengeance of the Queen's *ka*.

Soon afterwards the robbing was reported to the high official responsible for guarding the royal necropolis. With his staff he visited the tomb and found that the body had disappeared, but that most of the tomb furniture remained. No doubt he ordered a search to be made, but whether he found the robbers will never be known. However, he is certain, for his own sake, to have made an example of someone. Next came the delicate matter of informing the King that his mother's sepulchre had been violated. The official probably made as light of it as possible, minimising the damage done and *not daring to tell Cheops that Queen Hetephras' body had disappeared*. Enraged, the King ordered that the Queen and all her funerary equipment be brought to Giza and re-buried near his own pyramid. Perhaps he chose the site himself, and to make sure that there should be no second violation he ordered a secret tomb to be made. Work on the quarry was stopped, and the workmen began to sink their shaft. In his anger and impatience the King may have set them a time limit.

While arrangements were being made to collect the Queen's funeral furniture and bring it to Giza, the shaft was hurriedly cut. Probably the original intention was to sink it to a depth of 30 or 40 feet; but at this level the quarrymen struck a bad patch of rock and had to dig deeper in order to find a sounder stratum suitable for making the burial chamber. Still they were unlucky. Pressed for time they were unable to finish the sides of the shaft properly and narrowed its dimensions to hasten the work. At about 80 feet down they found better rock, and began excavating the burial chamber, but by this time the period allowed for making the tomb had almost expired.

Meanwhile, at Dashur, the necropolis officials gathered together the furniture and objects from the opened tomb, stuffing the articles hurriedly into boxes and getting them mixed with fragments of plaster and broken masonry left by the robbers. The canopy was dismantled, the bed and chairs removed and the whole transported by sledge or by boat from Dashur to the new tomb.

At Giza the foreman responsible for excavating the tomb, hearing that the sarcophagus and furniture were soon to arrive, gave orders for the hurried completion of the burial chamber. Originally he had intended to make it much larger; cuttings had been made in the east and west walls, and the workmen had commenced to sink a pit in one corner. Now orders were given to cease any further cutting and to seal up the gap in the walls with masonry. One gap only was left to receive the canopic chest. No attempt was made to give the walls of the chamber their normal smooth finish, and the accumulated rubbish was swept into the unfinished pit. No doubt the official responsible for the re-burial was anxious to have the sarcophagus lowered as soon as possible, for fear the King should take it into his head to look inside it.

The sarcophagus was lowered down the deep shaft, the lid replaced and covered with the rods from the dismantled canopy and the rest of the small chamber was filled with the remainder of the Queen's funerary equipment. Then the workmen began to refill the shaft. They were in such a hurry that they left their tools in the chamber where they were found incongruously mixed with the Queen's furniture. When they had practically refilled the shaft they found they had left out certain articles of red pottery brought from the original tomb. These they threw down and covered up with fresh rubble. Near the top of the shaft a sacrifice was made for the benefit of the Queen's *ka* and the remains buried in the wall-niche. While this was in progress some black basalt fragments from the pavement of Cheops' Mortuary Temple fell into the niche and were buried there. Then the rest of the shaft was filled, the entrance concealed with rough stones arranged to simulate the natural rock surface, and the work was almost complete. One can imagine the intense relief of all the officials concerned.

Later a street was laid above the site of the tomb, and as this thoroughfare would be in constant use by the priests of the necropolis the possibility of a second robbery was extremely remote. In any case the secret would be known only to a few, and they might not consider it worth their while to dig through 100 feet of masonry, knowing that the most valuable objects, those which had adorned the body, had already been taken. In time the secret would be lost, and so the burial survived intact down to the 20th century. One wonders if Cheops ever discovered that his mother's body was not in her sarcophagus, but that was probably the best-kept secret of all.

In clearing the tomb Reisner and his staff took 1057 photographs and covered 1701 foolscap pages with notes. Thanks to the painstaking method of work it was possible to reconstruct completely most of this unique Old Kingdom furniture, piecing together the thousands of minute gold fragments and re-laying them on a new wooden foundation. Dunham spent from 1926 to 1927 in reconstructing the wooden frames for the carrying chair, bed, head-rest and toilet box. Miss Thompson, another member of the expedition, set the gold hieroglyphs on the ebony strips, and W. A. Stewart continued the work. The rebuilding of the carrying chair alone took nearly two years, and Bernard Rise reconstructed the canopy, beginning in September 1930, and completing the work in September 1931.

To-day, if the shade of Queen Hetephras ever visits the Cairo Museum, she can see her furniture exactly as she saw it in life. Under the gold canopy, which her husband King Snofru gave her, stands the bed in which, perhaps, her son Cheops was born. Beside it stands her gold-encased armchair and her carrying chair with its long gold handles. Nearby is her make-up box with its neat alabaster jars in position, and the jewel-box containing her silver anklets. No one who has had the privilege of seeing this furniture is likely to forget its strength, simplicity and grace, so appropriate to the dignity of these Old Kingdom monarchs, the fathers of Egyptian history. In our view it is far lovelier than the tomb furniture of Tutankhamun, which, for all its lavishness and elaboration, has an air of decadence which is absent from the more ancient work.

CHAPTER VII

'THEBES OF THE HUNDRED GATES'

THE earlier part of this book has dealt chiefly with the Old Kingdom, when the centre of administration was in lower, *i.e.* northern Egypt. Most of the monuments and tombs of the Old Kingdom were discovered near the ancient capital of Memphis near Cairo, or in the pyramid fields of Giza, Sakkara, Dashur, Abusir, and other sites in lower Egypt. Now we have to make a big jump in time and space. Six hundred miles up river is Luxor (Plate 12), for many years the most important archaeological site in Egypt, though now almost worked out. Here stood the imperial city of No-Amun, later called Thebes, which for more than 1000 years ruled over the Egyptian Empire. It first figured in Egyptian history at the beginning of the Eleventh Dynasty (2100 BC) when, after a century of anarchy, a family of provincial nomarchs from Hermonthis gained power and established themselves on the site of the future capital. Besides its political and religious eminence, Thebes was also an important market. It controlled the routes to the gold mines in the Nubian mountains, and collected the produce of the Sudan, such as gums, ostrich feathers, gold dust and slaves.

However, the time of the city's greatest glory did not come until the Eighteenth Dynasty, about 500 years later, and it is chiefly the remains of this and later periods that the visitor to Thebes sees to-day. In the Eighteenth Dynasty, when the great warrior-kings who ruled from Thebes vied with one another in foreign conquest, rich tribute flowed into the city, enabling her monarchs to build those gigantic temples and monuments of which Champollion wrote:

> . . . No people, ancient or modern, has conceived the art of architecture on a scale so sublime, so great, so grandiose as the Ancient Egyptians. They conceived like men a hundred feet high, and the imagination which, in Europe, soars high above our portals, stops short and falls powerless at the foot of the one hundred and forty columns of the hypostyle hall of Karnak.

Champollion was one of a long succession of scholars, travellers, learned and unlearned, simple plunderers or scientific excavators who have visited Thebes. Even in Roman times it had become a 'showplace', but in the last two centuries it has attracted more attention than any other site in Egypt. Here some of the most romantic discoveries have been made, the finding of the thirty-six royal mummies at Deir-el-Bahri in 1881, and the opening of the kings' tombs in the Valley of the Kings, culminating in the discovery of the almost intact sepulchre of Tutankhamun. In fact so intimately is the site linked with great discoveries that the little town of Luxor has acquired a double fascination. There is not only the magnetic appeal of the place itself, its remote antiquity, the splendour of its temples on the east bank, the haunting sadness and mystery of that vast city of the dead hewn out of the western hills. There is also an atmosphere of more recent romance, of that period between the late 'eighties of the last century and the early 'twenties of this, when rich amateurs from Europe and America wintered in Luxor, living in the luxurious hotels which arose along the east bank, or in their private *dahabiyehs* on the Nile.

Looking westwards across the river they saw the rose-coloured cliffs of the Theban hills, burial-place of the Pharaohs at the height of Egypt's imperial power. The lure of Egyptology moved many of these men to obtain concessions to excavate. Usually they conducted their archaeological work in an elegant and leisurely manner, often employing professional archaeologists to do the actual excavation and thus leaving themselves plenty of time to enjoy the social amenities of Luxor. Those must have been good years for the professional Egyptologist, years when ample money was available for excavation and research, years when the Egyptian Government looked more kindly upon European excavators than it does to-day, and when peace seemed eternal. Something of the atmosphere of that period still lingers in those vast, half-empty hotels by the riverside. The tall Sudanese waiters in their white *gallabiyehs* and red sashes still glide among the wicker chairs on the verandas, but they no longer minister to rich and leisured gentlemen from the west. Instead there is an occasional American couple hurrying down the steps of the Winter Palace with sun-hats, cameras and a gaggle of long-legged, chattering daughters. Here and there a bored Pasha from Cairo fails to conceal an indifference to antiquity which he shares with most of his countrymen. Only these remain to mock the straw-hatted ghosts of forty years ago. Meanwhile the little donkey-drawn *arabiyas* still go clopping along the river-front towards Karnak, and at the landing-stages *dahabiyehs* with scimitar-like sails wait to take visitors across the Nile to explore the Theban Necropolis.

It is important to remember that in ancient times there were two cities of Thebes. On the east, *i.e.* the right, bank of the river was the city of the living, with the royal palaces, noblemen's houses and the towering temples of Amun-Re and the lesser deities. On the west bank was the city of the dead, for here, as at Memphis, the dead were believed to inhabit the west. On the east bank the site is still dominated by the great complex of temples which takes its name from the modern Arab village of Karnak, though in ancient times it was called 'The Most Perfect of Places' for here dwelt Amun-Re, king of all the gods. Amun, who from the Middle Kingdom onwards became the State God of Egypt, was originally an unimportant local god, but when a Theban family rose to rule Egypt, the Theban godling rose with them and soon he was identified with the other great solar deity, Re of Heliopolis, his name being changed to Amun-Re. He also had affinity with Min, the ithyphallic god of fecundity, whose home was at Kotpos, a town to the north of Thebes. His wife was the goddess Mut and his son was the god Khonsu, both of whom had their temples adjoining his at Karnak. Usually Amun is represented as a man wearing the royal *uraeus* or cobra on his forehead, and crowned with two plumes (Plate 3). Sometimes he is shown with the head of a ram, and the goose also seems to have been closely associated with him. These strange multiple identities, so perplexing to the modern mind, had their roots far back in pre-Dynastic times. The conservatism of the Egyptians prevented them from discarding ancient religious symbols even when their meaning had been lost. Hence a time came when even the systematising priesthood could not impose order on this theological chaos and the time was ripe for Akhnaten's religious revolution which we shall describe later. In the meantime all the general reader need remember is that, in whatever form he appeared, Amun, or Amun-Re, was the supreme god bearing in Egypt the title 'King of the Gods'. He took over the attributes of Re, the sun-god, with his solar barque in which he crossed the heavens by day and the underworld by night. His priesthood attained tremendous political power, rivalling that of the King himself, since the Pharaoh's right to the throne depended on his being accepted as the son of Amun. This was no mere mystical relationship which the literal-minded Egyptians would not have understood. The Queen was 'the Divine Consort'. On the temple reliefs at Karnak are scenes showing the divine birth of Queen Hatshepsut. First the god is shown revealing himself to Queen Ahmes, wife of Tuthmosis I, and the inscription states:

He (Amun) has taken the form of His Majesty King Tuthmosis I, he has found her asleep amid the beauties of her palace. She is awakened on becoming aware of the perfume emanating from the god. . . . He gave her his heart and he caused her to see him in his divine form. When he came to her, she rejoiced at the sight of his beauty and his love passed into her members at the same time as the perfume which emanated from the god . . .

Later scenes show the accouchement of the Queen, the birth, and presentation of the divine child to Amun by the goddess Hathor.

The importance of Karnak as the veritable home of the King of Gods explains why generations of Pharaohs lavished the wealth of an empire on the building and enlargement of its temples. These temples belong to that rare species of architectural marvels which, though they have been eulogised by writers until the mind is bruised by adjectives, still manage to exceed expectations. Even though one approaches them critically, noting that, though ponderously large, they are not as beautiful as Greek or Roman temples, one's judgment is finally overpowered by their titanic size and weight. They seem, as Champollion said, to have been "conceived by men a hundred feet high". Greatest of all is the famous Hypostyle Hall, the largest single chamber of any temple in the world, covering an area of 54,000 square feet (Plate 14). This, almost equal to the area of the whole of Canterbury Cathedral, is only the main chamber of a temple which, if it could be set down in London, would stretch from Piccadilly Circus to Hyde Park Corner. Each of the twelve nave columns is 69 feet high and nearly 12 feet thick, comparable with Trajan's Column in Rome, and it has been estimated that 100 men could stand on each of the capitals which these columns support. The guide books are full of these and similar facts; that, for instance, the outer wall surrounding Amun's temple complex would accommodate ten European cathedrals, and that within the walls of the temple itself there would be room for St. Peter's, Rome, Milan Cathedral, and Notre Dame in Paris.

But no facts, no dimensional comparisons can convey the atmosphere of the place itself, an atmosphere which, in this writer at least, induced both elation and depression, with depression predominating. Karnak is not beautiful; it has not the perfection of proportion of a Greek or Roman temple, or the delicacy and humanity of Egyptian tomb-paintings and sculpture. But it has terrifying strength, massiveness and power. One feels crushed by the weight of masonry, by the obese drum-columns, by the pylons which would dwarf the entrance to St. Paul's, by 64-foot obelisks carved out of a single block of granite and weighing 140 tons. Power, power, *power*! they shriek until one is deafened. The carvings and inscriptions reiterate the same monotonous message. Here is Queen Hatshepsut boasting to us about her obelisks:

> . . . and you who after long years shall see these monuments, who shall speak of what I have done, you will say, "we do not know, we do not know how they can have made a whole mountain of gold as if it were an ordinary task" . . . to gild them I have given gold measured by the bushel, as though it were sacks of grain. And when my Majesty had said the amount it was more than the whole of the Two Lands had ever seen. . . . When you shall hear this, do not say that is an idle boast, but "How like her this was, worthy of her father Amun!" . . .

Here, on the Seventh Pylon, is a gigantic carving of Tuthmosis III, his left hand grasping a group of bound captives, his right brandishing a mace with which he is about to dash out their brains as a sacrifice to Amun. Nearby is the vaunting inscription:

> From the mysterious lands as far as the boundaries of Asia . . . His Majesty brings back prisoners to make a great massacre of them. Never had any other king, save His Majesty, trodden them beneath his feet, and the renown of his exploits will never be annihilated in the land.

Three hundred and fifty-nine names of conquered peoples and cities have been deciphered, names from the southern Sudan to north of the Euphrates. Other kings added halls and pylons and obelisks in commemoration of their victories and as thank-offerings to their god: Sethi I, Ramesses I, and, of course, Ramesses II with his everlasting Battle of Kadesh. No doubt many of these oft-depicted conquests were symbolic. No doubt, too, these were not all wars of vainglorious conquest and aggrandisement but a necessary defence against encroaching enemies. None the less it is less easy for us than it was for an 18th-century author to write: ". . . When all these souvenirs recur to us, we admire the grandeur of the ancient kings of Egypt and the soul is lifted ever higher as she meditates upon a degree of magnificence which appears to be beyond human effort."

Magnificence, yes, but its motive was the same destructive lust for personal power which bedevils men and nations to-day.

Because the Karnak temples are too immense ever to have been lost and rediscovered, it might be thought that their interest to Egyptologists would be exhausted by now. This is far from being true. The knowledge still to be gained from them will keep scholars occupied for generations. First there is the necessity for repair and maintenance. In 1899, for instance, eleven of the columns in the Hypostyle Hall collapsed and were painstakingly rebuilt by the distinguished French Egyptologist M. Legrain, who also made a sensational find of over 1000 statues in the Temple. The Egyptian Government's Department of Antiquities is continually at work clearing sand from the ruins and copying inscriptions.[1] During this clearance interesting discoveries were sometimes made. In 1949 Zakaria Goneim, Chief Inspector of Antiquities for Upper Egypt, uncovered a fresh series of nine-foot sphinxes linked with the more famous Avenue of Sphinxes which led from the temple of Karnak to the Luxor temple two miles away. On the bases of these monuments, which are of late date, about 400 BC, is an inscription:

I, King Nechtanebis, made this road for the God Amun so that he might make good navigation from the temple of Luxor. Never before was such a beautiful road made.

Thus, even at this late period, when the royal capital at Sebennytos was 700 miles away, Thebes still retained its religious importance, and additions were still being made to the

[1] Owing to the later kings using the material of their predecessors, important reliefs and inscriptions come to light when pylons are pulled down for rebuilding. This fascinates philologists, one of whom remarked grimly to me "the whole of Karnak ought to be turned inside out!"—L. C.

temple. In fact Amun-Re was worshipped almost continuously on this spot for a period longer than the existence of Christianity. Even to-day traces of the old worship still linger among the nominally Moslem population. For instance, one of the most important religious ceremonies celebrated at Karnak was the carrying of Amun-Re's image, and those of his attendant gods in their sacred boats. There also remains, in the temple enclosure, the Sacred Lake on which this barque once floated. Now the local Moslem saint is Abu-el Hagag, and at his feast a sacred boat is still carried at the present day. M. Legrain, who devoted much of his life to the study of Karnak, tells a curious story about this event. He quotes from a document signed by three of the bearers in a procession which was carrying a descendant of Abu-el Hagag to his burial. They stated:

> During the procession we were carrying the bier upon our shoulders when, as we arrived near the Nile . . . we suddenly felt the bier become heavy. Not one of us could advance. We put down the bier and after reciting the *fatha*, we picked up the bier again, and we felt nothing. Then, as we were going along the road to the cemetery, on the west side, no one could walk, for the sheik was weighing heavily in the bier. . . . This is exactly what we were aware of and to what we can bear witness . . .

The strange point of this story is that the god Amun was believed to have guided the motion of his sacred boat by weighing on the shoulders of the porters in this way.

The late Professor Newberry, in his Presidential Address to the Anthropological Section of the British Association, said: "In almost every circumstance of daily life (in Egypt) we see the Old in the New. Most of the ceremonies from birth to burial are not Muslim, or Christian, or Roman, or Greek; they are Ancient Egyptian. . . . It was Lady Duff Gordon who said that Egypt is a palimpsest in which the Bible is written over Herodotus and the Koran over that; the ancient writing is still visible through all."

CHAPTER VIII

'CITY OF THE DEAD'

ALL the buildings of Luxor are on the east bank of the river. There the turbaned boatmen wait at the landing-stages to take one across the Nile as, no doubt, did their predecessors in Pharaonic times. Westward from the opposite shore a broad plain extends for about a mile, until it meets a range of limestone cliffs, worn, fissured and cracked into gullies by sun and wind. Their colour varies throughout the day. In the dawn light they are a ruddy gold. At noon they are a dull, whitish brown, blurred by the heat haze. In the evening they are a purple silhouette deepening to black. They are not very high, between 800 and 1000 feet, but to us the Theban hills have an impressiveness which is unparalleled anywhere in the world. For within them is a vast mausoleum. For 2000 years they received the embalmed bodies of seventy generations of Egyptians. Kings and queens, princes and nobles and citizens lay within their shadow, and their painted and sculptured tombs reveal a detailed picture of the daily life of this most ancient of civilisations.

Some of these tombs are as old as the Middle Kingdom, but the majority date from the time of the New Empire, *i.e.* about 1555 BC onwards. Unlike the Old Kingdom tombs previously described they were not concealed under massive *mastabas* but take the form of deep galleries and chambers hollowed out of the mountainside. In the hillside facing the river are the tombs of the nobles. The kings were buried in an isolated valley on the western side of the mountain, the famous *Biban-el-Maluk*, the 'Gate of the Kings'.

Although this was the region of the dead it also supported a large community of the living. Here lived the mortuary priests responsible for guarding and maintaining the tombs, conducting the funerary rites and making the regular ceremonial offerings. Here also dwelt the quarrymen who were constantly excavating new tombs, the carvers and draughtsmen who decorated them, the embalmers, and the makers of funerary furniture which as the centuries passed became increasingly elaborate. Near Medinet Habou, south of the Necropolis, M. Bruyère excavated the remains of the workmen's village which housed the men working on the great tombs of the Eighteenth Dynasty kings. Here are the foundations of scores of small compact mud-houses, built along regularly-spaced streets. Their occupants may not have been allowed to cross the river to Thebes but have had to live near their work. A track leading from the village over the hills to the Royal Valley can still be traced.

Apart from the royal tombs, which are in a class to themselves, the Theban tombs can be divided roughly into two main types. First there were the tombs of the nobles and high officials, usually consisting of an offering-chamber decorated with carved or painted scenes depicting the life which the deceased hoped to enjoy in the other world. Beyond was another chamber, or in some cases several chambers, containing the mummified body, and the funerary furniture, i.e. the dead man's bed, chairs, clothes, arms and beloved personal possessions, together with food-offerings.

The other and more common type of tomb was a communal catacomb in which men and women who could not afford individual tombs were buried in vast numbers, the mummies being stacked from floor to ceiling like bales of cloth in a storeroom. Most of the hundreds of mummies scattered about the world in museums and collections were taken from tombs of this type. From the time that mummies acquired a market value these tombs were ruthlessly robbed by the local Arab population, particularly from the village of Sheikh Abd-el-Gournah, which is on the site of the Necropolis. To-day most of these communal tombs are empty, but for a description of their condition a century ago there is no better guide than our friend Giovanni Belzoni, who visited Thebes in 1816 when this gruesome trade was flourishing.

Of some of these tombs [he writes], many persons could not withstand the suffocating air, which often causes fainting. A vast quantity of dust rises, so fine that it enters the throat and nostrils, and chokes the nose and mouth to such a degree that it requires great power of lungs to resist it and the strong effluvia of the mummies. This is not all; the entry or passage where the bodies are is roughly cut in the rocks, and the falling of the sand from the upper part of ceiling of the passages causes it to be nearly filled up. . . . After getting through these passages, some of them two or three hundred yards long, you generally find a more commodious place, perhaps high enough to sit. But what a place of rest! surrounded by bodies, by heaps of mummies in all directions; which, previous to my being accustomed to the sight, impressed me with horror. The blackness of the wall, the faint light given by candles or torches for want of air, the different objects that surrounded me seeming to converse with each other, and the Arabs with the candles or torches in their hands, naked and covered with dust, themselves resembling living mummies, absolutely formed a scene that cannot be described . . .

After the exertion of entering such a place . . . nearly overcome, I sought a resting place, found one and contrived to sit; but when my weight bore on the body of an Egyptian, it crushed like a band-box; I naturally had recourse to my hands to sustain my weight, but they found no better support; so that I sunk altogether among the broken mummies, with a crash of bones, rags and wooden cases, which raised such a dust as kept me motionless for a quarter of an hour, waiting till it subsided again.

In another paragraph, which would not have shamed Edgar Allan Poe, Belzoni describes his progress through

a passage about twenty feet in length, and no wider than that a body could be forced through. It was choked with mummies, and I could not pass without putting my face in contact with that of some decayed Egyptian; but as the passage inclined downwards, my own weight helped me on; however I could not avoid being covered with bones, legs, arms and heads rolling from above. Thus I proceeded from one cave to another, all full of mummies piled up in various ways, some standing, some lying, and some on their heads . . .

Fortunately the days of unrestricted plunder and exploitation are over, although much is still lost every year by clandestine digging. Fortunately, too, not all the tombs were ruined by the ruthless antiquity-hunters, but survived until the days of modern scientific excavation. Carefully excavated and lovingly restored by such men as Norman de

Garis Davies, Theodore Davis, Howard Carter and others, these tombs are now protected and guarded by the Antiquities Service. Although known as 'The Tombs of the Nobles', they are really mortuary chapels, and their paintings and inscriptions provide vivid pictures of the life of the Theban aristocracy and their dependants 3000 years ago.

We were fortunate enough to see some of the better-preserved tombs in the company of Zakaria Goneim, Chief Inspector of Antiquities for Upper Egypt. He is responsible for the care of the Theban Necropolis, which is his pride and delight. For Zakaria, a short, smiling Egyptian in his late thirties, has a quality which is rare among his countrymen, a genuine love of antiquity. He once said to us, "I divide mankind into two classes—those who are interested in the past and those who aren't. And the division between them cuts right across races, nations, and social groups. There are some who love the Necropolis. They may only be poor people, not learned, not even articulate, perhaps, but they *want* to learn. Some of your soldiers and airmen during the war came again and again and I loved to show them round. Then there are the others, some of them quite distinguished people, some of them quite charming people, but well . . ." and Zakaria broke off, flashed his white teeth and shrugged his expressive shoulders.

When we arrived at the Government Rest House, Zakaria's red tarbush was just visible above a crowd of white-turbaned Arabs, men of El-Gournah. They were trying to sell him something. "Ah, these people," he said. "Always they claim to have found some antiquity. I know it must be something pretty large if they come to me; probably a huge sarcophagus which they can't move. If it was something they could pocket they wouldn't come to the Department of Antiquities. No, they'd sell it to the Luxor dealers."

We pushed through the crowd, climbed into the Department's aged Ford and rattled off along the dirt road. A flood of derisive Arabic followed us. "These people," said the Chief Inspector, clasping and unclasping his hands and trying to look stern, "they are such rogues, and yet one cannot help liking them. I will tell you more about them later. But first, the tomb of Rekhmire." And we climbed out of the car into the blazing sun.

Professor Breasted described this tomb chapel as "the most important private monument of the Empire". Rekhmire was the Vizier, or Chief Minister under one of the most powerful monarchs of the New Empire, the great Tuthmosis III (1493–1439 BC). In his reign the Egyptian Empire had reached a high-water mark of power, and the Vizier was the most powerful man in the land next to the Pharaoh himself. The paintings on the walls of this chapel provide a unique picture of the life, duties and pleasures of a great official of this period.

The entrance opens into a narrow transverse hall, its walls painted with scenes showing Rekhmire receiving tribute from foreign delegations. There are Negroes from Nubia, bearded Asiatics from Syria, and others, the 'sea-peoples' from the islands of the Aegean, bearing vases of the distinctive Minoan type discovered by Sir Arthur Evans on the island of Crete. Row after row of men appear before the Vizier, some carrying necklaces of gold and silver, some wheat. Beyond this lateral hall is a long narrow passage, the roof of which rises steeply from the entrance to the rear wall, so that the whole chamber resembles a flattened funnel. The side walls are painted with vivid scenes showing incidents in the life of the Vizier. By virtue of his office he had authority over all the work performed in the temple of Amun.

Here we are shown the workshops in the temple, with Rekhmire looking on while lively red-brown figures in white kilts are fashioning statues, making chests and furniture, storing wheat and wine, while scribes record the store of wealth. On the other wall Rekhmire is being greeted by his relatives and friends as he steps off his boat on his return from an expedition to Middle Egypt.

Another painted scene shows Rekhmire's funeral procession with a long file of servants carrying articles of tomb furniture and chests of clothes, while others drag the cano-pied shrine containing the mummy.

Historically the most interesting scene represents the Vizier presiding over a court of law. Along the central aisle come the suppliants to plead before the great man. On either side stand officials waiting to carry out his orders while near-by lie what were once thought to be thirty rolls of law, but which are now known to be forty rods used for beating the witnesses! Every detail is included in these fascinating scenes; the messengers waiting outside, other people bowing deeply as they enter the presence. Rekhmire did not lack confidence in his own abilities, for he says of himself in an inscription, "There was nothing of which he (Rekhmire) was ignorant in heaven, in earth, or in any part of the under-world".

We move along and the scene changes. Now we are watch-ing the ladies of Rekhmire's household preparing for some social occasion. They sit in elegant attitudes, in their cling-ing white gowns, while young female slaves bring them their jewellery and perfume, arrange their hair and anoint their arms and shoulders with aromatic oils.

Another scene shows some of the pleasures which await the Vizier in the next world; for instance, there is a boat sail-ing on a pleasant lake surrounded by trees. There is no attempt at perspective, which the Egyptians hardly under-stood, but the pictures have vigorous life. In every scene the Vizier appears as a tall, dignified personage towering above the subordinate figures, as befits his importance. Sometimes his lovely wife accompanies him, wearing a close-fitting white gown falling in elegant folds, and leaving one shoulder bare after a more recent fashion.

Like the Old Kingdom tombs described in an earlier chap-ter the far wall has a 'false door' to permit the *ka* of the dead man to enter the offering-chamber, and high above in a niche was his statue, which has since disappeared. The total effect when the statue was in place, looking down from a height upon anyone entering the tomb, must have been deeply impressive. Beyond the wall should be the tomb shaft, but this, Zakaria Goneim told me, has never been discovered. He pointed with pride to the work being done by the Department of Antiquities, which was cleaning away a coating of soot from the paintings. "Until quite recently," he said, "a whole family had lived in this tomb, for years; this is from the smoke of their fires."

There are over 340 numbered and catalogued tomb-chapels on the eastern side of the cliffs, according to Baikie (*Egyptian Antiquities in the Nile Valley*), and most visitors are content to take his word for it, because to see all these places properly would take weeks. Those we saw were a small selection, skilfully chosen by the Chief Inspector for their special beauty and interest, but still only a selection. Those who would like a more comprehensive description should read Gardiner's *Topographical Catalogue of the Private Tombs of Thebes* (Bernard Quaritch). Largely through the generosity of Sir Robert Mond, hundreds of these fine tombs were excavated, copied and preserved. The principal workers were Mr. Arthur Weigall, Dr. (now Sir Alan) Gardiner, and Mr. and Mrs. N. de Garis Davies. It is mainly to them that we owe the preservation of what is left of these fascinating monuments.

But it is sad to think what has been lost for ever through the ignorance of the native tomb-robbers and the greed of the speculators who encouraged them to hack out the wall paintings and inscriptions to sell to collectors and European museums. Fortunately much still remains to be enjoyed, not only by the comparative few who can afford to visit Thebes, but by anyone who cares to consult the beautifully illustrated monographs written by the men who first excavated, drew and published the tombs in detail. For it is accurate *publication* which distinguishes scientific archaeology from mere curiosity-hunting and plunder. Much still remains to be done, the detailed copying and publication of existing monuments before they perish, and, of course, the excavation of undiscovered tombs. Sometimes a tomb is discovered and then lost, only to be rediscovered years later. Parts of the Necropolis are like a rabbit warren, and it is quite possible for an investigator to find his way to a tomb through a labyrinth of robbers' tunnels and later be unable to find his way back to it. This happened in the case of the Tomb of Kheruef, first discovered by Davies and Gardiner thirty years ago. After being 'lost' for many years it was rediscovered by Zakaria Goneim during the Second World War. This magnificent tomb belonged to a high official under Amenophis III, and we had the exceptional pleasure of being shown over it by its discoverer. Amenophis III, one of the greatest kings of the Eighteenth Dynasty (1555–1350 BC), was the father of the so-called 'Heretic King' Amenophis IV, who later changed his name to Akhnaten. Kheruef was Chief Steward to the wife of Amenophis, Queen Tiyi, and the scenes in his tomb are not merely painted but sculptured in fine relief. They have a delicacy, sweetness and sureness of line which are characteristic of the finest art of this period.

The principal scene, according to Zakaria Goneim, shows the King with the goddess Hathor and Queen Tiyi watching a processional dance in honour of the King's sed-festival (see description of *heb-sed* ceremony in Chapter IV). First come the eight slim and beautiful daughters of the King walking in pairs and carrying jars of water to purify the site of the festival. Behind them other girls are performing a graceful ceremonial dance suggesting the re-birth of life in the earth. Their bent arms and cupped hands suggest a ritual movement symbolising, perhaps, the scattering of seed and the growth of crops. In just the same way, the life of the King is to be ceremonially renewed. In other reliefs the King is seated with his lovely wife, Queen Tiyi, watching the erection of the 'djed-pillar' which symbolised the god Osiris; its erection represented the resurrection of the god. There is also a 'sham fight' between men armed with stems of papyrus, symbolising the conquest of Lower Egypt by the people of Upper Egypt. These ceremonies, still being performed 1400 years before Christ, had their origin far back in Egyptian pre-history. The figure of Kheruef himself has, in all but one instance, been erased by his enemies.

Mr. Goneim found the tomb when he was making a survey of other tombs which had been entered and mutilated by thieves. After crawling through underground passages for an hour he suddenly found himself near the ceiling of the large chamber, which was three-quarters filled with debris. It took him two months to clear the tomb and more remains to be cleared when money is available. For the time being, the Chief Inspector had to content himself with clearing the debris and carefully sealing the tomb to prevent the entry of thieves who might hack out the reliefs to sell to dealers. No objects have been found, as the tomb had been reopened in Ramesside and Ptolemaic times, and judging from the smoke-blackened walls, had at one time been used as living quarters.

After Kheruef we visited the mortuary chapel and tomb of Sennufer, not far from the workmen's village. He was a contemporary of Rekhmire, living in the reign of Tuthmosis III. He was 'Mayor of the Southern City' and 'Overseer of the Granaries and Fields, the Garden and Cattle of Amun'. A steep flight of steps leads down into the rock and turns half-right; Zakaria switches on a light, and—we are in a vine-yard! The ceiling of the chamber in which we stand has been left rough by the masons and then cunningly painted with hanging clusters of grapes to give the illusion of a canopy of vines. This, no doubt, is an allusion to part of Sennufer's office—'Overseer . . . of the Fields . . . and Garden of Amun'. Beyond is a much larger chamber, square, supported by four columns, with the walls finely painted, in which Sennufer appears with his wife Meryt, his sister Sent-nofret, and his daughter Mut-tuy, all of whose names are carefully inscribed over their figures.

Near the doorway leading out of the second chamber is a picture of Sennufer and his wife walking towards the door which leads from the tomb, and the inscription states, 'coming forth to earth to see the sun-disk every day', an echo of the text found in many Old Kingdom tombs. The pair are shown holding hands, and Sennufer wears round his neck an amulet with two arms, "which," says Zakaria, "the drago-man will tell you is a sign that they were in love . . . a pleasant theory unsupported by evidence".

Other scenes show Sennufer and Meryt in a boat making the voyage to Abydos, which was expected to take place after death as in life, and on the rear wall Sennufer is seated and receiving offerings. These pictures or sculptured reliefs were not intended as mere decoration. They had magical powers, and the fact that the same set of scenes recurs in tomb after tomb with slight variations, shows that they con-formed to a strict religious convention. They were, in fact, designed to ensure for the dead man or woman a continuance in the next world of the rank, privileges and pleasures which they had enjoyed on earth, and, above all, a never-ending supply of food offerings for the sustenance of the *ka*. Hence the groaning offering-tables piled with food and wine before which the dead man sits. Even if his descendants failed to keep up the regular offerings in his mortuary chapel, the picture of these offerings, as long as it survived, would ensure that the dead man continued to receive them.

As long as it survived, but what if it was damaged or des-troyed? Then, thought the Egyptians, the *ka* would suffer a like injury, and this gave the enemies of the dead an oppor-tunity to carry their malice beyond the grave. Not all the mutilation which these paintings have suffered is due to antiquity-hunters. Some of it was undoubtedly done by the Ancient Egyptians themselves in order to impair their enemies' prospects in the after-life. For instance, in the tomb of Menena, 'Scribe of the Fields of the Lord of the Two Lands', Menena cannot see his food offerings, as some enemy has hacked out his eye. Neither can he watch his fields being ploughed, nor see to spear the fish or aim his throwing-stick at the birds in these familiar scenes. The foe was very thorough. In the latter scene, he has cut through Menena's throwing-stick close to the thumb of his right hand and the same thing has happened to the fish-spear.[1] This unpleasant trait in the character of the Ancient Egyptians is one which even the kings shared, as they sometimes mutilated their predecessors' monuments in just the same way.

It is more pleasant to reflect on the Egyptians' obvious love of life and nature. Some of the tomb-chapels glow with colour, with vivid evocations of outdoor life. Papyrus skiffs sail among the bird-haunted reed marshes or on tree-fringed lakes. Cattle browse in the fields in high summer while a man sleeps beneath a tree. In spring, the ploughman drives his team of oxen along the furrows, and later we see brown-skinned figures in white loin-cloths, bringing down the ripe corn in swathes beneath their sickles. Here, the little brown men are treading the grapes while others draw off the juice for storage in jars, each marked with its vintage year. There, other men are catching wildfowl in nets, and here sits a man plucking them and preparing them for the table.

Although the same scenes occur again and again, the artist has found means, as artists will, of circumventing the religious convention which imposed a wearisome uniformity. Here and there he has contrived to introduce touches of individuality. For instance, in the tomb of the astronomer, Nakht, is a lively scene in which the nobleman is feasting his guests. While they recline in their rich apparel, slaves serve food and wine, and naked girls play and dance before them. Here sits the astronomer himself, smiling upon his guests, but what is that object under the great man's chair? It is his cat. Having stolen a chicken, she is now about to consume it out of sight of her master. The arched back and bristling fur of the animal are delightfully drawn.

In the same tomb, Nakht is standing in his papyrus boat hurling a throwing-stick at the wildfowl, a familiar scene in practically every nobleman's tomb. In the boat his daughter holds his legs to prevent him falling out, but his wife is tenderly holding an injured bird in her hand—again a human touch. In another tomb, the colours of which are as fresh as

[1] And the Coptic monks destroyed the girls' faces.—L. C.

if painted yesterday, we noticed, in the familiar scene in the fields, two little girls having an energetic quarrel and pulling each other's hair. There was also the tomb-chapel of a gentleman with the formidable name of Zeserkerasonb, who was steward in the house of a much more important man, the Second Prophet of Amun in the reign of Tuthmosis IV (1413 BC). Evidently the steward was rich enough to purchase a commodious tomb, which contains, besides the usual offering-scenes, some idyllic pictures of the country, with labourers working in the fields and sometimes pausing to refresh themselves from a water-skin hanging from a tree. There is also a feasting scene like that of Nakht, but including one touch of realism which is absent from that tomb. In the middle of the festivities one of the guests is quietly turning away to be sick. This was not, Zakaria assured us, an indication of the poor quality of the food, but of the abundance of the host's liquid refreshment. The same scene occasionally occurs in other tombs. Sometimes the unhappy guest is a woman, who is being assisted by a slave.

Then there is the so-called *Tombeau des Graveurs* which belonged to two sculptors of the late Eighteenth Dynasty, an indication that at this time a great artist could rise to a high rank. Their names were Nebamun and Ipuky, and the paintings in their tomb-chapel allow us a glimpse inside the great workshops which must have flourished in the Necropolis 3000 years ago. Some are carving emblems which are to be fitted into a portable shrine of a type which has been found in Tutankhamun's tomb. Others are weighing the precious metals from which they make collars and gold vessels. One man is carving a sphinx, another is soldering metal using a blow-pipe, while Nebamun examines specimens brought for inspection.

One quality seems to have been shared by all these tomb-builders—an unashamed delight in self-praise, a determination that their character and deeds should not go unnoticed by the Lords of the Underworld. There is a pathos in this; there is also, in some of the self-laudatory inscriptions, a certain unconscious humour. For example, in that of Ineni, who was Clerk of the Works during the reigns of five Pharaohs. He was the man who hollowed out the first tomb in the Royal Valley, that of Tuthmosis I, who set the fashion for succeeding monarchs. "It was", says Ineni in his inscription, "a job such as the ancestors had not done which I was obliged to do there. I shall be praised for my wisdom in after years, for who shall imitate that which I have done?" And he adds: "I continued powerful in peace and met with no misfortune; my years were spent in gladness. I was neither a traitor nor a tell-tale, and I did no wrong whatever. . . . I was foreman of the foremen, and did not fail . . . and I never blasphemed against sacred things." Of this Mr. R. Engelbach, who for years held high office in the Department of Antiquities, is reported to have said, "If he handled Oriental labour for some forty years without blaspheming, it was not the least of his achievements".

CHAPTER IX

THE ROYAL VALLEY

THE Valley of the Tombs of the Kings . . . "The very name", wrote Howard Carter, "is full of romance, for of all Egypt's wonders there is none, I suppose, that makes a more instant appeal to the imagination. Here, in this lonely valley-head, remote from every sound of life, with the 'Horn', the highest peak in the Theban hills, standing sentinel-like a natural pyramid above them, lay thirty or more kings, among them the greatest Egypt ever knew."

In fact the story of the Royal Valley (Plate 13) is superior to the most extravagant flights of romantic fiction. It out-Riders Haggard. It has drawn visitors over a longer period of time than any monument in Egypt except the pyramids.

The last Pharaoh to be buried there was laid to rest 3000 years ago. A thousand years later it had become a show place. Greek and Roman tourists carved their names in it. Medieval hermits made homes in its empty tombs. Eighteenth-century savants probed it, 19th-century archaeologists combed it from end to end. Yet it kept the greatest of its secrets until the twenties of this century; perhaps it is keeping some still.

Until the Eighteenth Dynasty (1555 BC) the Theban kings seem to have been buried on the eastern side of the mountain, as were the nobles. They still adhered to the pyramidal form for their tombs, but the pyramid had shrunk to a mere pigmy of 60 feet high, with the mortuary chapel closely adjoining. No doubt they were robbed as were their predecessors, and it was this which led later Pharaohs to seek to conceal their sepulchres. The chief difficulty was that it had always been considered necessary to build the mortuary chapel as near the tomb as possible, in order that the *ka* could have easy access to it from the burial chamber. As the mortuary chapel could not be concealed its presence naturally gave away that of the tomb. It is typical of the conservatism of the Egyptian mind that it took over 1000 years to recognise this fact and act upon it. The first Pharaoh to break with tradition appears to have been Tuthmosis I, the third king of the Eighteenth Dynasty, but it cannot be known whether the idea was his or that of his architect and Clerk of the Works, Ineni. This was the gentleman who never swore in his life, whose tomb-inscription we quoted at the end of the last chapter. "I attended to the excavation of the cliff tomb of His Majesty alone," he says, "no one seeing, no one hearing . . . I shall be praised for my wisdom in after years . . ." The side chosen was an amphitheatre in the hills, approached by a narrow valley-road which winds round the northwestern end of the Necropolis and then turns southward before debouching into the Royal Valley. "Although only screened from the teeming life of the Nile Valley by a wall of cliffs, it seemed to be infinitely remote and unearthly, a sterile, echoing region of the underworld or a hollow in the mountains of the moon."

Even to-day, when at the height of the season the valley teems with visitors and their attendant dragomans, it never loses its mystery, and in the evening, when the last tourists have streamed back to their hotels, the Eternal Habitation of the kings returns to its old silence and majesty. High above the deep, shadowed defile stands the highest point of the Theban hills, the Peak of the West (Plate 13), which the Ancient Egyptians believed was the home of a dreaded serpent-goddess, Meres-ger, the 'Lover of Silence'. Looking up at the lonely sentinel, golden in the sunset, one remembers the ancient text:

Beware the goddess of the Western Peak. She strikes instantly, and without warning.

From Tuthmosis I onwards through the Eighteenth, Nineteenth and Twentieth Dynasties, king after king had his tomb hollowed out of the cliffs of the valley, and as the years passed each Pharoah tried to make a more magnificent sepulchre than his predecessor. At first the chief aim was concealment. The tombs of the early Eighteenth Dynasty kings, Tuthmosis I, Tuthmosis III, Amenophis II and Queen Hatshepsut were sited in remote, mysterious recesses. Their entrances were inconspicuous. But when it became evident that even these precautions were of no avail against the thieves, aided as they probably were by corrupt officials and police, secrecy was abandoned. In the Nineteenth Dynasty the Ramesside kings (so called because most of them bore the name Ramesses) opened their tombs boldly on each side of the valley-road, tunnelled out long broad galleries which descended for hundreds of feet into the heart of the mountain, and relied for the protection of their bodies on concealed burial chambers, and massive granite sarcophagi. Meanwhile, on the other side of the cliffs, facing the Nile, rose the great mortuary temples of the kings whose bodies lay in the valley: the Ramesseum, the temples of

Sethi I, Amenophis III, Ramesses II, and Hatshepsut's terraced temple at Deir-el-Bahri. The spirits of the dead kings now had to pass through the mountain wall in order to receive the temple offerings, but this, apparently, was no longer considered a serious handicap.

"There must have been a time", writes Baikie, "when more wealth, both in sheer bullion and in artistic craftsmanship, was stored away in this desolate valley than in any other spot in the world; but it is highly improbable that it lasted for very long, or, indeed, that even all the treasures of a single dynasty remained intact at its close, or for more than a few years after. . . . Scheme after scheme failed in its turn; the gigantic pyramids of the Old Kingdom, the elaborate puzzle-passages of the modest pyramids of the Middle Kingdom, alike proved powerless against the hereditary skill of the native Egyptian tomb-robber."

After the Twentieth Dynasty (1200–1090 BC) no more kings were buried in the Royal Valley. Under the weak government of the later Ramesside kings the tomb robberies became even more frequent and daring, as we know from papyri describing the trials of some of these robber-gangs. Eventually the Valley, most of its tombs stripped and empty, was abandoned. The might of the Pharaohs, respect for the dead, fear of the gods, had all proved less powerful than mankind's eternal lust for gold. The Greeks and the Romans came; their historians Strabo and Diodorus Siculus came to the Valley, set down their careful observations, and went away. Some of their more careless contemporaries also came, and left their scribbled remarks, such as "I, Philastrios the Alexandrian, who have come to Thebes, and seen . . . the work of these tombs of astounding horror, have had a delightful day". When Christianity came to Egypt, the Copts built their monasteries nearby and some Christian hermits lived in the tombs themselves. Then the Arab invaders arrived, searching for buried treasure. Throughout all these invasions one people remained, the descendants of the Ancient Egyptians, a poor and conquered race now, their glory vanished, living among the ruins of their ancestors' monuments, and sometimes within their tombs. Throughout these many centuries the name of the valley survived, though now changed into Arabic, the Biban-el-Maluk, the 'Gate of the Kings'.

In the 17th and 18th centuries venturesome European travellers began to penetrate as far as Thebes and risked the violence of the wild men of 'Gournou' to examine the wonders of the Royal Valley. We have already encountered Richard Pococke who ventured here in 1745, and "viewed these extraordinary sepulchres of the kings of Thebes with the utmost pleasure" though worried lest "the people of Gournou might pay us an unwelcome visit . . .". But seventy years later, the invasion began in earnest. The deciphment of the hieroglyphs, the newly-awakened interest in Ancient Egypt, brought a succession of antiquity-hunters to Thebes, and sooner or later most of them dug in the Valley. Among them, of course, was Belzoni, who in 1817 discovered and cleared a number of tombs, including those of Ay, Mentuherkhepeshef, Ramesses I and Sethi I. All had been completely stripped in antiquity—coffins, mummies, funerary furniture had all disappeared. But in opening the tomb of Sethi I, the great Nineteenth Dynasty warrior king whose empire reached from the Fourth Cataract of the Nile to the sources of the Jordan, Belzoni revealed what is undoubtedly the most magnificent sepulchre in the Valley.

The discovery, he wrote:

has paid me for all the trouble I took in my researches. I may call this a fortunate day, one of the best, perhaps, in my life; I do not mean to say that fortune has made me rich, for I do not consider rich men fortunate [nevertheless he sold the sarcophagus for £2,000], but she has given me that satisfaction, that extreme pleasure, which wealth cannot purchase; the pleasure of discovering what has long been sought in vain, and of presenting the world with a new and perfect monument of Egyptian antiquity, which can be recorded as superior to any other in point of grandeur, style and preservation, appearing as if just finished on the day we entered it; and what I found in it will show its great superiority to all others.

There was a strong element of the showman in Belzoni. After opening the tomb he spent twelve months making drawings and wax impressions of the tomb paintings, and reliefs. These he took to England and with them produced a replica of the tomb in Piccadilly, London, which he called the Egyptian Hall. Here the fine alabaster sarcophagus of the Pharaoh was exhibited for some months before being sold to Sir John Soane, who placed it in the Soane Museum, Lincoln's Inn Fields, where it can still be seen.

When we visited Sethi's tomb, it no longer appeared "as if just finished" as it did to Belzoni. The torches of thousands of 19th-century visitors have begrimed the colour and sheen of its mural paintings, but the grandeur of the whole conception remains unimpaired. Although it is the grandest of the Nineteenth Dynasty hypogea, it has features which are common to practically all of them, and can therefore stand as a model of a Pharaoh's 'House of Eternity' in the great days of the Empire.

Sethi I, son of Ramesses I, was the third king of the Nineteenth Dynasty (1350–1200 BC). He came to the throne just after his thirtieth year, at a time when the turbulent Bedouin tribes, taking advantage of a long peace, had begun to stir up trouble in south-west Asia. The energetic young King led his armies into Palestine, scattered the Bedouin, restored order, then marched northward as far as the Lebanon, where he secured the allegiance of the Lebanese chiefs, who for half a century had not seen a Pharaoh at the head of his army in Asia. Later he campaigned vigorously and successfully against the Libyans, Egypt's western enemies, reopened the routes to the gold-mines in the south-east, and built magnificently at Karnak, where the temple reliefs record his victories. He reigned for over twenty years, during many of which his workmen must have been hollowing out his great tomb, which "descends into the mountain through a series of galleries and extensive halls no less than *four hundred and seventy feet* in oblique depth" (Breasted). Even this great length is exceeded in the tomb of Queen Hatshepsut, which extends for about 700 feet.

From the entrance a broad flight of stairs plunges into the mountainside. At the bottom of these we entered a long corridor which still sloped downwards, its walls covered with religious symbols. Above us rows of painted vultures stretched their wings; on each side were the symbols of Amun-Re, as a disc, as a beetle and as a ram-headed man. On we went, down another broad stairway, accompanied by painted bas-reliefs of Amun-Re in many varied forms, most of them hideous. The cold air, the gloom, after the sunlit Valley, the endless echoing galleries with their tribe of animal-headed gods made us feel that we were entering the Underworld. We descended another long corridor, on the walls of which the sun-god, in his sacred barque, was passing through the fourth and fifth divisions of the Underworld. At the end of this passage we found ourselves looking across a pit 40 feet deep, spanned by a modern bridge.

The pit had two functions, to trap any storm-water which might enter the tomb, and to baffle the thieves. Originally the entrance to the corridor beyond the pit was walled up, so that the tomb appeared to end at this point. But the robbers were not so easily deceived. They bridged the pit, burrowed through the wall and continued as we did, entering a four-pillared hall, in which was another picture of the sun-god's journey, a motif which is repeated again and again in this and other royal tombs. Beyond the hall, a doorway leads to a second hall, with two pillars, the walls being decorated with scenes which had been drawn but never finished. This again was a blind alley intended to fool the tomb-robbers, for the tomb seemed to end here. Once again, however, the thieves were suspicious. They sounded the walls, and finding the one on the left rang hollow, broke through and found *another* staircase descending further into the mountain. This staircase had been sunk in the floor of the preceding hall and then filled in flush with the floor. We continued our descent.

Still there seemed no end to the corridors and stairways which sloped deeper and deeper into the rock. We were now approaching the heart of the mountain. We entered an antechamber adorned with fine reliefs showing the Pharaoh being greeted by the deities with whom he was now co-equal; Hathor, the goddess of love; Anubis, the jackal-god, protector of the cemeteries; Osiris, god of the dead, and Horus, his son. A few steps further and the corridor suddenly opened into a huge square chamber supported by six pillars, all carved out of solid rock, and beyond it was a lofty hall, the 'Golden Hall' as it was called by the Egyptians. Under its high-vaulted roof, along which the gods and demons of the Underworld passed in procession, the Pharaoh himself had lain, and here Belzoni found the empty alabaster sarcophagus, its surface incised with hundreds of minute figures and religious texts. On each side other smaller chambers opened out, all glowing with painted and sculptured reliefs. These had once contained the funerary furniture, the royal thrones, the royal beds, the golden war-chariots, the jewel-chests of inlaid ivory and gold; the heaped-up treasure of a god-king who commanded the wealth of most of the known world.

All gone. Only an empty sarcophagus remains, blackening in the smoke of far-off London.

This is not the end of the tomb. Below the place where the sarcophagus stood, another passage dives into the rock and penetrates for another 300 feet before a fallen roof bars further progress. "Among the men of Gourna", said Zakaria Goneim, "are some descended from those who assisted Belzoni. They will tell you that their ancestors allowed the Italian to believe he had found the burial chamber, but that in reality it lies even deeper under the mountain, at the end of this passage." His shoulders made an expressive comment. ". . . Still, there is no doubt that this passage goes much further. Perhaps at one time it passed right through the mountain and connected with Sethi's mortuary temple on the other side. Maybe, some day, one of us will find it."

Although no two tombs in the Valley are alike, most conform to a pattern of which Sethi's tomb is a highly-developed example. There are a number of descending passages linked by staircases, there is the pit, the bricked-up walls and concealed stairways intended to deceive the robbers. Finally there is the burial hall with the sarcophagus which once contained the body, and adjoining smaller chambers for tomb furniture. There is, moreover, another way in which the royal hypogea resemble each other and differ markedly from the tombs of the nobles described in the last chapter. *They do not contain scenes of everyday life.*

The ordinary mortal, whether he was a nobleman, merchant or citizen, hoped to enjoy in the next world the happiness he had experienced in this. He could not conceive a different form of existence, only a perfection of earthly pleasures, perfect hunting, perfect fishing, perfect harvests, an assured supply of the good things of life. True, he would have to appear in the Judgment Hall of Osiris where his heart would be weighed in the balance while Thoth, the ibis-headed god of truth, recorded the result (Plate 2). There were also trials through which he must pass before he reached the hall, many gods who would ask awkward questions, many demons to be outwitted or placated. But by the time of the New Empire the priesthood had produced lengthy and elaborate books of magical spells, 'manuals of infernal geography' by the aid of which the soul might make the journey through these perilous regions unscathed. There the dead man or woman would find all the questions they would be asked, and the correct answers to give.

These scrolls, complete with the judgment scene which included the inevitable verdict of acquittal, were sold by the priestly scribes to anyone who could afford to buy them. One version was called the *Book of what is in the Duat* (the Underworld). Another was the *Book of the Gates* and purported to describe each of the twelve divisions of the Duat through which the boat of the sun-god passed, with the gates or portals which divided them. The *Book of what is in the Duat* was derived from spells which were painted inside the coffins of the Middle Kingdom. These products of the priestly imagination side-tracked the development of Egyptian religion into dubious byways. Though crude and primitive, the ancient Osirian doctrine did contain some elements of ethical belief. There were the so-called 'negative confessions' in which the dead man affirmed that "I have never taken a thing belonging to another person . . . I never oppressed one in possession of his property . . . never was there one fearing because of one stronger than he . . ." and sometimes more positive statements such as "I gave bread to the hungry and I clothed him who was naked . . ." Such moral compulsions must have weakened considerably when it was possible, by buying a book of spells, to put the gods in one's pocket.

So, in the the time of the New Empire, the nobleman and private citizen, after filling in his name in the space provided, had his scroll of magic placed in an appropriate niche in his tomb, or on his mummy. That, he hoped, would look after his welfare in the Underworld. Meanwhile, on the walls of his tomb, he caused to be painted scenes which affirmed his position in society and reproduced the earthly pleasures he hoped to enjoy in a future existence. Not so the Pharaoh. Being himself a god, and the son of Amun-Re, he did not need to re-live his earthly life. On the walls of the royal tombs we find no scenes of fishing and fowling, hunting and feasting. The only exception is in the tomb of Ay, who was not of royal descent or even of high rank. He was a priest who seized power after the death of the boy-king, Tutankhamun, and in his tomb there is a curious mixture of both types of tomb-paintings, the familiar scenes of daily life and the ritual scenes in which the Pharaoh consorts with his fellow gods.

But in other royal sepulchres the walls of the long corridors are covered with paintings copied from one of the magical books, the *Book of what is in the Duat* and the *Book of Gates*. These show the progress of the sun-god's sacred barque through the twelve divisions of the Underworld, corresponding to the twelve hours of night. The king, as a god, hopes to be admitted to the sun-god's boat, to pass with him in safety through the dread Underworld where ghostly creatures lie in wait to trap unwary spirits who do not know the magical formulae. Having passed through the Duat, the king hopes to be re-born each morning like Re himself, and to journey with him in his boat across the sky. These two books were compiled by the Theban priests who hoped to prove thereby the omnipotence of their god, Amun-Re, but the more ancient Osirian doctrine was so deeply rooted in the minds of the people, that Osiris, as god of the dead, had also to be incorporated in the revised theology. He ruled over one of the divisions of the Duat, and even Amun-Re could not pass through his region without the use of the requisite 'words of power'.

It is in the light of these beliefs that we must try to understand the meaning of such great tombs as that of Sethi I. The long corridors joined by staircases seem to have represented the caverns or regions into which the Underworld was divided, and the funeral ceremony was probably an imitation of the journey which the dead king would have to make. It must have been a dreadful ritual in which the royal coffin, carried on the shoulders of the chanting priests, moved slowly from chamber to chamber while other priests re-enacted the scenes in which friendly or hostile spirits helped or tried to hinder its progress. Here is an example of the questions which the dead man was expected to answer. Actually they are taken from an even earlier document, the *Book of the Dead*, but they are equally characteristic of the later books. The translation is by Sir Peter Page Renouf and Sir Wallis Budge.

The king has arrived before the Hall of Righteousness and speaks to its guardian gods:

KING: Hail, ye gods. I know ye, and I know your names, let me not be stricken down by your blows; report not the evil which is in me to the God whom ye follow . . .

127

QUESTIONER: Who, pray, art thou? What is thy name?

KING: "He who groweth under the Grass and dwelleth in the Olive Tree" is my name.

QUESTIONER: Pass on then.

KING: I pass to a place north of the Olive.

QUESTIONER: What didst thou see there?

KING: A thigh and a leg.

QUESTIONER: And what said they to thee?

KING: That I shall see the greetings in the land there of the Fehkhu.

QUESTIONER: What did they give thee?

KING: A flame of fire and a pillar of crystal.

QUESTIONER: And what didst thou to them?

KING: I buried them on the bank of the lake of Maait as Provision of the Evening.

QUESTIONER: And what didst thou to the flame of fire and to the pillar of crystal after thou hadst buried them?

KING: I cried out after them and drew them forth, and I broke the pillar and made a tank.

QUESTIONER: Thou mayest now enter through the door of the Hall of Righteousness, for thou knowest us.

Along the walls of the corridors marches a procession of nightmare creatures which like surrealist paintings, seem to have been dragged from the depths of the unconscious (Plate 15). Between them moves the barque of the sun-god with its attendant gods, while on the banks of the Underworld river wait the strange demons and monsters who have survived from the depths of Egypt's pre-history. Here is another quotation from the *Book of the Dead* called 'The knowing of the pylons of the house of Osiris, in the Garden of Aarru'.

. . . The fifth pylon; the flame, the lady of the words of power, who gives joy to him who addresses his supplications to her, to whom no one who is on earth will come near. The name of the doorkeeper is: he who coerces the rebels . . .

. . . The eighth pylon; the burning flame whose fire is never quenched; she who is provided with burning heat, who sends forth her hand and slaughters without mercy . . .

. . . The fourteenth pylon; the lady of fear, who dances on the impure, to whom the Haker festival is celebrated on the day of the hearing of yells . . .

. . . The fifteenth pylon; the evil one, with red hair and eyes, who

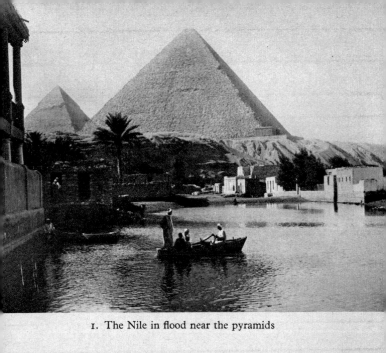

1. The Nile in flood near the pyramids

2. A scene from the *Book of the Dead*. *Left*, the dead man, Ani, and his wife watch Anubis, the jackal-god, weighing their souls against a feather. *Right*, Thoth, the ibis-headed God of Writing, records the judgment, and behind him a crocodile-headed monster waits to devour condemned souls

3. Amun-Re, King of the Gods

4. One of the Amarna Letters: a baked-clay tablet with cuneiform writing

5. The Rosetta Stone

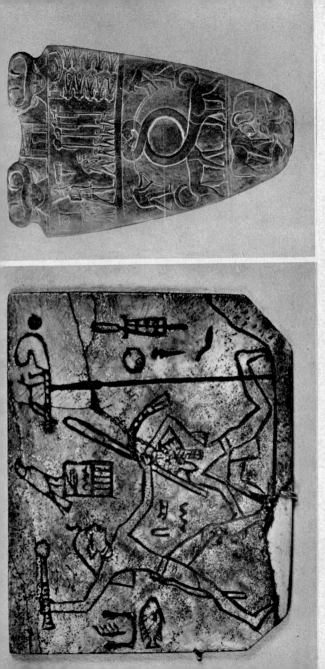

6. Ivory plaque, found in the royal tombs at Abydos, showing King Udimu smiting the Asiatics. 7. Slate palette commemorating the victories of Narmer (Menes), founder of the First Dynasty. The top register shows him in triumphal procession. Note decapitated enemies

8. Painted siliceous limestone figure of King Djoser, found in a small stone chamber on the north side of the Step-Pyramid

9. Sekhmet, the lioness-headed Goddess of War

10. King Djoser's Step-Pyramid, the oldest of the pyramids and the first large stone building in the world

11. King Djoser's Temple

12. Luxor from the air

13. The Valley of the Tombs of the Kings, with the Peak of the West, home of the goddess Meresger, 'the lover of silence', in the background. The low wall with standing figures covers the entrance to Tutankhamun's tomb. Above it is the larger entrance to the tomb of Ramesses VI

15. Wall-painting from the tomb of Ramesses IX depicting the boat of the sun-god (represented as a beetle) passing through the underworld preceded by serpents. *Below*, the serpent-goddess

14. The temple of Amun-Re at Karnak: part of the Hypostyle Hall, built by Sethi I

16. Tomb of Tutankhamun: the Ante-chamber, stacked with the King's furniture. In the background, gold-encased couches with animal heads, a bed (on top of couch), boxes containing garments and personal belongings, stool (bottom left), and wooden cases containing mummified birds (under couch)

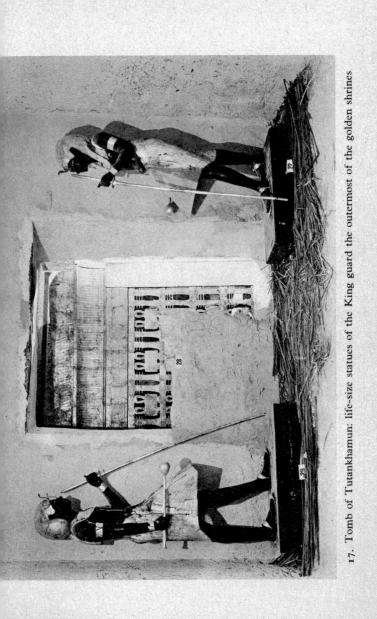

17. Tomb of Tutankhamun: life-size statues of the King guard the outermost of the golden shrines

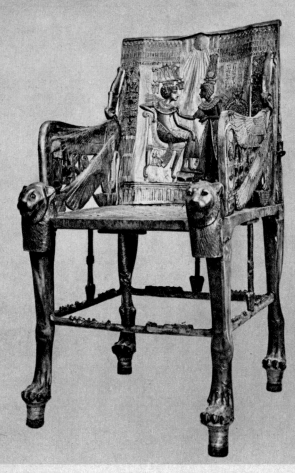

18. The golden throne of Tutankhamun. The back-rest relief, worked in gold, silver and coloured stones, shows the Queen anointing the King's shoulder. Above them is the Aten disk, with descending rays

19. Tutankhamun's solid gold innermost coffin, inlaid with carnelian and lapis-lazuli. Eagles' wings enfold the upper part of the coffin, winged goddesses the lower part

20. Nefretiti,
wife of Akhnaten

21. Akhnaten

22. Detail of a painting from the tomb of the Vizier Nakht (18th Dynasty), showing guests at a feast. *Top right*, the blind harper

23. An amusing detail from another 18th-Dynasty tomb-painting. *Above*, two girls quarrelling in a cornfield. *Below*, a girl removing a thorn from another's foot

24. Sculptured relief from the tomb of Ramose, an 18th-Dynasty nobleman. He is shown with his wife seated before an offering table

25. Karnak: the Sacred Lake

comes out at night, who binds her enemy all round, who puts her hands over the god whose heart is motionless, in his hour (of danger).

... The eighteenth pylon; she who likes fire, who washes her knives, who loves cutting heads, the welcome one, the lady of the palace, who slays her enemies in the evening ...

Even to-day there are some who would endow this gibberish with a mystical significance, but it is doubtful if it had any for the civilised Egyptians of the New Empire. It seems to us that these unintelligible spells were part of an elaborate trick by which the Egyptians hoped they could hoodwink the menacing powers which would try to deny them survival in the after life. The meaning of the words was unimportant. It was their effect which mattered, like the combination which opens a safe. Read them again. Are they not like the nightmare fantasies of childhood, or those grim 'fairy-stories' which, according to psychologists, embody fragments of the remote pre-history of the human race? The tomb paintings in the Royal Valley are more than 3000 years old, but they open a window on a world compared with which they are modern. In them are embedded scraps of belief which have survived from an incredibly far-off epoch, before the first civilisation grew up along the Nile Valley. In that world the savage ancestors of the Ancient Egyptians lived in fear, surrounded by hostile forces which had to be outwitted by magic or placated by blood-sacrifice.

What didst thou see there?
A thigh and a leg ...

Is it too fanciful to see in those words a sinister connection with those pre-dynastic graves which Petrie found at Nagadeh, with their strangely dismembered bodies?

CHAPTER X

THE LOST PHARAOHS

". . . but it was found to have been robbed in antiquity". How often one finds that rueful little phrase in the record of modern excavators! Their ambition is to find an intact burial. Sometimes they seem to be within sight of their goal. The original entrance is found untouched, and their hopes rise, only to be dashed when on penetrating to the central chamber, they find that the ancient tomb-robbers have been here before—by another route. To be the first to enter at sepulchre since antiquity is the rarest of experiences, but one which compensates the archaeologist for all his previous disappointments. We remember the late Professor Newberry describing to us how he entered a Theban tomb which escaped the attentions of thieves, and found, on the dusty floor, the footprints of the last person to leave it—3000 years ago. There is also this memorable passage from Howard Carter's book, *The Tomb of Tutankhamun*.

> For a moment, time as a factor in human life has lost its meaning. Three thousand, four thousand years may have gone by, and yet, as you note the sign of recent life around you—the half-filled bowl of mortar before the door, the blackened lamp, the farewell garland dropped upon the threshold, you feel it might have been yesterday. The very air you breathe, unchanged through the centuries, you share with those who laid the mummy to its rest . . .

But such romantic sentiments are uncommon among Oriental peoples. Before the growth of the European antiquity-cult, the Egyptians had one simple motive for entering a tomb—to get at the gold, silver and precious stones it contained. This single-mindedness has sometimes worked to the advantage of later archaeologists, as the looters often overlooked objects of great artistic worth because they had no financial value.

But, in the main, the tomb treasures suffered badly, and the mummies worst of all, as they were often adorned with precious ornaments. Such robberies were inevitable from the nature of Egyptian burial customs. The very presence of great wealth underground was bound to attract daring and determined thieves. In Thebes, for example, the Necropolis police had to protect not only the tombs of the nobles but even those of the kings and queens from these enterprising robbers, who were drawn from the great numbers of artisans who lived near the Necropolis. These men made the tombs and knew what was buried in them. They formed themselves into bands, and with the complicity of the guards and local officials, penetrated into the underground chambers, opened the sarcophagi, cut up the mummies and took away the valuable objects.

When the Pharaoh was powerful the royal hypogea would be reasonably safe, but under a weak and corrupt administration the robbers became more daring. We know that under the Ramesside kings of the Twentieth Dynasty the robbers had already begun to attack the pyramid tombs of the Eleventh Dynasty kings on the eastern side of the hills, facing the Nile. By a fortunate chance rolls of papyri have survived from this period describing the trials of certain of these robbers, and revealing in addition an amusing political intrigue. The story of how the two halves of one of these papyri were brought together is in itself one of the romances of Egyptology.

Part of the papyrus, brought from Egypt nearly 100 years ago, belonged for a time to Lord Amherst of Hackney and is called the Amherst Papyrus. But it was incomplete; only the upper half remained. (Arab treasure-seekers, when they find a roll of papyrus, frequently break it in half and sell the halves separately in order to get a bigger price.) Such was the position until one February morning in 1935, when Monsieur J. Capart, the distinguished Belgian scholar, arrived at the Royal Museum of Art and History in Brussels. He had come to examine a collection of Egyptian antiquities, part of the royal collection which had been presented to the museum. They had been brought from the Nile Valley by the Duke of Brabant in the 'sixties and, from Capart's account, seem to have been quite an average collection such as wealthy travellers made in those days: a few bronze figures and statuettes of faience, some vases and so on. Among them he found a wooden funerary statuette with a painted inscription giving the name Khay, superintendent of works and royal scribe in the temple of the king. Such figures are often hollow, and originally contained funerary papyri, so Capart was not surprised to find a roll of papyrus inside this one. Naturally he thought it was an ordinary funerary papyrus and did not even bother to unroll it until he had had lunch. What happened afterwards is best described in his own words:

> I began by raising the outer fold of the roll with the point of a knife. My readers will understand the peculiar sensation which came over me as I read, for the benefit of those present, the date of Year Sixteen of Ramesses the Ninth (c. 1126 BC). This year is famous in the annals of Egyptology. It is that of the celebrated Abbott Papyrus, which has been in the British Museum since 1857 . . .

He goes on to describe how, after laying the roll on damp blotting-paper, the outer layer peeled off, and Capart recognised the cartouches of King Sekhemre-shedtaui, son of Re Sebekemsaf. Hurriedly he sent to the library for the catalogue of Lord Amherst's papyri as edited by Professor Newberry. This catalogue contains a facsimile of the Amherst Papyrus.

> One can judge my surprise, indeed my stupefaction, as a single glance at one of the plates of the catalogue revealed the fact that the lower edge of the new papyrus fitted exactly the upper edge of the Amherst, and that where the latter only showed fragments of signs, the piece we were in the course of unrolling gave their missing portions.

After nearly a century a miraculous chance had brought together the two halves of this most valuable document, from which we can read the whole story of a robbery which took place in the Twentieth Dynasty and the trials which followed. The Abbott Papyrus in the British Museum tells the first part of the story. The Leopold II–Amherst Papyrus completes it. The two principals in the drama are Pesiur, the Mayor of Thebes, and his rival Pewero, who, as Prince of the West, was responsible for the safety of the royal tombs. It seems that Pesiur had alleged that certain tombs in the Royal Valley had been violated. His motive in making this accusation may have been loyalty to the Pharaoh, or personal hostility to Pewero. At any rate the latter immediately took steps to meet the accusation by forming a commission to inspect the tombs and report on their condition. The Abbott Papyrus contains the report of this Commission, which found, no doubt to Pewero's relief, that most of the tombs were intact. But not all:

> The pyramid-tomb of King Sekhemre Shedtaui, son of Re Sebekemsaf. It was found to have been violated by the thieves tunnelling in . . . from the outer hall of the rock-tomb of Nebamun, Overseer of the Granary of King Menkheperre. The burial chamber of the King was found empty of its lord and likewise the burial chamber of the great royal wife, Nubkhaas, his consort, the thieves having there laid hands upon them. The Vizier, the notables and the butlers investigated the matter, and the nature of the attack which the thieves had made on this king and his consort was discovered . . .

Pesiur had made further accusations concerning robberies in the Valley of the Queens, known as the 'Place of Beauty'; he even named the robbers. So next day, day nineteen, the Commission set out to examine the queens' tombs, taking with them the suspected men, the leader of whom was a coppersmith named Peikhar. The Abbott Papyrus continues:

> . . . Now the Vizier and the butler had this coppersmith taken in front of them to the tombs, blindfolded as a close prisoner, and he was given his sight when he reached them. Then the notables said to him, 'Go before us to the tomb from which you say you brought these things.' And the coppersmith went before the notables to a tomb of certain of the royal children of King Usimare Setpenre the Great God, in which no burial had been made and which had been left open, and also the house of the workman Amenomone, son of Hui, of the Necropolis, saying, 'behold the places where I was . . .'

After severe 'examination' in the Great Valley, the unfortunate coppersmith is alleged to have said: "I take my oath on pain of being beaten, of having my nose and ears cut off, and of being impaled, that I know of no place here among the tombs save this tomb which is open and the house I pointed out to you."

Delighted with the result of the inquiry, Pewero's friends crossed over to Thebes and staged a demonstration to annoy Pesiur. They met the Mayor near the temple of Ptah at Karnak and a noisy altercation took place. In the Abbott Papyrus we can read the actual words of this 3000-year-old quarrel. "You have rejoiced over me at the very door of my house!" shouts Pesiur. "What do you mean by it? For I am the Prince who reports to the Ruler! If," he roars above the jeers, "you are rejoicing concerning this tomb . . . which you have found intact, yet King . . . Sebekemsaf has been violated, together with Nubkhaas, his royal wife. A great ruler he . . ."

Userkhepesh, chief of the workmen, denies this, affirming that "all the kings and their royal wives and royal mothers and royal children . . . are intact. . . . The sage counsel of Pharaoh, their child, guards and examines them strictly!"

"Your deeds belie your words!" retorts the angry Mayor, and goes on to speak of five very serious charges "involving mutilation or the severest penalties," which, he says, he is reporting "to Pharaoh my Lord, to cause him to send servants of Pharaoh to deal with you".

On hearing of this threat Pewero played his cards skilfully. He informed the Vizier, or Prime Minister, Khaemwese, of Pesiur's intention to report "certain serious charges" to the Pharaoh, well knowing that, in his own interests, the Vizier would wish to hush the matter up. A tribunal met two days later but the only evidence considered was that concerning tombs which had *not* been robbed. In this way Pewero no doubt hoped to throw ridicule on Pesiur's accusations and draw attention away from the fact that several tombs, including that of King Sebekemsaf, *had* suffered violation.

Pesiur, who was present at this tribunal, had to sit impotently by while the Vizier reprimanded him.

So far we have quoted from the Abbott Papyrus. The Leopold II–Amherst Papyrus, as the other is now called, describes the trial of the men accused of robbing the pyramid-tomb of King Sebekemsaf. It is pleasant to record that the much-abused Pewero was present on this occasion. The most interesting part of this document is the confession of one "Amenpnufer, the son of Anhernakhte, a stonemason of the house of Amun-Re, King of the Gods". He begins by stating quite boldly that "I fell into the habit of robbing the tombs in company with the stonemason Hapiwer, the son of Meneptah", and that "when the Year Thirteen of Pharaoh our Lord had begun, four years ago, I joined with the carpenter, Setekhnakhte . . . the decorator, Hapio . . . the field labourer, Amenemhab, the carpenter, Irenamun, the water-pourer, Khaemwese . . . and with the boatman of the Mayor of Thebes—in all eight men".

Then the Vizier says, "Describe how you came to rob the tomb of this god."

"Well," replies Amenpnufer, "we went to rob the tombs in accordance with our regular habit, and we found the pyramid of Sekhemre Shedtaui, the son of Re Sebekemsaf, this being not at all like the pyramids and tombs of the nobles which we habitually went to rob." Here is an inindication that at this time the Theban robbers had only begun to turn their attention to the kings' tombs.

Amenpnufer goes on to describe how, with their copper tools, he and his companions forced their way into the pyramid.

Then we broke through the rubble . . . and found this god lying at the back of his burial-place. And we found the burial-place of Nubkhaas, his queen, situated beside him. . . . We opened their sarcophagi and their coffins in which they were, and found the noble mummy of this King equipped with a falchion; a large number of amulets and jewels of gold were upon his neck, and his head-piece of gold was upon him. The noble mummy of this King was completely bedecked with gold, and his coffins were adorned with gold and silver inside and out and inlaid with all kinds of precious stones.

We collected the gold we found on the noble mummy of this god ... and we collected all that we found on her (the Queen) likewise; and we set fire to their coffins. We took their furniture ... consisting of articles of gold, silver and bronze, and divided them amongst ourselves. ... Then we crossed over to Thebes. And after some days the District Superintendent of Thebes heard that we had been stealing in the west, and they seized me and imprisoned me in the office of the Mayor of Thebes. And I took the twenty *deben* of gold which had fallen to me as my portion and gave them to Khaemope, the scribe of the quarter attached to the landing place of Thebes. He released me, and I rejoined my companions, and they compensated me with a portion once again. Thus I, together with other thieves who are with me, have continued to this day in the practice of robbing the tombs of the nobles and the people of the land who rest in the west of Thebes. And a large number of people of the land rob them as well, and are as good as partners of ours.

The rest of the document records the condemnation of the thieves and that a report was sent to the Pharaoh.

To us the confession of the stonemason, Amenpnufer, is one of the strangest and most moving documents which have come down to us from the ancient world. Anyone who has visited the sepulchral chambers of the Egyptian kings will remember the awe with which they strike even the least sensitive modern traveller. Imagine, then, the feelings of Amenpnufer and his seven companions, fearing the terrible punishment which awaited them if they were caught, but fearing even more the wrath of the King whose tomb they were violating. For to them he was a god. In the flickering light of their torches they would see, on the walls of the burial hall, the carved and painted figures of the denizens of the Underworld, and of the dread gods who were now the companions and protectors of the King. Perhaps some would hesitate, afraid, until greed and desperation drove them on, and the bolder spirits rallied the faint-hearted. Then ... the ringing blows of the hammers on copper, the splitting open of the sarcophagus, the breaking of the triple coffins, and the tearing of the funereal wrappings. Finally flames and smoke from the burning mummies blackening the sacred inscriptions as the thieves struggled back through their tunnel, clutching the gold and silver ornaments which had adorned the royal bodies.

This particular robbery took place in the time of the Ramesside kings of the Twentieth Dynasty, but later, under the weak rule of the Twenty-first Dynasty kings, the robbers became even more audacious and penetrated into the Royal Valley itself. The priests of the Necropolis seemed powerless to protect even the great Pharaohs of the Empire whose names and deeds were fresh in memory. Again and again the tombs were entered, though sometimes the thieves were interrupted before they could complete their work. When this happened the Necropolis priests would re-wrap and re-coffin the mummies, supply fresh adornments and furniture and re-bury them; but sooner or later the thieves struck again. Finally the priests gave up trying to protect each individual tomb. There were too many, and probably an insufficient number of reliable police to guard them. Their chief concern was to ensure the safety of the mummies themselves, for once these were destroyed all hope of their royal owners' survival would vanish. But where could they find a place which the robbers would not discover? Eventually they hit on a plan.

As absolute secrecy was essential the operation was almost certainly carried out at night, possibly in one night. All the royal mummies were collected from their hiding-places and brought together in the Royal Valley. They were then divided into two groups. The smaller group of thirteen mummies was hidden in the tomb of Amenophis II in the Valley. The remainder, some thirty-six Pharaohs, queens, princes and princesses, were carried up a bridle-track over the mountain to the western side, where the cliffs recurve in a series of natural amphitheatres. In one of these, at the foot of a deep crevice in the cliff-face, a shaft had been sunk 30 feet into the rock, with a horizontal gallery branching out from its base and ending in an oblong chamber. Into this, their last hiding-place, the mummies were lowered from above, carried along the gallery and crammed into the small chamber, which was barely large enough to hold them. Then the shaft was sealed, and before daybreak the priests and their helpers had dispersed. Though they may not have known it at the time, they had won the last trick. The secret died with the men who had buried the kings, and the royal dead lay undisturbed for 3000 years.

The secret shaft was eventually re-discovered in 1871, by descendants of the ancient tomb-robbers. The finder was one Ahmed Abderrasul, a native of El-Gournah, who survived until the early years of this century. The late Professor Percy Newberry, who knew him personally, gave me the following account of how Ahmed found the Pharaohs.

Accompanied by his elder brother Mohammed and a stranger, Ahmed was indulging in a little illicit digging in the Theban hills when they found the shaft. Ahmed volunteered to explore it. He was lowered by a rope, and found himself facing a sealed passage which, when he had broken through the sealing, led him to a burial chamber full of mummies. Ahmed realised that the secret must be kept at all costs from the stranger, or the rest of El-Gournah would soon know of it. He hurried back to the bottom of the shaft and called to his friends in an agitated voice to draw him up at once. He told them that he had seen an *afrit*—an evil spirit, and they all hurriedly left. To make doubly sure of keeping unwelcome inquirers away Ahmed returned that same night with a donkey, which he killed and hid in the shaft. *Afrits* are always recognisable by their evil smell, and in a few days' time there could be no doubt that a particularly noxious specimen lived in the shaft. Then, after allowing a decent interval to elapse, Ahmed again descended, removed the donkey, and made a more thorough search. He discovered that most of the mummies were covered with cartouches and had an *uraeus* (royal cobra) on the forehead.

The diggers of Thebes [writes Maspero in *Les Momies Royales*] had known for a long time that these were the marks of kingship. Our man knew his craft too well not to recognise that chance had delivered to him a full tomb of Pharaohs. Never had anything similar been seen within the memory of men, but the find, though very valuable, was difficult to exploit. The coffins were many and heavy, a dozen workmen were not too many to move them, and it would be necessary to set over the opening of the shaft a structure of beams and ropes which would be impossible to conceal.

The Abderrasul family therefore decided not to attempt to remove the mummies for the time being, but to content themselves with selling the more portable objects, which could easily be concealed. First they took away a number of funerary statuettes, some scarabs, canopic jars, figures of Osiris and some half a dozen funerary papyri. Every winter they sold to tourists some of their loot, and it was this which eventually put the Department of Antiquities on their track; though not for many years.

In 1881 the Keeper of the Cairo Museum was the famous Sir Gaston Maspero, perhaps the greatest of a long list of scholars who had held this distinguished post. From the nature of the objects, all of the Twenty-first Dynasty, which came on the market in that year he realised that the natives had found one or more tombs of that period. Inquiries were begun, and after long and patient research certain of the objects were traced to Ahmed Abderrasul, his brother Mohammed and a certain Mustafa Aga Ayat, Consular Agent at Luxor of Great Britain, Belgium and Russia. The latter could not be sued, being covered by his diplomatic immunity, but orders were given for the immediate arrest of Ahmed Abderrasul. Maspero, with Emil Brugsch, the Assistant Keeper, interrogated Ahmed without success. "Abderrasul denied all the actions which I imputed to him following the unanimous testimony of the tourists, and which fell directly under Ottoman law, namely clandestine digging, unauthorised sale of papyri and funerary statuettes, breaking up of coffins and objects of art belonging to the Egyptian State . . . softness, threats, offers of money, nothing succeeded."

One of the reasons for Ahmed's obduracy was that Mustafa

Aga Ayat had persuaded him and his associates that under his protection they would be untouchable by the officers of the local administration. It was noticed that Abderrasul pointed out several times that he was a servant of Mustafa, living in his house. In this way the Consular Agent had succeeded in getting his hands on most of the trade in antiquities on the Theban plain. However, Ahmed was soon to be disillusioned when he was handed over to the local authorities for examination. The *Mudir*, *i.e.* the Turkish Governor, of the province was noted for his severity. Many years after Ahmed pointed out to Newberry the scars on the soles of his feet.

After two months' imprisonment Ahmed returned to his family, an angry and embittered man. He had kept the secret, and in return demanded from Mustafa a larger share of the treasure. At first he had wanted a fifth. Now he demanded a half, and threatened to give away the secret to the authorities if this was refused. Quarrels broke out between the brothers and their associates. Mohammed, realising that disclosure was imminent, decided to take the matter into his own hands. On June 25th he went to the *Mudir* and told him he knew the whereabouts of the tomb.

Maspero was in Paris. The Assistant Keeper, Emil Brugsch, on receiving the message, set out from Cairo, and arrived at Keneh on July 4th, when he was handed a parcel of antiquities thoughtfully presented by Mohammed Abderrasul. It contained four canopic jars of Queen Ahmes Nefetari, and three funerary papyri of other queens. Encouraged by this start, Brugsch and his companions set out for Deir-el-Bahri, led by Mohammed Abderrasul. It was in the sweltering heat of July, a time when, normally, all archaeological work has ceased, that the expedition entered the narrow alley and Brugsch was lowered into the shaft. What he found there is best described in his own words.

After telling how he crawled with difficulty along the narrow gallery crammed with coffins he entered the main burial chamber, where, he says:

. . . every inch . . . was covered with coffins and antiquities of all kinds. My astonishment was so overpowering that I scarcely knew whether I was awake or whether it was only a dream. Resting on a coffin, I mechanically cast my eyes over the lid, and distinctly saw the name of King Sethi I, father of Ramesses II . . . a few steps further on, in a simple wooden coffin, with his hands crossed on his breast, lay Ramesses II, the great Sesostris himself. The further I advanced, the greater was the wealth displayed—here Amenophis I, there Ahmes, the three Tuthmoses, Queen Ahmes Nefetari—all the mummies well-preserved, thirty-six coffins, all belonging to kings or queens or princes or princesses . . .

The bodies were not, of course, in their original gold coffins, as most had been disturbed and re-buried in ancient times. On the wrappings the priests had left dockets on which they had recorded the names of the dead, their successive re-burials, and the places in which they had been hidden before they reached this final repository. Ramesses III, for instance, had been re-buried three times. "These successive records," writes Breasted, "in which one may trace their transfer from tomb to tomb in the vain effort to find a place of safety, form perhaps the most eloquent testimony of the decadence of the age. . . ."

Not all the lost Pharaohs were present, however, Hatshepsut was missing; so were Amenophis II and Amenophis III and Meneptah. Great significance was attached by Christians to the absence of Meneptah, as he was believed at the time to be the 'wicked Pharaoh' of the Exodus who had been drowned in the Red Sea. For the time being, however, these absences did not worry the Department of Antiquities, which was fully occupied in putting the newly-found Pharaohs out of reach of the robbers. In two days Brugsch had cleared the shaft, an extraordinary feat. Maspero writes:

Two hundred workmen were gathered through the effort of the *wakîl* of the *mudîriyah* and began to work . . . forty-eight hours of relentless effort sufficed to take everything out, but only half the task was accomplished. It was necessary to transport the objects across the plain of Thebes and across the river of Luxor. Most of the coffins were lifted with great difficulty by twelve to sixteen men and it took seven or eight hours to transport them the distance between the

141

mountain and the bank; it can be imagined what that journey must have been in the dust and heat of July. . . . Three days later the ship *El Menshiya* arrived; after the necessary time had been spent in loading she was again at full steam on the way back to Bulak [in Cairo].

Then a strange thing happened, perhaps the strangest incident in the whole story. From Luxor down to Kuft on both banks of the Nile the fellahin fired guns, as is customary at funerals. Fellah-women with loosened hair followed the steamer, sending up the old wailing cry for the dead which has probably come down from Pharaonic times. Many of these people were robbers and had lived for years by despoiling the tombs of their ancestors. But they were also descendants of the Ancient Egyptians. The foreigners had found their kings and were taking them away. This was their last instinctive act of homage.

This story, which has been told many times, came back to us vividly when Zakaria Goneim took us to the actual shaft where the royal mummies were found. It was evening. The valley lay below, lonely, deserted and in shadow. We sat beside the deep rock-cut shaft, while the setting sun tipped the distant cliffs with gold, and from the high desert behind us a jackal barked.

"Even now very few people know where this place is," he said. "The dragomans usually point out another place much lower down, but they're quite wrong. I only discovered it myself by studying the old records."

We asked him if the rest of the missing mummies were found.

"Yes," he said, "by Monsieur Loret in 1893. He opened the tomb of Amenophis II in the Royal Valley and found thirteen more royal bodies."

"Including Meneptah?"

"Including Meneptah, but by that time it had been decided that he was not, after all, the Pharaoh of the Exodus, so his discovery did not cause the stir it would once have made. But Loret found the warrior-king, Amenophis II, still lying in his own sarcophagus, and beside him lay the

142

great bow which, Amenophis boasts on his monuments, no one else in his army could draw. Loret also found Tuthmosis IV and his son Amenophis III, the father of Akhnaten."

One sometimes hears the Department of Antiquities criticised for taking the royal mummies to Cairo instead of letting them remain in their own tombs. Actually only two kings were discovered in their original sarcophagi, Amenophis II and Tutankhamun, and these have been left where they were found. Even so the risk is great, because tomb-robbery is by no means a dead art, nor are some of the Necropolis guards any less susceptible to corruption. For instance, after Loret's discovery of the tomb of Amenophis II, it was decided to let the body of the King remain in his sarcophagus, as it was found. Two years later, on November 24th, 1901, the night guards at the tomb reported that they had been overpowered by armed men who had entered the tomb, stripped the body and stolen its funerary furniture. Howard Carter, who was then Inspector of Antiquities, hurried to the spot and made an examination. The King had been tumbled out of his coffin and thrown on the floor. "The bandages", writes Carter in his official report, "had been ripped open, but the body not broken. This had evidently been done by an expert, as only the places where objects are usually found had been touched. The boat in the ante-chamber had been stolen, the mummy that was upon it was lying on the floor and had been smashed to pieces. I carefully examined the wrappings of the royal mummy to see if there were any signs of their having contained jewellery but could find no traces . . ."

Alas for the hopes of the robbers! Their ancestors, 3000 years before, had done the job only too well.

Carter, who had had long experience of the inhabitants of El-Gournah, examined the padlocks of the tomb and found that "they had been stuck together and made to look all right with little pieces of lead paper", which pointed to the tomb having been robbed with the connivance of the guards. Within the tomb Carter took measurements of bare footprints left on the floor and with the aid of a "spoorman" tracked similar footprints to a house in Gournah, that of Soleman and Mohammed Abderrasul—a name we seem to have heard before. Measurements of Mohammed's footprints were taken and found to agree to a millimetre with those in the tomb, but the charge could not be brought home to him and the missing boat was not found.

Back at the Department's rest-house Zakaria Goneim talked to us about the present-day inhabitants of Gournah.

"When I first came to Thebes," he said, "I hated them bitterly. I took every possible means to rescue the ancient tombs from their hands. But having worked among them for so long, I have come to like them, in spite of myself. Some are rogues, I admit, and yet . . . well, they are the only living link with the people of Ancient Egypt. They are directly descended from the embalmers, craftsmen, painters, sculptors and artists who lived here 3000 years ago."

We asked him what else they did besides tomb-robbing.

"*Everything!*" he exploded, with a helpless gesture. "You saw how they hovered round me when we arrived at the rest house. They said they had found some antiquity which I must see—found it quite by accident, of course. Well, maybe they have, maybe not. But if they don't find anything, then they're quite capable of making it. I remember during the war an English airman coming to me with a nearly perfect statue of Queen Nefretiti, of the so-called Amarna period of Egyptian Art. It was beautifully done, an exquisite piece of work. He told me he had bought it in a shop in Luxor for forty pounds, and asked if it was authentic. I looked at it, and told him that there is not one statue of the Amarna period in so perfect a state. Even some museums do not own so perfect a statue of the Amarna period, and if they did it would be worth many thousands of pounds. The statue was a fake, made at El-Gournah."

Some of the Gournah craftsmen are so skilful that their work has deceived experts. Goneim told us another story of a distinguished English excavator, who, many years ago, came to dig in the Necropolis. He was rich and paid his workmen well, but although he dug energetically for months he found nothing of importance. This worried the work-men, who reasoned that if the effendi did not find anything soon he would lose heart and they would lose their jobs. So they decided that he *should* find something. One morning the English excavator called excitedly to his head workmen to help him to clear the sand from an object he had found. The workmen gave a cry of joy. The effendi had found a marvellous figure of the Eighteenth Dynasty. Other fellahin gathered round, wildly excited. They formed a procession and marched to the rest-house, shouting and singing, and carrying the statue before them. Encouraged by this success, the excavator continued to dig, and though no more valuable finds were made, he was satisfied. It was not until years later that a discrepancy in the headdress worn by the figure proved that it was a fake, specially buried for the Englishman to find.

Customs and religious beliefs inherited from the ancient Egyptians still survive among these people, as do a number of ancient Egyptian words which are found nowhere else in Egypt. For instance, in Pharaonic times the mountain peak which dominates the Necropolis was believed to be the home of the goddess Meres-ger, the 'Lover of Silence'. She was greatly feared by the inhabitants and may have had a shrine on the hill opposite the peak. To-day there is a Moslem shrine on the summit of this hill and there the people of the Necropolis place offerings, although such offerings are not a part of the Moslem religion. The people are following an ancient tradition; they are still making their offerings to the Peak of the West.

Music plays a great part in the life of the people of the Necropolis. Living, as they do, among the bones of their ancestors one might imagine them to be a melancholy race, but the reverse is true. They have songs for every occasion, and most of them are gay. In their songs for springtime and harvest, love songs and feasting songs, aspects of a remote past still survive, as vivid and sparkling as ever. The harvest song begins:

> The grain has ripened, and it says to us, "harvest me".

In the 3000-year-old tomb of Menena, over a painting of men and women in the harvest fields, is a harvest song:

> Oh, men, women and children, rejoice in the produce of the fields at this time. Rejoice in the glory of Menena . . .

The Department of Antiquities has put a ban on all unlicensed digging, and to-day it is said to have almost ceased. The Necropolis guards patrol the area, and the Inspector and his staff keep constant watch. Even so there are times when the people of El-Gournah still manage to outwit the authorities. The Department realised that the only way to prevent further robberies was to remove the inhabitants from their old homes under the cliff face, and allow no one but the guards to live in the Necropolis. When we were at Luxor the authorities had almost completed building a new model village for the inhabitants at a safe distance from the tombs.

"But", concluded Zakaria with a smile, "when we have moved these people from their mud-houses on the cliff-face to the modern village on the plain, I am not sure whether I shall be glad or sorry. The antiquities will be much safer when these rascals have gone, but, when they leave, a 3000-year-old link with the past will be broken, and the Necropolis will become truly a place of the dead."

CHAPTER XI

THE GREATEST DISCOVERY

IN 1817, when Belzoni had finished his investigations in the Royal Valley, he wrote: "It is my firm opinion that in the valley of Biban-el-Maluk there are no more tombs that are not known, in consequence of my late discoveries. For previous to quitting that place, I exerted all my humble abilities in endeavouring to find another tomb, but could not succeed."

Subsequently more investigators dug in the Valley, Champollion, Burton, Rosellini, Rawlinson, Lepsius and others. They, too, left with the conviction that the Valley was exhausted. Then in 1898 came Loret's surprising discovery of the tomb of Amenophis II with its hoard of royal mummies, and this convinced other would-be excavators that there were still tombs to be found. Wealthy amateurs became interested in Egyptology and applied to the Egyptian Government for permission to excavate. In 1902, an American, Theodore M. Davis, obtained the concession. He provided the funds, but the actual work of excavation was carried out by the staff of the Antiquities Service, among whom were Arthur Weigall, Edward Ayrton, J. M. Quibell, and a young man named Howard Carter.

Carter entered the ranks of the Egyptologists by a curious route. His father was a professional 'animal-painter', an art of which there are fewer exponents now than in Victorian times, when thousands had their favourite pets recorded in this way. The young Carter inherited his father's skill in draughtsmanship and in 1891 he came to the notice of Professor Percy Newberry, who had just returned from Egypt with a mass of pencil tracings from the tombs at Beni Hasan. Carter was employed for three months at the British Museum inking in these tracings. He did the work so well that in the following year the Committee of the Egypt Exploration Fund agreed that young Howard Carter should accompany Professor Newberry to Egypt. During the next eight years Carter became absorbed in Egyptological work. He obtained his first experience of digging under Petrie, and worked as a draughtsman to the Archaeological Survey under Newberry. Then in 1899, when Maspero entered on his second term as Director-General of the Antiquities Department of the Egyptian Government, he appointed Carter Inspector in Chief of the Monuments of Upper Egypt and Nubia with his headquarters at Thebes.

It was during this period that he helped to carry out excavations for Davis, discovering, in 1903, the tomb of Tuthmosis IV. In subsequent years Weigall, Ayrton and Davis found further tombs, including that of Prince Yuia and his wife Tjuiu, which yielded the best-preserved specimens of chariots and funerary furniture discovered up to that date. In 1907 Ayrton and Davis opened a small tomb in which were fragments of a large gilded wooden shrine bearing the name of Queen Tiyi, wife of Amenophis III, together with a damaged royal coffin containing the mummy of a young man. This caused considerable excitement at the time, as it was thought that the body might be that of Akhnaten, the so-called 'heretic' son of Amenophis III and Queen Tiyi. From later investigations, chiefly by Mr. R. Engelbach, it now seems fairly certain that the body is that of Akhnaten's half-brother, Smenkhkare.

In the same year Lord Carnarvon arrived in Egypt and began an association with Egyptian archaeology which was to have great consequences. He was recovering from a serious illness following a motor accident, and had decided to winter in Luxor. Like others before him he became interested in Ancient Egypt, and hearing of the finds which had been made at Thebes, obtained permission to excavate, though not at first in the Royal Valley, where Theodore Davis still held the concession. "After Carnarvon had completed a short season alone," writes Professor Newberry,

"Maspero insisted that if another permit was granted an expert excavator must be employed, and Carter was recommended." Thus began a collaboration which lasted many years.

Meanwhile the indefatigable Davis and his helpers continued to probe the Biban-el-Maluk, until in 1914, after twelve seasons digging, he stated that in his view there were no more tombs to be found. Carnarvon, who, with Carter, had waited long for an opportunity to dig in the Valley, took over the concession from Davis, though Maspero, who signed the authorisation, agreed that the site was exhausted. Owing to the First World War, Carter was not able to commence serious work until 1917. Mr. Charles Breasted has an interesting note on Carter's working methods in *Pioneer to the Past*, his biography of his father, Professor James Breasted. "To make absolutely certain", he writes, "that not a square inch of [the Valley] floor should escape examination, he [Carter] made a large-scale map of it upon which he subdivided the terrain into convenient sections; and as his excavations of an actual area progressed and he had satisfied himself that it contained nothing of value, he checked off the corresponding sections on the map."

The 1917 season yielded nothing of importance. Neither did 1918. It began to look as if Davis and Maspero were right. Still Carnarvon had faith, and Carter continued his patient search. Most of the Pharaohs had been accounted for, it is true, yet there were still gaps which might be filled. 1919 . . . 1920 . . . 1921 passed but still without result. So, in the summer of 1922, Carnarvon, back in Britain, summoned Carter to his home at Highclere Castle to discuss whether or not they should continue this apparently hopeless task. Breasted describes this meeting:

When they met at Highclere, Lord Carnarvon reviewed the history of the work, expressed his appreciation of the years of effort Carter had given to it, then said that in view of post-war economic stringency he would find it impossible to support this obviously barren undertaking. . . . Carter said that their consistent failure to find anything

149

had not weakened his conviction that the valley contained at least one more royal tomb, probably that of Tutankhamun, the existence of which was strongly supported by circumstantial evidence.

Tutankhamun, like the ephemeral Smenkhkare whom he succeeded, was an obscure boy-king who reigned briefly at the very end of the Eighteenth Dynasty. He was one of the few Pharaohs of this period whose tombs had not been accounted for.

The evidence on which Carter pinned his hopes was a small cache of baked clay jars which Davis had found in the Valley fifteen years previously. These jars were full of bundles of linen and small objects known to have been used in funeral processions; and on the clay sealings to some of these jars was the cartouche of Tutankhamun. This seemed to indicate that the King himself must have been buried somewhere in the Valley. Still Carnarvon seemed doubtful. Carter then produced his map of the Valley floor on which, season after season, he had systematically recorded the progress of their excavations. He spread it out on the table before Carnarvon. At first glance it appeared that every inch of the Valley had been examined. There was, however, a small triangular area in front of the tomb of Ramesses VI which had not been tackled because work there would temporarily have barred visitors to the Ramesside tomb. Until this area had been dug, said Carter, they could not say that they had exhausted every possibility. He added that if Carnarvon would allow him to use his concession, he, Carter, would himself bear the cost of another season's excavation. Carnarvon was a sportsman, and this offer appealed to him. He agreed to another and final season of investigation at his own expense.

The two men shook hands on it, and in that autumn of 1922 Carter returned to Egypt for what was to be his farewell season in the Valley of the Kings' Tombs. He arrived at Luxor on October 28th. Nine days later, on November 6th, Dr. (now Sir Alan) Gardiner and his wife were sitting down to dinner in London when the telephone rang.

Dr. Gardiner picked up the receiver and heard Lord Carnarvon's excited voice. "Listen to this," he said. "It's a cable I've just received from Carter . . . 'At last you have made wonderful discovery in Valley; a magnificent tomb with seals intact; re-covered same for your arrival. Congratulations.' "

*　　*　　*　　*　　*

What had happened in those nine days? Here are Carter's own words (*The Tomb of Tutankhamun*):

> By November 1st I had enrolled my workmen and was ready to begin. Our former excavations had stopped short of the north-east corner of the tomb of Ramesses the Sixth, and from this point I started trenching southward. By late afternoon of the third, my men had laid bare the foundation stones of a row of ancient workmen's huts beneath which we had never probed. Hardly had I arrived . . . the next morning, than the unusual silence, due to the stoppage of work, made me realise that something out of the ordinary had happened. . . . The workmen had discovered a step cut in the rock immediately under the first hut to be attacked. It seemed almost too good to be true, but a short amount of extra clearing revealed the fact that we were actually in the entrance of a steep cut in the rock some thirteen feet below the entrance to the tomb of Ramesses the Sixth.

Later, when describing this moment to Charles Breasted, Carter said: "Think of it! *Twice* before I had come within two yards of that first stone step. The first time was years ago when I was digging for Davis, and he suggested we shift our work to some more promising spot! The second was only a few seasons ago when Lord Carnarvon and I decided to reserve clearance of this area for a time when we wouldn't interfere with visitors."

The step was the first of sixteen leading down into the hillside. At the bottom was a doorway, blocked and sealed with the seal of the Necropolis.

"It was a thrilling moment for an excavator," wrote Carter. "Alone, save for my native workmen, I found myself after years of comparatively unproductive labour on the threshold of what might prove to be a magnificent discovery. Anything, literally anything might lie beyond that passage, and it needed all my self-control to keep from breaking down the doorway and investigating then and there." But instead, he filled in the entrance stairway again, posted a strong guard over it, and despatched a cable to his patron.

*　　*　　*　　*　　*

Sir Alan Gardiner, the distinguished philologist, is one of the few surviving members of the small band of men and women who were directly associated with the discovery; we are indebted to him for some of the personal details which follow.

"When Carnarvon had told me the news," he said, "his first question was, 'Do you think this could be the tomb of Tutankhamun?' I said I had no detailed knowledge of the close of the Eighteenth Dynasty, but that it did seem probable. Then Carnarvon said, 'Well, this is all most exciting. I'm arranging to go out to Egypt with Evelyn (Lady Evelyn Herbert, his daughter) as soon as possible. Will you come out with me? There are almost certain to be inscriptions for you to study.' I regretted that I couldn't go until the New Year as I wished to spend Christmas at home with my children, but that I would try to get out to Luxor early in the next year. In the meantime Lord Carnarvon travelled to Egypt with Lady Evelyn, arriving at Luxor on the 23rd of November."

By the afternoon of the 24th the staircase was clear again and the excavators were able to examine the whole doorway. On the lower part were the unmistakable seal impressions of Tutankhamun. But side by side with this confirmation of their hopes, they discovered something more disquieting. Careful examination of the walled-up entrance showed that the plaster bore two sets of seal impressions: (*a*) of Tutankhamun and (*b*) of the Necropolis priests who were responsible for guarding the royal tombs. There had in fact been *two* successive openings and reclosings of the entrance, and the Necropolis seal was on the re-closed part of the door. The tomb, therefore, was not absolutely intact, as Carter had hoped. At some time in antiquity thieves had entered it, but they could not have rifled it completely or it would not have been re-sealed. Still, it was a severe disappointment, and as Carter broke down the first sealed doorway and began removing the rubble beyond, doubt was mingled with hope.

Throughout the next two days the work continued. Beyond the first sealed doorway was a sloping entrance passage filled with stone chippings which had to be removed. On November 26th, 30 feet from the outer door, the excavators found a second sealed and plastered doorway.

"At last", writes Carter in a most memorable passage of his book, "we had the whole door clear before us. The decisive moment had arrived. With trembling hands I made a tiny breach in the upper left-hand corner. Darkness and blank space, as far as an iron testing-rod could reach. . . . Candle tests were applied as a precaution against possible foul gases, and then, widening the hole a little, I inserted the candle and peered in, Lord Carnarvon, Lady Evelyn Herbert and Callender standing anxiously beside me to hear the verdict. At first I could see nothing, the hot air escaping from the chamber causing the candle-flame to flicker. But presently, as my eyes grew accustomed to the light, details of the room emerged slowly from the mist, strange animals, statues, and gold—everywhere the glint of gold. For a moment—an eternity it must have seemed to the others standing by—I was struck dumb; then Lord Carnarvon inquired anxiously, 'Can you see anything?'

" 'Yes,' I replied, '. . . wonderful things . . .' "

CHAPTER XII

'ALL THE WORLD WONDERED'

MORE than a quarter-century has passed since Carter's trembling hand pushed its way through the broken wall and his candle shone on treasures which had lain in sealed darkness for 3000 years. The sensational headlines which greeted the discovery now lie in the yellowing files of newspaper offices. The wild Press surmises, the wrangles of scholars, the argument and controversy are almost forgotten. There has been another and greater war, and if such another discovery were made to-day it is doubtful if our anxious world would be as stirred as it was in 1922. Yet the story remains, for those who care to read it, one of the greatest romances of the 20th century. Carter's pages, and those of his colleagues, still have power to quicken our hearts.

"We saw an incredible vision," wrote one of them, "an impossible scene from a fairy tale, an enchanted property room from an opera house of some great composer's dreams. Opposite us were three couches on which the King had lain, all about us were chests, caskets, alabaster vases, gold-embellished stools and chairs—the heaped-up riches of a Pharaoh who had died . . . before Crete had passed her zenith, before Greece had been born or Rome conceived, or more than half the history of civilisation had taken place. . . . Against the white limestone wall, the colours of all these things were vibrant yet soft—a medley of brown, yellow, blue, amber, gold, russet and black."

This was several days later, when Carter had broken down the second sealed door and entered the room which became known as the Ante-chamber (Plate 16). The first objects which drew the excavators' attention were the three great couches of wood encased in gold, ornamented with grotesque animal heads whose eyes seemed to watch the intruders.

Beneath them, insecurely resting on other treasures, was a rich throne, encased in solid gold and embellished with silver and semi-precious stones in an intricate and charming design which showed the King seated in a garden with his slim young Queen Ankhesnamun (Plate 18). There were hundreds of objects, large and small, chests of inlaid ivory ornamented with hunting and battle scenes, golden bows, staves, but in no kind of order. "The objects", said Sir Alan Gardiner, "were piled up like furniture in a warehouse; tidily, but not arranged in any kind of artistic grouping; except for two life-sized figures which stood to the right, on either side of a sealed and plastered door. They were of wood, coloured black and gold, each wearing the royal serpent on the forehead and each carrying a gold wand" (Plate 17).

The significance of this guarded door became clear to Carter and Carnarvon after their first bewildered examination of the objects in the Ante-chamber. "Behind the sealed door there were to be other chambers, perhaps a succession of them, and in one of them, beyond any shadow of doubt . . . we should see the Pharaoh lying." Then they began to notice other things. The room showed clear traces of having been hastily tidied after the disorderly retreat of the thieves. Evidently they had been surprised before they could do much damage; perhaps they were caught in the very act. Working in desperate haste, they had snatched as many portable objects of value as they could find. They had snapped off the gold struts under the seats of one of the royal thrones (Plate 18). They had opened the chests and tumbled out the King's clothes on the floor in their search for objects of value. The priests had hastily stuffed these clothes back in the boxes without bothering to fold them, and packed with them an assortment of small objects which had obviously come from other boxes. Most significant of all, one thief had picked up a royal headcloth and knotted within it a handful of gold rings, then flung down the treasure in his hurried exit. To the left of the entrance doorway, under one of the animal-headed couches, was an opening leading to another smaller chamber where the objects were lying as the thieves left them, in utter confusion.

It was fortunate for the science of Egyptology that this, the greatest single discovery (artistically) in the history of excavation, should have been made by a man who combined a profound knowledge of Ancient Egypt with extraordinary practical ability. Sir Alan Gardiner, who knew him well, describes him as "a strange fellow in many ways. He had a lot to contend with—official interference, irritating delays, misunderstanding and a surfeit of unwelcome publicity, and perhaps he was not the best-tempered of men. But he had great gifts. He was a superb draughtsman. He was nearly a genius in the practical mechanics of excavation, and in the recording and preservation of fragile objects of antiquity. But his greatest gift was patience."

This gift was put to its severest test when Carter opened the Ante-chamber. He had found the outer-chamber of what was almost certainly the intact tomb of a Pharaoh— the first ever found. Beyond that room, crowded with precious things, lay further chambers. One can imagine the temptation to break down that sealed door immediately. But Carter decided at the outset that he would remove the objects from the tomb only when he was ready, after every precaution had been taken to preserve them. Only then would he consider opening the second chamber. Of this preliminary work, which took two months, he wrote:

> It was slow work, painfully slow, and nerve-racking at that, for one felt all the time a heavy weight of responsibility. Every excavator must, if he has any archaeological conscience at all . . . the things he finds are not his own property to treat as he pleases. They are a strict legacy from the past to the present age, and if by carelessness, slackness or ignorance he lessens the sum of knowledge that might have been obtained from them he knows himself to be guilty of an archaeological crime.

Carter obtained permission from the Department of Antiquities to use the tomb of Sethi II as a laboratory and workshop. To this laboratory, one by one, the objects were removed for treatment before being packed for transport to Cairo. He called in other archaeologists, each an expert in his field: Lythgoe, Curator of the Egyptian Department of the Metropolitan Museum of Art, New York; Burton, their photographic expert; Winlock and Mace, also of the New York Metropolitan Museum; Hall and Hauser, draughtsmen; and Lucas, Director of the Chemical Department of the Egyptian Government. Sir Alan Gardiner was invited by his friend Lord Carnarvon to help in deciphering the inscriptions, and Professor Newberry's task, as a botanist, was identifying the floral wreaths and other plants found in the tomb. All these and other specialists gladly gave their help.

Every article, however small, was entered by Carter in a card-index file, in which every detail was recorded. These records, in Carter's small meticulous handwriting and illustrated by his beautiful line drawings, are now in the Griffith Institute at Oxford, still awaiting an individual or institution wealthy enough to pay the high cost of adequate publication.[1] Here is a typical specimen, picked out at random by the writer; one item out of more than 600 in the Ante-chamber alone. He is describing one of the king's walking-sticks:

> 48D. Stick with crook composed of Asiatic and African prisoners. Dimensions of stick proper, 2.2 centimetres. But for handle and head and arms and legs of prisoners, stick entirely covered in gold leaf on gesso.
> (a) Handle of ivory.
> (b) Plain bands with five incised lines.
> (c) Chevron pattern all the way down.
> (d) As (b).
> (e) Feather pattern on three sides; on top is relief running entire length.
> (f) An Asiatic and an African prisoner bound back to back. Binding shown as raised bar.
>   Cleaned with damp brush, sprayed with celluloid in amyl acetate and treated with melted paraffin wax.

---

[1] Since the First Edition of this work was published, an excellent new book, based partly on these notes, has been written by Miss Penelope Fox of the Griffith Institute. Its title is *Tutankhamun's Treasure*.

Reading those careful observations one sees Carter, after another exhausting day's work, bending over his notebook in that lamplit 'laboratory', tired but thankful for a little rest from the visitors who crowded the Valley in the daytime. For the world-wide publicity which the discovery had received brought with it problems which no archaeologist had had to face before. "All day long", writes Breasted, "a continual procession of messengers brought him sacks of telegrams, letters and messages from hundreds and hundreds of people entreating or demanding the privilege of entering the tomb. Each day hordes of visitors swarmed across the river and into the Valley, where they gathered round the pit at the opening of the tomb."

With the visitors came representatives of the world's Press. Hoping to simplify matters Lord Carnarvon had given to *The Times* newspaper of London a world copyright in all news and photographs. He was strongly criticised for this by other newspapers who accused him of commercialism. It is hard to realise at this distance of time the bitterness of the controversy which raged around the discovery, but the columns of contemporary newspapers bear witness. Under the heading TUTANKHAMUN LIMITED the *Daily Express* of February 10th, 1923, stated:

> While we have admiration for the faith and persistence which have brought so magnificent a reward to the labours of Lord Carnarvon, it is difficult to approve the manner in which he has seen fit to exploit his discovery . . . The tomb is not his private property. He has not dug up the bones of his ancestors in the Welsh mountains. He has stumbled on a Pharaoh in the land of the Egyptians . . . By making an exclusive secret of the contents of the inner tomb he has ranged against him the majority of the world's most influential newspapers.

To which *The Times* replied, on February 16th :

> Discreditable and unfounded aspersions have been cast on Lord Carnarvon's work. He has been charged with creating a monopoly of news from Luxor, and even commercialism . . . No charge could be more false. He supplied the news through *The Times* solely because he thought it would be the best way, in fact the only practical way, of

supplying it fully and independently to all newspapers throughout the world who wanted to take it. The character of the work compelled him to distribute news of it through an agent.

To us it seems difficult to escape the logic of this argument. To be compelled to admit *every* newspaper representative into the tomb while the delicate work was in progress would be like trying to conduct a surgical operation with the Press of the world at one's elbow.

How Carnarvon came to give the copyright to *The Times* was explained by Sir Alan Gardiner: "After Carnarvon's return from Egypt in December 1923," he said, "I saw quite a lot of him. One day, at lunch, he told me how much worried he was by Press publicity. 'I can't get a night's rest,' he complained. 'As soon as I am in bed there are telephone calls. If I walk out of my house I am stopped by some pressman.' I sympathised, but pointed out that in view of the enormous public interest in the discovery such incidents were bound to occur. The newspapermen were, after all, only carrying out their duties. While we were having lunch, Dawson, the Editor of *The Times*, called to see him. Carnarvon asked me to have a preliminary talk with Dawson, who explained, when Carnarvon had joined us, that he had come to ask him to give *The Times* exclusive rights in the story. Carnarvon said he'd never been in such a position before, but Dawson pointed out that by making *The Times* his sole agent for the distribution of news and pictures he would be saved an enormous amount of trouble. Carnarvon said he'd think about it. Later we saw the Secretary of the Royal Geographical Society and asked his opinion. He said that the Society had made a similar arrangement in connection with the Mount Everest Expedition and that it had worked very well. As a result of this, Carnarvon decided to give *The Times* the agency."

Thus the quarrel started, a quarrel which may seem trivial now but which had an important bearing on what followed. Denied access to the tomb itself, newspaper representatives hung around the Valley and the Luxor hotels trying to pick up a morsel of information which could be expanded into a cable:

> The scene at the tomb [wrote the *Daily Telegraph* correspondent on January 25th] awakened memories of Derby Day. The road leading to the rock-enclosed ravine . . . was packed with vehicles and animals of every conceivable variety. The guides, donkey-boys, sellers of antiquities, and hawkers of lemonade were doing a roaring trade. . . . When the last articles had been removed from the corridor to-day the newspaper correspondents began a spirited dash across the desert to the banks of the Nile upon donkeys, horses, camels and chariot-like sand-carts in a race to be the first to reach the telegraph offices.

No archaeologist had ever had to cope with such a situation. Carter, by nature nervous and highly strung, was now working long days at top speed under an inhuman stress. Carnarvon, too, though less actively involved, began to suffer from frayed nerves, which were not improved when he became the subject of Press attacks. Meanwhile, as the newspaper battle raged, Carter had other difficulties caused by streams of unwelcome visitors. The excavators were accused of ill-manners, selfishness and boorishness in refusing admittance to many who wished to visit the tomb. But, as Carter explained in his book, there were two dangers: first, that to admit large numbers of visitors would risk serious damage to the precious objects, and second, that to do so would involve serious loss of time. In the limited season, during which excavation was possible, every hour was important. "There were many days last season", he wrote, "in which we actually had ten parties of visitors, and if we had given way to every demand there would not have been a day in which we did not exceed the ten. In other words there would have been weeks at a time when no work would have been done at all."

Finally the Ante-chamber was cleared and Carter was ready to break down the sealed door leading to the second chamber. This was the day for which the newspapers of the world had prepared their readers; on the day of the opening pressmen and visitors were massed at the entrance to the tomb. Only *The Times* correspondent was allowed inside. The scene outside was described by the representative of the *Daily Telegraph*, who wrote:

Mr. Callender opened the massive dungeon door leading from the entrance to the steps and a number of chairs were taken down. [The chairs were for the distinguished guests, Government Officials and others who had been invited to watch the opening of the second chamber]. 'We're going to have a concert! Carter's going to sing a song!' said Lord Carnarvon very audibly, glancing up at the pressmen whose presence seemed to disconcert him. For the next three hours every sound and every incident were noted and interpreted. Sometimes it was a piece of masonry that was brought up, sometimes we heard Lady Evelyn's exclamations, sometimes the sound of chisel blows or the hammering of wood. The excitement of the watchers on the parapet grew intense as they saw labourers carrying out blocks of masonry and baskets of minor debris.

Meanwhile, within the cleared Ante-chamber, the twenty privileged guests sat watching Carter and his assistants as they broke down the sealed door between the two guardian figures. Among them was Sir Alan Gardiner, who has kindly given us this eye-witness account:

As Carter removed the upper part of the wall we saw beyond it what seemed to be a wall of solid gold, but as the rest of the masonry was taken away we realised we were looking at one side of a vast outer shrine [Plate 17]. We had seen such shrines depicted in ancient papyri, but this was the real thing. There it was, splendid in its blue and gold, and almost filling the entire space of the second chamber. It reached nearly to the ceiling, and the space between it and the walls at the sides was not more than about two feet.

First Carter and Carnarvon went in, squeezing their way through the narrow space, and we waited for them to return. When they came back they both lifted their hands in amazement at what they had seen. Then the rest of us entered, two at a time. I remember Professor Lacau saying to me jokingly, "You'd better not attempt it; you're much too stout." Anyway, when it came to my turn, I went in with Professor Breasted. We pushed our way through and then turned left, so that we were opposite the front of the shrine, which had two great doors. Carter had drawn the bolt and opened these doors, so that we could see that inside the great outer shrine, which was 17 feet long and 11 feet wide, was another, smaller shrine, also with double doors, with the seal still unbroken. In fact there were in all four of these gilded shrines, one inside the other like a Chinese nest of boxes, and within the fourth was the sarcophagus, which we were not to see until a year later.

Of this sealed door, Carter wrote:

I think at the moment we did not even want to break the seal, for a feeling of intrusion had descended heavily upon us, heightened, probably, by the impressiveness of the linen pall which drooped above the inner shrine. We felt that we were in the presence of the dead King and must do him reverence.

Sir Alan Gardiner continues:

There is one fact which it is difficult to realise at this distance of time. If you go to the Cairo Museum to-day you can see these objects. They are still magnificent, of course, but some of the gold has a slightly jaded appearance. Now when we first entered the tomb the gold shrines glittered with the greatest possible brilliancy, preserved for 3000 years in the dry atmosphere. Beyond the Burial Chamber we found on the right the entrance to another room. . . . It was full of marvels. There was the King's canopic chest guarded by four delicate little golden goddesses; there were more golden chariots, a great effigy of the jackal-god Anubis and many other precious things. There were also a number of caskets. Carter opened one of these and on the top lay a beautiful ostrich-feather fan. The feathers were perfect, fluffing out just as if they had recently been plucked. Those feathers completely annihilated the centuries for me. It was just as if the King had been buried a few days before. Of course, in a few days the feathers began to perish and had to be preserved artificially, but when I first saw them they were perfect, and they made on me an impression such as I had never experienced before and never shall again.

*   *   *   *   *

This was in February 1923. During this and the following month the excavators were faced with problems quite unconnected with archaeology. First there was the question of the so-called Press monopoly. There was also the problem caused by the increasing numbers of visitors, and thirdly the problem of the disposal of the objects themselves. Lord Carnarvon claimed that under the concession signed by the Department of Antiquities, a proportion of the finds belonged to him. With this Carter disagreed, believing that all the objects should go to the Egyptian State. In March he quarrelled with Carnarvon. Breasted writes:

> Bitter words were exchanged and in anger Carter requested his old friend to leave his house and never to enter it again. Soon after this Lord Carnarvon fell ill with fever brought on by an infected wound. For some time he had been in poor health. Pneumonia set in, and on 5th April, 1923, at the age of 57, he died. The press attributed his death to an ancient curse, and sensationalised this superstition until it became a legend.

But what are the facts? Ten years after the opening of the tomb all but one of the five men who attended the opening were still alive. Carter survived until 1939, dying at the age of sixty-six. Burton and Engelbach also lived the normal span of years. Lady Evelyn Herbert, now Lady Beauchamp, is still living, so are Mr. Winlock and Sir Alan Gardiner. Professor Percy Newberry died in August, 1949, shortly after his eightieth birthday; Dr. Derry, who performed the autopsy on the royal mummy, is over eighty. So much for the 'Curse of Pharaoh'.

The following season, 1923–24, was devoted to dismantling, preserving and removing the four golden shrines which occupied nearly all the space in the Burial Chamber. There were a bare 24 inches to spare on each side. To dismantle and remove the enormous gold-encrusted sides without damaging them taxed all Carter's skill and patience, but the job was done magnificently. On February 14th, in the presence of leading officials, the lid of the sarcophagus was raised, and the onlookers saw for the first time the splendid outer coffin of the Pharaoh, untouched since it was placed there. Professor Breasted left his sick bed to attend the ceremony. He wrote:

> There at last was the King who had slept thus in the silent heart of the mountain for some three thousand and fifty years. So he lay at rest when his girl-wife, Akhnaten's third daughter, stepped down into the burial chamber for the last time. . . . Did she perhaps, with her own fingers, gently draw over him the shrouds beneath which he

had ever since lain asleep? And in a final gesture of affection and grief, had *she* placed beside the entrance to the Ante-chamber a bouquet of delicate wild flowers, just as we had found it standing?

Then came a dramatic development. On the same day on which the sarcophagus was opened, the following notice appeared in the principal hotels of Luxor:

> Owing to the impossible restrictions and discourtesies on the part of the Public Works Department and its Antiquities Service, all my collaborators in protest have refused to work any further on the scientific investigation of the discovery of the Tomb of Tutankhamun. I am therefore obliged to make known to the public that immediately after the press view of the tomb this morning between 10.0 a.m. and noon the tomb will be closed and no further work carried out.
>
> (Signed) HOWARD CARTER.

This was the culmination of a long and bitter dispute between Carter and the Department of Antiquities of the Egyptian Government. There were two main points at issue. The first was a dispute between the Egyptian Government and the Carnarvon Estate as to whether or not Lady Carnarvon, to whom the concession had passed, was entitled to a proportion of the objects found. In this Carter tended to agree with the Government that the articles should remain in Egypt. Secondly, Carter complained that, by harassing him with minute instructions as to the manner in which he conducted the work, and particularly by sending to the tomb a stream of visitors, the Government was making it impossible for him to carry out his delicate and exacting task. In this he was supported by the other distinguished archaeologists who were working with him.

The Egyptian Government countered by cancelling Lady Carnarvon's authorisation, taking over the tomb and forbidding Carter to enter it. Carter left for Cairo to fight the case in the courts. Meanwhile the Government itself reopened the tomb to visitors, marking the occasion by a large official celebration to which hundreds of officials and their wives were invited. The proceedings were rounded off by fireworks. The correspondent of the *Egyptian Gazette* reported:

> A pathetic note was provided by two of Mr. Carter's trusted Egyptian foremen faithfully guarding a heap of their master's property, not far from the mouth of the tomb for the discovery of which they had served him with such unflagging fidelity and perseverance. Their saddened faces left no doubt as to their thoughts . . . at seeing the careless throng passing into the tomb which to them and their master represented the almost sacred crowning of the labour of a lifetime.

After the persecutions of officialdom, Carter must have found consolation in the loyalty of his Egyptian workmen, who had a high regard for him. In his book he reprints a charming letter from one of his foremen.

> Mr. Howard Carter,
> Honourable Sir,
> Beg to write this letter hoping you are enjoying good health, and ask the Almighty to keep you and bring you back to us in safety.
> Beg to inform your excellency that Store No. 15 is alright, the Northern Store is alright. Wadain and House are alright, and in all your work order is carried on according to your most honourable instructions. Rais Hussein, Gad Hassan, Hassan Awad Abdelal Ahmed and all the ghaffirs of the house beg to send their best regards.
> My best remarks to your honourable self,
> Longing to your early coming,
> Your most obediant servant,
> RAIS AHMED GURGAR.

A long legal battle followed. At one time it seemed that agreement was in sight and that Carter would be given permission to continue his work. Unfortunately, at this stage, Carter's counsel, Mr. Maxwell, in an exchange with the judge stated that "the Egyptian Government went down like a bandit and broke into a tomb". Although Maxwell withdrew the remark, the Government broke off all further negotiations and Carter returned to England more embittered than ever. Possibly he would never have gained permission to work on the tomb but for the political upheaval which followed the murder of the Sirdar in November 1924. The Nationalists fell from power, Great Britain tightened her control on Egypt, and while public attention was thus occupied, the Government allowed Carter to open the tomb.

So began the last stage of his task, the opening of the three coffins, each enclosed within the next like the four outer shrines which had enclosed the sarcophagus; the unwrapping and examination of the royal mummy, lying within the inner coffin; and the preservation and removal of the precious objects in the third chamber, which he called the 'Treasury'. The opening of the three coffins taxed all Carter's resourcefulness and skill. They nested within each other so tightly that it was hardly possible to pass a finger between them, and the funeral libations poured over them had solidified like cement. Professor Breasted, who was present when the third and last coffin was revealed, described it vividly:

> Within the second was the third and last coffin, of solid gold so heavy that four men could hardly lift it. The lid of this coffin represents the King in all his splendid regalia. The face is a portrait . . . his garments above his crossed arms are encrusted with many coloured precious stones such as carnelian, turquoise and lapis-lazuli; while below his crossed arms he is enfolded by the protecting wings of guardian goddesses whose lovely forms are elaborately graven in gold and envelop him with a net of gold plumage . . . (Plate 19).

Inside the coffin the royal mummy was adorned with an exquisitely wrought portrait mask of solid gold polished to a mirror-like sheen. The sensitiveness of the modelling, the grace and serenity of the whole conception cannot be conveyed in words, but this work by an unknown artist of 3000 years ago will stand comparison with the finest products of the European Renaissance. No doubt he was the master craftsman of his time, for no one else would have been entrusted with the task of modelling the sacred features of the Pharaoh (see cover). On the mummy were gold trappings, the finger and toe nails were covered with golden sheaths, the breast adorned with jewelled necklaces, the fingers with enjewelled gold rings. Heavy gold plaques bore welcoming speeches of the gods, addressed to the King as he entered the Underworld:

166

"My beloved son [says Geb, the god of the earth], inheritor of the throne of Osiris, the King Nebkheperre; thy nobility is perfect; thy Royal Palace is powerful; thy name is in the mouth of the common folk, the stability in the mouth of the living, O Osiris, King Tutankhamun!"

And Nut, the Divine Mother, says: "Thy members are firm; thou smellest the air and goest out as a God, going out as Atum, O Osiris Tutankhamun!"

After that it would seem almost a sacrilege to probe among the pitiful human remains which were the core of all this magnificence. But Science is implacable. The last decayed bandages were stripped from the body, which was not as well preserved as other royal mummies owing to the chemical action of the funerary libations which had been poured into the coffin before it was closed. In his report Dr. Derry, who performed the autopsy, writes:

> The effigy of Tutankhamun on the gold mask exhibits him as a gentle and sensitive young man. Those who were privileged to see the actual face when finally exposed can bear testimony to the ability and accuracy of the Eighteenth Dynasty artist who had so faithfully represented the features and left for all time, in imperishable metal, a beautiful portrait of the young King.

After examination, the King's body was replaced within the outer coffin inside the stone sarcophagus in the Burial Chamber. There it still lies. The rest of the contents were put on permanent display in the Cairo Museum. This work of clearance, preservation and removal occupied Carter for ten seasons. Some of the objects found in the tomb were in pairs or larger numbers and it was therefore suggested that an appropriate way of rewarding Carter and his American collaborators would be to present duplicate objects to the British Museum and the Metropolitan Museum of New York. The suggestion was not adopted; the Egyptian Government gave none of the treasure to either Museum.

Looking back over a quarter of a century, how does Carter's achievement appear to-day? Was it as valuable as it appeared at the time? Did the discovery add materially to our knowledge of this period of Ancient Egyptian history? When we put these questions to Sir Alan Gardiner he replied:

"I would say that the discovery has added very little to our knowledge of the history of the period. To the philologist the tomb was disappointing, as it contained no written documents. Of Tutankhamun himself we know little beyond the fact that he succeeded to the throne after the death of his father-in-law, Akhnaten, that he reigned only for a few years and that he died while still a youth. He was succeeded by Ay, an elderly priest who had been an Atenist under Akhnaten, and on the walls of Tutankhamun's burial hall he is shown officiating at the funeral ceremonies of his predecessor. There is also the interesting fact that the mummies of two stillborn infants were found in the tomb, probably his children by his young wife, Ankhesnamun.

"But as a revelation of the *artistic* achievement of the period, the discovery was quite unparalleled. Nothing like it had been discovered before, and, in my opinion, it is extremely doubtful if any comparable discovery will be made in the future. The fact that, after a superficial looting, it remained untouched for 3000 years was probably due to a lucky chance. When, many years after Tutankhamun's burial, the hypogeum of Ramesses the Sixth was being tunnelled out of the hillside above the tomb, the stone chippings from the excavation buried the entrance to Tutankhamun's much more modest sepulchre, which thus escaped [Plate 13]. The value of the discovery to archaeology lies not only in the wealth of objects it revealed, but in the fact that these lovely things were recorded and preserved with such consummate skill.

"This, the greatest discovery in the history of Egyptology, was made by an Englishman. Yet the sad fact is that the results have never been properly published in the scientific sense; that is, with a detailed description of *every* object found, illustrated by coloured plates. In 1926 Carter told me he estimated that such a publication would cost £30,000. To-day it would cost little short of £100,000. All Carter's notes exist together with his photographs and drawings. But who will finance such a publication to-day?"

CHAPTER XIII

JOURNEY TO AKHETATEN

THE train comes slowly to rest beside the long, low platform above which hangs the name MELLAWI. Doors bang open. There is a babble of excited Arabic as alighting passengers pour on to the packed platform. Coffee-coloured faces shine beneath white headcloths; bare brown feet stir the dust. You climb down, clutching your bag and looking anxiously among the crowd of chattering figures for someone who looks as though he might be the Chief Inspector of Antiquities for Middle Egypt. Could that be him at the back of the crowd, also looking anxiously around; that small, dark man in European dress and a red tarbush? It is. He's seen you, and, smiling, he comes forward, accompanied by a tall, fierce gentleman in a blue gallabiyeh and a turban with a rifle slung from his shoulder. You introduce yourselves. He is indeed the Chief Inspector. His armed attendant? That's Ahmed, one of the *ghaffirs* (guards) responsible for protecting the antiquities under their master's charge. Ahmed takes your bag and leads the way out of the station.

A cup of coffee would be welcome? Of course. You sit at a dirty marble-topped table in a wooden café beside a canal. At a nearby table two men are playing tric-trac and the clatter of the pieces keeps up a monotonous background to your conversation. Outside in the sun, the road is a river of black dust churned up by the feet of the passers-by. Above it rises the huge, vulgarly ornate 19th-century palace of the Sheikh, all pointed arches like a bastard child of the

Brighton Pavilion. At the open door of the café squats a black-robed woman, her head covered by a hood which hides most of her face. A brown, dirty child with black curly hair squats beside her. Flies cluster round its eyes and it chews a lump of mouldy bread. Heat, dust, smells, and swarming, indifferent life. You've left the clean, swept tourist-track now. This is Egypt.

But how kind is the Chief Inspector! His round brown face radiates goodwill. He takes your arm. He talks excitedly, incessantly. You have come to see Tell-el-Amarna, the city of Akhnaten, the 'Heretic King'. Well, to-morrow you are going to see it. He has arranged *everything*. It is not easy to get to the site. One must go part of the way by car, then by donkey, and it is necessary to arrange for a boat to cross the Nile, but he has arranged it all. You will see. In the meantime, you are to be his guest at the nearby town of Minya.

Here you are joined by the Assistant Inspector, who has much to discuss. How is England? He had many English friends at the University of Cairo. Professor So-and-So; do you know him? A fine man, a great scholar. And young Professor Blank who lectured on English literature. He read English Lit. himself. Your Lord Byron; now there was a poet! And your Keats and Shelley. He had a friend in Hampstead, London, who lived near Keats' house; but what about archaeology? Oh, that can come later. Talk, talk, talk, far into the night, about literature, politics, and very occasionally about Akhnaten and Ancient Egypt. That night, in your host's house at Minya, you go to bed mentally exhausted but happy. Cairo with its bitter Anglophobia seems a million miles away. You are an Englishman, and yet they seem to like you here. You feel you are among friends and that even if you never get to the city of Akhnaten it will have been fun.

Next morning you breakfast early and set off with your host for Tell-el-Amarna. It is a complicated journey. First by crowded train back to Mellawi, where you are met by an assistant and two ghaffirs. An ancient Ford car appears. You all climb in; the ghaffirs stick their rifles out of the windows to make more room. A bumping, jolting, rolling, talkative journey along grey dirt roads which run for miles alongside the sky-reflecting canals and through mud-brick villages where naked children rush out, like children anywhere in the world, and shout after the car. On you go, with Ahmed's rifle-butt between your knees, through green bean-fields and under avenues of date-palms, while your host discourses endlessly on Lord Byron. Then a flood of Arabic accompanied by large Oriental gestures; what's happened? Nothing, except that we've made contact with the party which is to take us on to the river. Liaison has been accomplished! The donkey-boys are here, on the spot, on the hour, and their beasts with them. Could organisation go further?

We all pile out of the car and warm greetings are exchanged. The donkey-boys and their friends, the ghaffirs, behave like small boys at a picnic. There is much amusement as the English effendi is helped on to his donkey. Put your foot in the stirrup; no, *not* that way! The Chief Inspector and his assistant, already mounted, look on indulgently. You note with satisfaction, however, that they look just as ridiculous seated on donkeys as you feel. And you set off in procession, riding in single file along the narrow dirt paths between the fields, the donkey-boys trotting beside you. As you accustom yourself to the pace of the surefooted little beast you lose your sense of the ridiculous. Snatches of the Old Testament float into your consciousness . . . "riding upon an ass" . . . where had you read that? Of course, Balaam in the Book of Numbers:

> And Balaam rose up in the morning, and saddled his ass, and went with the princes of Moab. And God's anger was kindled because he went; and the angel of the Lord stood in the way for an adversary against him. Now he was riding upon his ass, and his two servants were with him . . .

Once again you feel that sense of timelessness which is

171

part of the fascination of Egypt. As your beast picks its way
delicately along the narrow path, climbs mounds and skirts
walls, always avoiding grazing your knees, you remember
Balaam's ass, which saw "the angel of the Lord standing in
the way, and his drawn sword in his hand; and the ass turned
aside out of the way, and went into the field . . ." With the
timelessness comes a feeling of serenity. Padding softly
along the dusty path between the bean fields, the merry-
eyed boy beside you, you suddenly realise that you are completely happy and relaxed. There steals over you that con-
tentment which comes so rarely to us Europeans but of
which Orientals have the secret. You want to laugh and
sing with the others, for no reason at all except that the air
is sweet in your nostrils, the sun warm on your shoulders,
and you are with people you like.

* * * * *

"And what camest thou forth to see?" Not the monumental ruins of temple, of pyramid. Nothing to strike the
eye with grandeur of an obvious kind. Only a desert plain
beside the Nile, enclosed in a semi-circle of barren hills.
This, more than any other visit described in this book, is a
romantic pilgrimage, a tribute to the spirit of the place.
You are drawn, not by marvels of architecture or artistic
craftsmanship, but by a human personality, by a man who
stands out, in the words of Mr. J. D. S. Pendlebury, as "the
first rebel against the established order of things whom we
know, the first man with ideas of his own which ran counter
to all tradition, *who was in a position to put those ideas into
practice*" (my italics). Within this crescent of hills, remote
from any town, Akhnaten built his holy city of Akhetaten—
'The Horizon of the Disk'. Here began what some believe
to have been a noble attempt to emancipate the human spirit.
At a single stroke the gross polytheism of the ancestral
Egyptian religion was to be replaced by a simpler, purer
faith. Akhnaten, according to these believers, was the first
monotheist, who recognised but one god, a divine spirit,

172

"the creator and preserver of all things", who manifested himself in the life-giving heat of the sun. But not all scholars take this view. Akhnaten is an enigma. More has been written about him than any other Pharaoh, and authorities are as sharply divided in their view of him as, to take a much more recent example, the supporters and opponents of Charles the First of England. Readers will find in the Appendix a survey of the conflicting opinions. But whatever view one finally takes, and that can only be decided by the reader after he has studied the views of both schools, Akhnaten can never be a shadow like most of the Pharaohs. He is a man of flesh and blood, one of the most interesting personalities of the ancient world.

*   *   *   *   *

The donkey-boys ahead of you raise a shout, and your own boy quickens his pace. You have reached the Nile, and there moored at the foot of the steep clay bank is the old *felucca* which is to take us across, complete with our donkeys. Congratulations are given and exchanged. Everyone is pleased, most of all the Chief Inspector, who has thus shown that Oriental powers of organisation are not to be despised. Happily we sit down on the bank while the donkeys are led on board. On the far side of the broad yellow river, palm groves stand around the mud-brick village of El Till. Beyond you can see the brown cliffs curving away eastward, Akhnaten's 'Eastern Mountain' in which he wished to be buried. And as you sit there, with the river flowing at your feet, the story re-forms in your mind, as you first read it in the pages of Petrie, Peet, Woolley, Pendlebury and the others who have dug there in the past sixty years.

*   *   *   *   *

The Eighteenth Dynasty, Egypt's Imperial Age, began some 1580 years before Christ, 2000 years after the beginnings of Dynastic history in the Nile Valley. Its founder, Amosis I, a Theban princeling, drove out the Asiatics, the Hyksos kings, who had dominated Egypt for a century and

a half. He pursued them into Syria, and returned in triumph
to become King of Egypt, with his capital at Thebes.
Throughout most of her history Egypt has not been a particularly warlike nation, but in the reaction which followed
her humiliation under the Asiatic domination, she became
militantly aggressive. After the energetic Amosis, a succession of kings carried her conquests further into Palestine and
Syria. Greatest of these was Tuthmosis III, the redoubtable
Menkheperre, the ablest general Egypt produced; he reigned
for fifty-four years and fought many successful campaigns
against the Nubians of the south, the Asiatics of the north
and east, and the Libyans of the Western Desert. In about
1467 BC, in his eighth campaign, Tuthmosis crossed the
Euphrates. That was the high-water mark of Egyptian conquest.

Province after province was subdued and brought under
Egyptian rule, and rich tribute flowed into Thebes, especi-
ally into the treasury of the god Amun. Successors to
Tuthmosis, Amenophis II (of the famous bow) and Tuthmosis IV maintained Egypt's position, but did not extend
her power, and when Amenophis III (the Magnificent) succeeded them, he saw no reason to fight any further campaigns. After the seventh year of his reign he never again
led his armies out of Thebes but spent the rest of his life
living luxuriously in his capital with his chief wife, Queen
Tiyi (see page 196), of whom he seems to have been fond.
Her name appears beside his in most of his inscriptions, a new development which was to be carried even
further in the reign of his son and successor. At the same
time Amenophis maintained an extensive harem, including
the daughter of the King of Mittani, who brought with her
"the chief of her harem ladies, namely 317 persons". There
was considerable Asiatic influence at the Egyptian court and
indeed throughout Egyptian society at this time. The King
himself was born of a Mittanian mother, and in the past
century officers serving in the Pharaoh's foreign campaigns
were in the habit of bringing back the most handsome female

captives, whom they then married. The change in Egyptian physiognomy can be clearly traced in the tomb-paintings and reliefs of the Eighteenth Dynasty.

Egypt, no longer isolated in her river valley as in the days of the Old Kingdom, had become a great international power, enjoying trade and cultural intercourse with the other great nations of the ancient East. These nations were the Minoans, the great island civilisation of Crete, and whose successors were the Greeks; the Babylonians, in the lower plain of the Euphrates; the kingdom of Mittani, an Aryan people whose land lay within the great bend of the Euphrates; and the Hittites, whose land lay to the north and west of Syria, in Asia Minor (modern Turkey). There was also a lesser power over which, at this time, both Mittani and Babylon claimed a vague suzerainty, but which was destined to grow more powerful than either: Assyria, the northernmost country of the Mesopotamian plain. These territorial divisions are extremely rough, and intended only to enable readers to pick out the approximate positions of these ancient states on a modern map.

This was the position when the sybaritic Amenophis ruled from Thebes, living in his palace on the western bank, with its pleasure lake, on which, according to a commemorative scarab, he was wont to sail with Queen Tiyi in their royal barge named *The Aten Gleams*. The name is significant. The Aten, which means 'the Disk', was an aspect of Re, and at this time the King, concerned at the growing power of the Amun priesthood, was tending to favour the priests of the Heliopolitan sun-god. In fact the movement can be traced back even further, to Tuthmosis IV, the preceding ruler. His son, Amenophis III, was the first Egyptian king to be worshipped as a god *in his own lifetime*. The view generally held by most modern Egyptologists is that the origin of the cult was political, and arose (*a*) because of the need to set up a rival to Amun, whose priests were becoming too powerful, and (*b*) because of the need for a *universal* god who would be recognised not only in Egypt but in the Pharaoh's foreign dominions. One theory is that Amenophis hoped that by being deified and worshipped as Nebmare, the 'Great God', he would hold the allegiance of his subject peoples without the need for frequent displays of force. It certainly fits in with what we know of his sagacity—and his indolence. However, Amenophis III did not go so far as to identify himself with the Aten.

In about the fourth year of his reign Tiyi bore him a son, who at first had the same name as his father.

Strung along the shore of the eastern Mediterranean, in what are now Palestine and Syria, lay the Pharaoh's vassal states, the rulers of which, as princes, had been educated at the Egyptian court. From these, and from the kings of the great neighbouring states which bordered them, letters flowed into the Foreign Office of Amenophis, letters which still survive. Tushratta, brother of the Mittanian princess whom Amenophis had married, writes of an attempted invasion by the Hittites, which he had repulsed:

Teshub, my Lord, gave my enemy into my hand, and I routed him. There was none among them that returned to his own land . . .

Aki-izzi, lord of Katna, another Egyptian province, warns the Pharaoh of a threat to his own and neighbouring vassal states by Aziru the Amorite, of whom we hear more later:

O my Lord, if the trouble of this land lies upon the heart of my Lord, let my Lord send troops, and let them come!

Already trouble had begun within the Egyptian Empire, but it had not yet reached serious proportions. Most of these early letters are unashamed requests for gold.

"Send me much gold, more gold [writes Tushratta of Mittani], for in my brother's [i.e. Amenophis'] land, gold is as common as dust . . . Send me a great deal of gold [writes the King of Babylon, adding], if, during this harvest, you send the gold concerning which I wrote to you, then I will give you my daughter."

It was not for nothing that the Pharaohs controlled the

gold-mines of Nubia. Gold was a powerful instrument of diplomacy.

When the Crown Prince Amenophis was twenty-one he married the lovely Nefretiti, a name which means "the-beautiful-woman-has-come" (Plate 20). She is the queen whose features have become famous through the sculptured head which was found by the German expedition at Amarna. She was almost certainly the daughter of Amenophis III and therefore sister to the Prince Amenophis. At his sed-festival, *i.e.* the thirtieth anniversary of his accession, the King appointed his son co-Regent, and thereafter the young Amenophis IV ruled Egypt jointly with his father. We will not be tempted to speculate on how the Prince's character may have developed during his childhood and adolescence at the Theban court, nor how much he was influenced by his mother, Queen Tiyi. All these possibilities, and others, such as the extent of Syrian influence at Thebes, have been discussed *ad infinitum* by the many who have written about the 'Heresy Period'. Here we will only give the bare facts.

During the first four years of the co-regency with his father the young Pharaoh ruled from Thebes. Then he began to build an entirely new capital city on a virgin site, over 200 miles down river from the capital. In the sixth year of his reign he left Thebes and established himself in his new city which he called Akhetaten (the 'Horizon of the Disk'). He then changed his name from Amenophis, which means 'Amun-is-satisfied', to 'Akhnaten', meaning 'It is well with the Aten', and afterwards ordered that the name Amun be struck out of every tomb, temple and monument on which it appeared throughout the length and breadth of the land; even on the monuments of his father.

Those are the facts, but what drama lies behind them and what questions they pose! What manner of man was this young king, and what had caused him to make so profound a change? Having taken the step, how did he come to choose this lonely site? One imagines the royal barge with its attendant craft, leaving the crowded quays of imperial

Thebes, the sun catching the gold and silver of its mount-
ings, the brown backs of the sweating rowers, and the bright
awning under which the King sat with his Queen, his
counsellors and friends. It glided past the many-pillared
temple of Amun, the god whom the King hated so bitterly,
past the docks and wharves thronged with foreign shipping,
and so downstream for 200 miles. Several days passed and
then the cliffs which had hugged the eastern bank curved
away from the river in a great bow enclosing a broad sandy
plain, several miles wide, with the river, like the string of the
bow, flowing along its western side. And Akhnaten knew
that he had found the site of his city.

Then, in a short time, hurried on by the impatient King,
workmen laboured to build the new capital. Overlooking
the broad main street, the King's Way, rose the official
palace linked by a bridge with the King's house. Near it was
the Temple of the Aten. In the residential quarter rose the
houses of the nobles with their fine pillared halls, their
granaries and stables. Where the royal fleet had moored,
quays jutted into the river; where formerly there was barren
desert, gardens bloomed, bright with the flowers which
Akhnaten loved and shaded by rare trees brought from Asia.
Here in the sixth year of his reign, with his Queen, his three
daughters, and the court, Akhnaten declared war on Amun
and began his experiment.

*　　*　　*　　*　　*

You are nearly across the river now. The felucca has to
tack sharply to avoid two huge barges, lashed together and
piled high with bales of straw, which are drifting downstream under no apparent guidance. Behind them trails a
dinghy, with a man in it, asleep. The boatmen do not seem
concerned but merely laugh at the sleeper as they haul on
the ropes. *Maleesh* . . .

A ragged fusillade of rifle-fire crashes out from the eastern
bank as you approach, but there is no cause for alarm. It is
merely the young men of El Till firing a salute. Stand up

178

and try to look dignified. You are being accorded the
honours of a sheikh. Ashore, more handshakes and smiling
salutations. You mount and move on again through the
village and its palm grove and out towards the desert. The
sun burns your back. The slow pace of the donkeys, the
rhythmic patter of their footsteps on the sand induce a mood
of reverie. Once again the ancient drama returns to your
mind.

*   *   *   *   *

For eleven years Akhnaten ruled from Akhetaten, which
was now the capital of the Egyptian Empire, abounding in
wealth. To it came envoys from the furthermost limits of
the known world and in the King's Foreign Office near his
palace were stored the royal letters from the foreign kings.
They were very like those they wrote to his father; requests
for gold, and sometimes, from Akhnaten's Syrian and
Phoenician vassals, urgent demands for military aid. The
Hittites, ancient enemies of Egypt, were beginning to
penetrate southward. Some of the King's vassals remained
loyal, but others began attacking the coastal cities of Tunip,
Simyra and Gebal, ostensibly to prevent their falling into the
hands of the Hittites, but in reality as an advance guard of
the invaders. Of these Quislings, the most notable were
Abdashirta and his son, Aziru, the Amorite. The governor
of the threatened city of Tunip, wrote to Akhnaten:

> My lord, Tunip, thy servant, speaks, saying; who formerly could
> have plundered Tunip without being plundered by Menkheperre
> [the great Tuthmosis III—Akhnaten's ancestor]? The gods of the
> King of Egypt, my Lord, dwell in Tunip. May our Lord ask his old
> men if it is not so.
> Now, however, we belong no more to our Lord, the King of
> Egypt. If his soldiers and chariots come too late, then the King of
> Egypt will mourn over these things which Aziru has done, for he will
> turn his hand against our land. And when Aziru enters Simyra he will do
> as he pleases in the territory of our Lord the King . . . and now Tunip,
> thy city, weeps, and her tears are flowing, and there is no help for us.
> For twenty years we have been sending to our Lord the King, the
> King of Egypt, but there has not come to us a word, no not one.

On the northern and eastern frontiers, new tides of population, moving down from northern Mesopotamia, were lapping against the bastions of the Egyptian Empire. Already the outer walls were crumbling, but the sound of their fall was only a far-off murmur to the Pharaoh. Within his pleasant city, locked within its crescent of hills, he devoted his time to the things nearest his heart: to extending his palaces, pleasure houses and temples, to encouraging a new realism and humanism in art and to the inspired worship of the one good god to whom he was dedicated. For by this time Akhnaten had shed the last vestiges of the older faiths. Beginning with the hated Amun, he had moved on to forbid the worship of all other gods. Isis, Osiris, Hathor, Ptah and the entire pantheon of lesser deities were swept away. The demons and monsters which inhabited the Underworld found no place in the tombs of his nobles which were now being hewn out of the eastern cliffs behind the city. Instead there appeared the great Hymn to the Aten, the most exalted expression of Akhnaten's faith, probably composed by the King himself.

Thou risest beautifully in the horizon of heaven,
O living Aten who creates Life!
When thou risest in the eastern horizon
Thou fillest every land with thy beauty.
Thou art beautiful, great, gleaming and high over every land.
Thy rays, they embrace the lands to the limits of all thou hast made.
Thou art Re and bringest them all,
Thou bindest them (for) thy beloved son.
Thou art afar off, yet thy rays are on the earth;
Thou art in the faces (of men), yet thy ways are not known.

When thou settest in the western horizon
The earth is in darkness after the manner of the dead;
They sleep in their rooms,
Their heads are covered
And the eye sees not its fellow.
All their possessions are stolen from under their heads, and they know
     it not.
Every lion cometh forth from its lair,

All snakes bite, for darkness is a danger (?)
The earth is silent, for he who created it rests in his horizon.

Day dawns when thou risest in the horizon.
Thou shinest as Aten in the sky and drivest away darkness.
When thou sendest forth thy rays the Two Lands are in festivity,
The people awake and stand on their feet, for thou hast raised them,
Their limbs are washed and they take their clothing,
Their arms are (raised) in adoration at thy appearance.
The whole earth does its work,
All cattle rest in their pastures,
The trees and herbage grow green,
The birds fly up from their nests,
Their wings are (raised) in praise of thy *Ka*,
All goats jump on their feet,
All flying and fluttering things live when thou hast shone upon them.
The boats sail up-stream and downstream likewise,
And all ways are open because thou hast appeared.
The fish in the river leap before thee,
Thy rays are in the midst of the Sea.
Creator of germ in woman, who makest seed in men,
Who givest life to a son in his mother's womb,
Who pacifiest him so that he may not cry,
A nurse (even) in the womb,
Who givest breath to vivify all that he has made.
When he comes forth from the womb . . . on the day of his birth,
Thou openest his mouth duly (?) and suppliest his needs,
The chick in the egg that chirps while in the shell,
Thou givest him breath therein to let him live.
Thou makest for him his appointed time that he may break it in the
    egg.
He comes forth from the egg at the appointed moment to chirp,
And he runs on his feet as soon as he comes from it.

How manifold are thy works!
They are hidden from the face of men, O sole god,
Like unto whom there is none other.
Thou madest the earth at thy will when thou wast alone:
Men, cattle, all animals, everything on earth that goes on its feet,
Everything that is on high that flies with its wings,
The foreign lands, Syria, Kush, and the land of Egypt.
Thou settest every man in his place, and suppliest their needs.
Each one has his food, and their days are numbered.
Their tongues are diverse in speech, and their forms likewise,
For thou has differentiated the peoples.

Thou makest the Nile in the Underworld;
Thou bringest it at thy will to cause the people of Egypt to live,
For thou hast made them for thyself, O Lord of them all,
Who growest tired through them,
O Lord of every land who shinest for them,
Thou Disk of the Day, great of dignity.
All the distant lands, thou makest their life.
Thou settest a Nile in heaven that it may descend for them
And make floods on the mountain like the sea,
In order to water their fields in their towns.
How excellent are thy plans, thou Lord of Eternity!
The Nile in heaven is thy gift (?) to the foreign peoples
And all herds that go on their feet,
But the (real) Nile comes from the Underworld for Egypt.

Thy rays nourish every field.
When thou risest, they live and flourish for thee.
Thou makest the seasons in order to create all that thou hast made;
Winter to cool them, and the heat (of summer)
That they may taste thee.
Thou hast made heaven afar off in order to shine therein
And to see all thou hast made, thou alone, rising in thy form as the
      living Aten,
Appearing and shining, afar off and yet close at hand (?)
All eyes see thee before them, for thou art the Aten of the day over
      (the earth) . . .

Thou art in my heart,
There is none that knoweth thee but thy son
Nefer-kheperu-Re, Wa-en Re,
And thou hast made him wise in thy plans and in thy might.
The earth exists in thy hand, just as thou hast made them;
When thou risest they live; when thou settest they die.
Thou thyself art length of days, by thee do men live.
Eyes see beauty until thou settest,
But when thou settest on the right hand
All work is laid aside;
When thou riseth thou makest . . . to grow for the king;
Movement (?) is in every leg since thou hast founded the earth.
Thou hast raised them up for thy son, who came forth from thy
      flesh,
The king of Upper and Lower Egypt, who lives on truth,
The Lord of the Two Lands,
Nefer-kheperu-Re, Wa-en-Re; son of Re, who lives on truth,
Lord of Diadems, Akhnaten, whose life is long:

And for the great royal wife, his beloved,
The Mistress of the Two Lands,
Nefer-Neferu-Aten, Nefretiti,
May she live and grow young for ever and ever!

(*Translation by H. W. Fairman*)

Putting aside for the moment all commentary and speculation, that superb hymn is all we have by which to interpret Akhnaten's religion. As critics have pointed out it contains no moral teaching. "The Aten", writes Pendlebury, "is purely a creative god. He has made all things living and provided for their wants, but there his work ends. There is no feeling that he will reward good or punish evil. There is no sense of sin or even of right or wrong."

This is undeniable, though the absence of ethical teaching from this one surviving religious document does not prove that it was not present in the fully developed creed. But if Akhnaten's theological stature is uncertain, there can be no doubt of his stature as a poet and visionary. Perhaps even more significant than what he says is what he leaves out. Gone is the meaningless magic, the hundreds of anthropomorphic gods surviving from a savage past. More remarkable still is the *absence of fear*. The destructive aspects of the sun are never mentioned. "The deity is presented as confessedly beneficent; not fear, but gratitude and a sense of dependence are regarded as the natural motives to piety" (Peet). There is no glorification of power, as in the hymn to Amun quoted in an earlier chapter. The god sheds his beneficence on all lands alike. He is universal.

Their tongues are diverse in speech, and their forms likewise,
For thou has differentiated the peoples.
All the distant lands, thou makest their life.
Thou settest a Nile in Heaven that it may descend for them
And make floods on the mountain like the sea,
In order to water their fields in their towns.

The wondering Egyptian, seeing rainfall in the mountainous lands of the north-east, could only interpret it by imagining another Nile in the sky. But, he adds, the Egyptians' own Nile comes from the Underworld.

This stress on universality has been called by the "hardheaded" school as evidence that the Aten was merely a unifying political symbol. But might not the lines be simply a recognition that the Egyptian mind had at last learned to look beyond its own valley?

Accompanying the religious revolution (if it was religious) came an even more astonishing development in art. For thousands of years Egyptian art had been bound by strict religious conventions, particularly in respect of royalty. There was only a limited number of postures in which the Pharaoh could be represented, and these were repeated through century after century. He was a god, and in art, particularly sculpture, his power and regal dignity were always emphasised. As for his queen, only rarely was she shown with him and then in an equally dignified pose. It was true that there had been a slight relaxation of this rigid role during the preceding reigns. The modelling of the Eighteenth Dynasty reliefs had become more flexible and sensitive, but the essential dignity remained.

During the reign of Akhnaten all these conventions were abandoned. Apparently under the King's own direction (for no one else had the power to abolish so deeply-rooted a convention) artists were encouraged to set down honestly what they saw before them. There was to be no flattering concealment of physical deficiencies. If a man was fat and old he was not to be represented as slim and young, no matter how important his position. The King himself seems to have suffered from a physical deformity. He had a swollen belly and an elongated skull poised on an unusually long neck. All these peculiarities, including feminine characteristics to which medical authorities have drawn attention, he caused to be faithfully reproduced. He allowed Nefretiti equal prominence beside him, and even more revolutionary, encouraged his artists to show him in the most natural and intimate attitudes, sitting with his child on his knee or even

184

kissing his wife. For a brief flash of time, eleven years out of three score centuries, the god stepped down from his pedestal and became a human being.

*   *   *   *   *

Your donkeys patter up the last few yards of steeply sloping track beneath the palm groves and out on to the sunbaked, sandy plain beyond. To the south the dusty, pebbly, desert surface is scooped into hollows, corrugated by mounds of crumbled mud-brick and broken pottery, the debris of half a century's excavation. Your eyes gradually make out the outlines of foundation walls and, visible through this confusion, the broad central street, the *Sikkit es Sultan*, which once ran through Akhnaten's city. The donkeys stop. One of the ghaffirs raises his rifle and fires into the air. The report slams back from the distant cliffs. There is a pause. Then, from one of the black tomb entrances high up in the cliff-face a distant blue-smocked figure appears, one of the ghaffirs who guard the tombs. Crash comes his answering salute, and its echoes rumble back and forth across the plain as the Chief Inspector turns to you with a smile and an outstretched arm. "The city of the Aten," he says.

CHAPTER XIV

CITY OF THE SUN-KING

> Those golden pallaces, those gorgeous halles,
> With fourniture superflouslie faire,
> Those statelie courts, those sky-encountering walles
> Envanish all like vapours in the aire . . .

AWAY to the south, in a dark, irregular strip between river and mountain, straggle the half-buried ruins of Akhnaten's holy city. Apart from a Roman encampment, and one or two small Arab settlements, the city of Akhetaten has had no successor since Tutankhaten took his court back to Thebes. Akhetaten was built, occupied, and deserted within a generation.

The wind blows grit in your eyes, the reflected glare beats into your face from the hot yellow sand into which your donkey's feet sink. Your little cavalcade wheels to the north led by the Chief Inspector.

"To the Northern Palace," he calls, melodramatically.

But you know that at the most you will see only a few pitiful mud-brick walls. Were you, after all, rather foolish to come so far to see so little? And then you remember something. The Northern Palace . . . what had H. W. Fairman told you, in Cairo—Fairman who had dug at Amarna with Pendlebury immediately before the war, and had filled you with something of his own enthusiasm for Amarna? You feel in your pocket for the crumpled sketch and notes which he had made for you. The Northern Palace was Akhnaten's pleasure palace, and beyond it the special palace to which the Queen had retired after her quarrel with the King. Now you remember, and as your donkey picks his way over mounds and ditches you piece together in your mind the dramatic story of Akhnaten's last years and the intrigues which followed his death.

From the beginning Queen Nefretiti seems to have been a devotee of the new faith. Akhnaten loved his beautiful wife, and her influence over her sensitive husband was great. Like Akhnaten's mother, Queen Tiyi, she was given equal prominence beside her husband in his inscriptions and monuments; in fact the feminine influence at the court of Akhnaten appears to have been even greater than that existing in the reign of Amenophis III. A curious fact, noted by Pendlebury, is that whereas the sculptures of previous reigns showed the Pharaoh with one foot forward, and the Queen with her feet together, in the Amarna period the reverse was true. Nefretiti and her daughters (Akhnaten had no son) are shown striding forward, but the King has his feet together. In the reliefs showing Akhnaten making offerings in the temple of the Aten Nefretiti is there beside him, shaking the *sistrum*. In the inscriptions showing the King honouring his nobles the Queen is also there, with her daughters, who hand to their father the gold collars with which he decorated his followers.

Meanwhile, from the Pharaoh's threatened Asiatic dominions the pleadings of the harassed but loyal vassal-princes swelled to an agonised chorus. From the east the Habiru, whom some historians have identified with the Jews, were pressing into Canaan. On the north the wily Hittite King Shubbuliliuma spun his web, intriguing with the petty kings of the Pharaoh's northerly provinces and inviting them to break away from Egypt. The Quisling Aziru was becoming increasingly dangerous, and while protesting his loyalty in fulsome letters to the perplexed Akhnaten, was attacking the King's Phoenician cities.

Simyra was one of the threatened towns. South of it lay the port of Gebal (Byblos), which had been loyal to Egypt for centuries, even as far back as the Old Kingdom. The governor of Gebal, Ribbadi, wrote to Pharaoh a series of vivid letters which were discovered at Amarna over fifty years ago. In one of these he writes:

> Behold Aziru has fought my chiefs, and the chiefs whom I despatched to the city Simyra he has caused to be seized in the city. Both the city Beruta and the city Ziouna are sending ships to the city. All who are in the land of the Amorites have gathered themselves . . . I need men to save the rebellion of this land . . . Give me soldiers!

No effective help was sent and Simyra fell. The loyal Ribbadi wrote again:

> Grievous it is to say what he has done, the dog Aziru. Behold what has befallen the lands of the King on account of him; and he cried peace unto the land, and now behold what has befallen the city of Simyra—a station of my Lord, a fortress . . . and they spoil our fortress . . . ah, the cries of the place . . . a violent man and a dog . . .

Few documents have such power to stir our hearts as these little tablets of baked clay in which Ribbadi's cuneiform scribe set down the angry, passionate messages of the stubborn old warrior. "Now Abdesherah is marching with his brethren," he warns Pharaoh in another letter, and appeals to him to

> ... march against him and smite him ... the land is the King's land; and since I have talked thus and you have not moved the city of Simyra has been lost. There is no money to buy horses, all is finished, we have been spoiled ... give me thirty companies of horse with chariots, men, men ... there is none of this for me ... not a horse ...

Reading these and other letters discovered in Akhnaten's Foreign Office one wonders why the King neglected these appeals. Did he not realise that the empire his ancestors had won was collapsing? Was his a deliberate policy of non-violence? Was he the first pacifist? Or was his inaction due simply to lethargy and indifference? We may never know the answer to these questions, but in fairness to Akhnaten it should be remembered that there is no certainty that he ever saw these letters. A letter from the traitor Aziru to Akhnaten's Foreign Minister, Tutu, suggests that there may have been a secret understanding between them:

> Thou art in that place (Egypt) my father [writes Aziru], and whatever is the wish of Dudu my Father, write it and I will surely give it. Behold, thou art my Father and my Lord ... the lands of Amor are thy lands, and my house is thy house; and whatever thou desirest, write, and lo! I will assuredly grant thy wish. Lo, now! thou sittest before the King, my Lord, and my enemies have spoken slanders of me to my Father before the King, my Lord. Do not thou allow it to be so ...

Perhaps the King only saw such portions of his foreign correspondence as Tutu thought fit to show him.

Again, it is easy for us, with the whole course of subsequent history before us, to be wise after the event. But what seems obvious now would not be so to the King, who was receiving from Aziru letters which passionately protested his loyalty. Allowing for the distances involved, and the slowness of communication, there is perhaps some excuse for Akhnaten.

One certain fact is known. In the twelfth year of his reign the King received his mother, Queen Tiyi, who paid a special visit to Akhetaten. The occasion was marked by a 'Pageant of Empire', depicted on the walls of the tomb of Huya, in which representatives of the King's foreign dominions are shown bringing tribute to their lord. Aware of the dangerous situation within the Empire, and also, perhaps, within Egypt itself, the Queen-Mother may have persuaded her stubborn son to come to terms with the priests of Thebes. All that is certainly known is that in the fifteenth year of his reign Akhnaten married his half-brother, Smenkhkare, to his daughter Meritaten, and made Smenkhkare his co-regent, just as his own father, Amenophis III, made *him* co-regent during the latter years of his reign. But the most significant fact is that Smenkhkare and Meritaten returned to Thebes and ruled there, while Akhnaten continued to rule from Akhetaten.

Akhnaten's life-history had been one of rebellion. He had abjured the old gods and forbidden their worship; he had deserted his ancestral capital and built a new city dedicated to his 'sole God'. After such a life any kind of compromise would have galled him bitterly. Unless, and it is a fascinating possibility, *the fanatical force behind Atenism was Nefretiti and not the King*. In such a case her subsequent quarrel with him after the compromise would become intelligible. Egyptologists digging and sifting among the foundations of Akhetaten have unearthed evidence which at least suggests this as a possibility. A summary of the evidence will be found in the Appendix, but for the present we will merely put forward the conclusions which have been drawn from it.

In about the fourteenth year of his reign, Akhnaten seems to have quarrelled with Nefretiti, who then retired to a palace in the northern part of the city, cut off from it by a high wall. She took with her Akhnaten's other half-brother, the child Tutankhaten, whose name occurs with hers on objects found on that site. At the same time, in a series of

monuments, expecially at Maruaten, the Southern Pleasure
Palace at Amarna, her name was erased and replaced by that
of her daughter Meritaten. The quarrel may have arisen
over Akhnaten's attempted compromise with Thebes.
Nefretiti remained a convinced Atenist, perhaps from religious conviction but more likely because she knew that her
political future depended on preventing the return to power
of the Amun priesthood. Her ruthless feminine intelligence
may have appreciated the logic of the situation, whereas
Akhnaten did not. At any rate Smenkhkare returned to
Thebes to prepare for the swing back to Amunism. Akhnaten, left alone in his Southern Palace, married his own
daughter Ankhsenpaaten and had a daughter by her.

In the seventeenth year of his reign Akhnaten died, at the
age of forty-one, and almost simultaneously Smenkhkare
also died, leaving the throne vacant. This gave Nefretiti her
chance. She produced Tutankhaten and married him to the
heiress Ankhsenpaaten, Akhnaten's widow. In this way she
legitimised his succession, and Tutankhaten, still a child,
reigned for a short time from Akhetaten, under Nefretiti's
guidance. Later, however, the boy-king was persuaded to
return to Thebes, the most likely reason being that Nefretiti
was now dead. At Thebes he changed his name to Tutankhamun (it was his tomb which Howard Carter discovered)
and his wife became Ankhesnamun. Thus the wheel had
come full circle. The great adventure was over, and the
priests of Amun returned to power.

Later they revenged themselves in full. Just as Akhnaten
had caused the name of Amun to be erased from every
monument on which it appeared, they in turn hacked out
the name of the heretic. Gangs of workmen descended on
the half-empty city of Akhetaten. Wherever they found the
name and features of Akhnaten and his Queen, in tombs,
temples, and private houses, they obliterated them. The
temples of the Aten were thrown down and buried. Akhnaten's mummy has never been found and presumably his
tomb was violated and his body destroyed. But this came

later. The priests still had to wait a little time for their vengeance. Tutankhaten was closely associated with the heresy, and while he lived the memory of Akhnaten would not be openly scorned. Even when he died, after a short reign of nine years, the drama was not over. Some years ago, at Boghaz Keui in Turkey, archaeologists discovered a cuneiform tablet which has caused much controversy among Egyptologists. It is an account by one of the Hittite kings of certain letters received by his father, Shubbululiuma, from an Egyptian Queen whose name is given as Dakhamun. It was translated by Professor Sayce. After describing the sack of Amka (on the plain of Antioch) the Hittite king goes on:

Then their ruler [*i.e.* of the Egyptians] namely *Pip-khurru-riya*—just at that moment died; now the Queen of Egypt was Dakhamun . . . she sent an ambassador to my father; she said thus to him: "My husband is dead; I have no children; your sons are said to be grown up; if to me one of your sons you give, and he will be my husband, he will be a help; send him accordingly, and thereafter I will make him my husband. I send bridal gifts."

Shubbululiuma was cautious, over-cautious in this instance, since a marriage alliance with Egypt would have been greatly to his advantage. But he wasted too much time in making inquiries. Again the Queen wrote, and there is desperation in her words:

What is this you say, 'She has deceived me'? . . . now you say to me thus, 'there is thy husband'; but he is dead; I have no son; so I have taken a servant . . . and to another country in this matter I have not written; to you, however, I have written; your sons are said to be grown up; so to me one of your sons give, and he as my husband in the land of Egypt shall be king.

Now, one of Tutankhamun's names was Neb-kheperu-Re, which is not unlike *Pip-khurru-riya*, and Dakhamun might be Ankhesnamun, the widow of Tutankhamun. For many years philologists puzzled over these two names. Now at last the facts have been definitely established by Herr E. Edel.[1] It is now certain that Pip-khurru-riya was

[1] See his article in the *Journal of Near Eastern Studies*, Vol. VII, pp. 11–24.

Tutankhamun, and so another vital piece can be added to the jig-saw puzzle of Egyptian history.

The story which this letter reveals adds a note of pathos to the closing scenes of the drama. Ankhesnamun was not more than twenty-four when she wrote that letter. She had already been married twice, once to her father Akhnaten, and a second time to Tutankhamun when he was a child of seven or eight. She was the heiress, and she must have known that the elderly courtier-priest, Ay, who had held high office under her father, was planning to marry her and so ascend to the throne. In desperation the young queen sent her messenger to the far-distant King of the Hittites, 800 miles to the north, asking if one of his sons might marry her. She knew that time was short. Probably she had only seventy days, the time taken for the embalmment and burial of her husband's body. But for once the Hittite King was too clever. By the time he was convinced of the genuineness of the Queen's request it was too late. Ankhesnamun was married to Ay, and the Hittite prince, though he set out for Egypt, never reached Thebes; Ay would see to that. And with his short reign the Eighteenth Dynasty, which had begun in a blaze of glory, guttered out like a spent candle.

*   *   *   *   *

So, with the story of the Amarna Age in your mind, you have arrived at Akhetaten. Without that background, built from the researches and discoveries of such men as Petrie, Woolley, Pendlebury and others, the place would mean very little. It has none of the monumental attractions of Giza, Karnak, or Thebes, and yet in many ways it is the most romantic site in Egypt.

Of Akhnaten's Northern Palace only the foundations are left. You wander from pillared hall to colonnaded court, through corridors along which Akhnaten and Nefretiti must have passed, and over churned-up sand where once were tree-shaded, bird-haunted gardens. Part of the grounds seem to have formed a zoological garden where the King could watch birds and animals and indulge his passion for nature. There are remains of stone mangers, some carved with reliefs of cattle and antelopes. There are remains of aviaries. There are even remains of aquariums. In the Water Court, a long pillared hall, are a series of T-shaped tanks, with the pillar-bases between. "The sloping sides of the tanks", writes Pendlebury, "were painted white up to the surface of the water and above this with brightly-coloured water plants, lotuses and water lilies which must have looked as if they were actually growing out of the water. The low parapets were similarly decorated, while the pavement itself consists of a series of frescoed panels showing all kinds of wild plants from which startled flights of duck arise, and brakes of papyrus among which cattle are plunging."

The whole gives the impression of a pleasure-palace with formal gardens surrounding a large ornamental lake with islands and pavilions. But not all the rooms were large and formal. There were the smaller, more intimate apartments. You see the King's retiring room with a dais for his throne, and a bedroom and bathroom opening on to a small central court.

Nor were Akhnaten's pleasures entirely spiritual and contemplative. In this palace were found wine-cellars with the sealing of wine-jars marked with such inscriptions as 'very good wine of the House of Akhnaten'.

Beyond the Northern Palace, still further north, you are shown the remains of a thick wall beyond which lie the scanty foundations of Nefretiti's place of retirement. Little remains above ground to stir the imagination. The party is getting restless. The Chief Inspector waves his hand towards the cliffs, and you turn eastwards, away from the city, to explore the tombs.

The site of Akhetaten is roughly the shape of the letter *D* with the cliffs forming the curved side of the letter. But it is not a perfect *D*. About half-way along the curved side there is a break in the cliffs where a *wadi* (dried-up water-course) enters the plain from the high desert. The tombs of the nobles are in two groups, one cut out of the cliffs over-looking the plain on the northern side of the wadi, the other group on the southern side. And 4 miles up the wadi itself is the lonely tomb which may be that of the 'Heretic King'.

As your party rides across the hot, gritty plain towards the cliffs you shade your eyes and look up at the sun which rides almost vertically overhead. So the worshippers in the open courtyard of the Aten Temple must have gazed at the fiery disk, and seen, as you can see, the bright rays which seem to stream from it. The donkeys stop near the base of the cliff. You dismount and scramble up the steep slope to-wards the square black hole in the cliff face which is the entrance to the tomb of Huya, Superintendent of the Treasury and Household of Queen Tiyi. As you pass from the hot sunlight into the cool stillness of the rock-cut chambers you see nothing at first, not even the faces of your companions. Then, gradually, as your eyes grow accus-tomed to the gloom, a picture forms.

You are looking at a great carved relief which occupies most of the wall. The Royal Family are entertaining the Queen-Mother to dinner. (This was in Year Twelve, when Tiyi paid her state visit to Akhetaten on the occasion of the Pageant of Empire.) Near the centre of the picture sits Akhnaten, leaning back comfortably in his chair and gnaw-ing a large broiled bone which he holds in his right hand, his left resting negligently on the arm of his chair. Near him sits Nefretiti, also holding in her right hand a roast duck which she is attacking with as much grace as is possible in the circumstances. Although knives and forks were not in use, it appears that etiquette prescribed the use of the right hand only, to judge from this picture; so that the scene is not quite as inelegant as its sounds (see page 196).

On the right, facing the King and Queen, sits Queen Tiyi, who eats more delicately. Beside her is her young daughter Beketaten, and with her left hand the Queen is handing the little girl some tit-bit from the table. Beside Nefretiti are two of her daughters, Meritaten and perhaps Nefer-nefreu-

Aten. Each diner has his or her own table piled high with delicacies, and nearby stand wine-jars.

Huya, owner of the tomb, was the Queen's majordomo and as such would have had a hand in these proceedings, but his figure is so small and inconspicuous that it could pass unnoticed. This is the first and most striking difference you notice between the Amarna and the Theban tombs. At Thebes the scenes depict incidents from the life of the owner, and he is usually in the centre of the picture. In all the Amarna tombs the scenes of the royal family occupy the most prominent places, and the object of the owners was to show how high they stood in the King's favour.

Norman de Garis Davies, who devoted years to studying and copying these scenes, wrote: "They reveal only one personality, one family, one home, one career, and one mode of worship. This is the figure, family, palace and occupations of the King, and the worship of the sun—which also was his, and perhaps, in strictness, of no one else."

On the east wall Akhnaten conducts his mother to the Aten Temple. On another wall the King and Queen are carried on their great state palanquin to "receive the tribute of Syria and Ethiopia, the West and the East. All countries", says the inscription, "collected at one time, and the islands in the midst of the sea, bringing offerings to the King on the great throne of Akhetaten . . ." Akhnaten and Nefretiti sit side by side, but even on this solemn occasion she has her arm round his waist. And always overhead is the shining disk of the Aten with its down-stretched rays, each terminating in a hand which seems to caress the royal couple.

You go back blinking into the sunshine. From the ledge outside the tomb you can look across the plain and see the outlines of the ancient roads which led from the city to the tombs. Behind and above you, running along the top of the cliffs, is the track along which the sentries passed, guarding the city against the raiding Bedouin of the desert. You return to the base of the cliff, mount, and move southward, skirting the hills, and occasionally dismounting to visit one

of the tombs, each of which is sealed by an iron gate and guarded by an armed ghaffir. To-day, as the Chief Inspector is with us, the ghaffirs are eager to demonstrate their efficiency and alertness.

You visit the tomb of Ahmose, which contains a moving prayer in which the Veritable Scribe of the King prays that the Aten will bestow on the King

> very many jubilees, with years of peace. Give him that which thine heart desireth, to the extent that there is sand on the shore, that fishes in the stream have scales, and cattle have hair. Let him sojourn here until the swan turneth black, until the raven turneth white, until the hills arise to depart . . . while I continue in attendance on the Good God [*i.e.* the Pharaoh] until he assigns me the burial that he granteth.

Did Ahmose ever suspect, when he caused that prayer to be inscribed, how short would be the duration of the Aten faith? In the same tomb is a lively relief of Akhnaten and Nefretiti in their chariot. They are on their way to visit the Temple, as in so many scenes. The King and Queen are facing each other and chatting, completely disregarding where they are going, although the King is holding the reins. Between the royal couple, and just able to peep over the edge of the chariot, is little Meritaten, greatly interested in the prancing horses.

The King and Queen in their golden chariot must have been a common sight in Akhetaten, but one doubts if it was always as graceful as would appear from the tombs. In one of the workmen's houses in Akhetaten excavators discovered a child's toy in the form of a model chariot driven by a monkey with a monkey passenger. The horses are rearing and the driver is having great difficulty in controlling them, while in the front is a monkey-groom trying desperately to hold the horses' heads. This charming little model, which is on view in the Cairo Museum, looks suspiciously like a caricature.

Opposite: carved relief from the tomb of Huya, superintendent of the treasury and household of Queen Tiyi.

As you leave the tomb of Ahmose you see on the wall something which brings home to you the immense age of these sepulchres, and the centuries during which they have been known to sightseers. There were no iron gates on the tombs when Ptolemaic soldiers came here two centuries before the birth of Christ. They were therefore able to leave their names scrawled clumsily in Greek on the ancient plaster. One says:

> Having ascended here, Catullinus has engraved this in the doorway, marvelling at the art of the holy quarriers.

And nearby is another inscription which simply states:

> Aulutrales . . . I have been here.

Nowhere in these tombs appears any god but the Aten. Nowhere appear the gods and demons of the Underworld. Re in his sacred barque, Osiris and Isis, Nephthys, Hathor, all are banished. The inscriptions record only the honouring of the noble owners of the tombs by the King, they describe his offices, and sometimes include fragments of the Aten-hymn. Few of the tombs are complete, and all bear evidence of very hasty construction. In some only half of the pillared halls have been completed. In others the scenes have only been roughly sketched in, but not carved. When every noble was hurrying to complete his Eternal Habitation, competition for workmen must have been acute and no doubt they were hustled from one tomb to another, leaving much skimped and faulty work. Altogether there is something jerry-built about Akhetaten.

Now you are approaching the great wadi which interrupts the line of cliffs and which leads to a solitary tomb which may be that of Akhnaten; he gave orders that on his death he should be buried "in my sepulchre in the Eastern Mountain". You travel for 4 miles along the rough, rocky track between the desert hills, until you reach the entrance to a smaller wadi opening into the main valley. The royal tomb is a grim and depressing place. There is no inscription above the entrance. A sloping passage and a steep flight of steps leads to the burial pit where the sarcophagus once lay. Beyond is a hall with badly-damaged reliefs showing the royal family worshipping the Aten. Opening from the top of the stairs are smaller tomb chambers made for Princess Meketaten, who died young. No trace of Akhnaten's body was found, though Professor Sayce, who watched the excavation of the royal tomb, saw the corpse of a man which had been burned some time after mummification. Professor Fairman has noted that the surviving inscriptions refer more to Nefretiti than Akhnaten, and that as there is an emplacement for only one sarcophagus the so-called tomb of Akhnaten may well be that of Nefretiti. No traces of the bodies of the royal couple have ever been found: nor is it likely that they will ever be found.

You return to the plain; your companions seem tireless, but, recognising that you are not, they dismount, and settling down comfortably in the shadow of a rock, produce a picnic lunch of fish sandwiches. The rest is blessedly welcome. Afterwards the Chief Inspector gathers the fragments and tucks them out of sight beneath a rock, remarking, "We must not spoil the desert." Then he rises and points upwards to a place high on the cliff face where the rock has been smoothed to a height of 20 feet and covered with an inscription in deeply-cut hieroglyphs. "That", he says, "is one of the boundary marks of Akhnaten's city." You all look up to the great *stele* as he translates:

> As my father the Aten liveth, I will make Akhetaten the City of the Horizon of the Disk, in this place. I will not make him Akhetaten to the south of it, north of it, west of it, or east of it ... And the area within these four stelae is Akhetaten in its proper self; it belongs to Aten the father; mountains, deserts, meadows, islands, upper and lower ground, land, water, villages, men, beasts and all things which the Aten my father shall bring into existence eternally for ever ...

"Come," says your guide, "we have still much to see." You mount and ride on again, towards the southern tombs. Now you enter the tomb of Tutu, chief mouthpiece of the land, the Foreign Minister with whom Aziru was on such friendly terms. Here is Nefretiti, sitting, this time, with her two baby daughters on her knee, while beside her Akhnaten rewards his faithful Minister. Nearby stand the representatives of the foreign lands, Syria, Ethiopia, Mittani and others bearing tribute.

> O great ones who stand before the King [says Akhnaten in the inscription], my purpose is to confer an exceptional reward equal to a thousand of which are done to men. I give it to the Chamberlain, Tutu, because of his love for the King his Lord.

And Tutu replies:

> O my good Lord, a ruler of character, abounding in wealth, great in duration, rich in monuments! Thy every command is done; they come to pass as in the care of Aten, the Lord, the living Aten . . . Thou controllest the entire land; Syria, Ethiopia, and all the nations. Their hands are outstretched in praise of thee . . .

Beside that fulsome declaration one should read Ribbadi's letter after the fall of Gebal:

> Ribbadi to the King, my Lord, at thy feet seven times I bow . . . Lo, it is not granted to my sons to take root of me, as the prophets have perceived of old. Behold my brother has commanded, he went out as my deputy. It is no use, the soldiers of the garrison failed with him, and so the evil is done, and they made me flee from the city. It is not defended from the enemy . . .
> Behold the city of Gebal was a city truly like our eye; there was plenty of all that was royal in her midst. The servants of the chief city were at peace, the chiefs were our well-wishers when the King's voice was for all . . . It is the chief city of the land, they have wasted for me. But the King my Lord will protect me, and restore thou me to the chief city, and to my house as of old.
> O King my Lord, O King my Lord, save the city from shame . . .

Further south you approach the tomb of Mahu, Chief of Police. You have read about this tomb in de Garis Davies' great book, and you are particularly anxious to see it because it contains one of the finest scenes of the King and Queen riding in their chariot, with the King kissing the Queen, and Meritaten poking the rumps of the horses with a stick. The tomb has a low entrance and is quite small, but the reliefs are charming. The ghaffir opens the iron door, and you stumble gratefully out of the sunlight into the white coolness of the inner chamber. Then the Chief Inspector shouts, and turns angrily to the ghaffir, pointing to the carved relief on the far wall. Where the picture of Akhnaten and Nefretiti had been is a deep hole, and below it lies a heap of white dust.

When the altercation has died down a little you ask what has happened. "The ghaffir", says the Inspector, "says this is the work of an enemy who has done it to spite him. It is not the first time," he sighs. "A man is dismissed, a new one is appointed in his place, and the old one damages the tomb in order to get the new man into trouble." Again he turns to the luckless guard and harangues him in loud, angry Arabic. His assistant, trying to be helpful, joins in, and the clamour of their voices fills Mahu's little chamber. Meanwhile you examine the other reliefs which fortunately have escaped damage.

Mahu, the owner of the tomb, was the Chief of Police for Akhetaten, responsible for the protection of the temple and palace and the defences around the city. In one of the reliefs, after being honoured by the King, he is shown kneeling at the gate of the temple while his men raise their arms and shout their praises of 'the Good Ruler'.

The police of Akhetaten sing and shout the refrain, "He promotes, in masses, in masses. He shall live eternally like the Aten."

In another relief the royal family drive out to inspect the defences. This is the relief of which the most important scene has been destroyed. In front of the chariot run Mahu and fifteen policemen, and with them runs the Vizier, and his deputy. The plump Vizier, no longer in his first youth, is having a job to keep up with the younger men. The artist, true to the realistic Amarna tradition, has not spared the great man.

In this scene the ubiquitous Mahu is not only waving good-bye to the royal couple as they leave the palace, but he is the first to greet them on their arrival. He is seen at his best in yet another relief, which shows him performing his official duties.

First he is called out of his house, apparently at night, to hear a report by his officers. They are on the track of certain malefactors. With an armed escort Mahu drives off in his chariot to capture these men. In the last scene he proudly hands them over to high officials, including the Vizier, with the remark, "Examine ye, O Princes, these men whom the foreigners have instigated," which suggests that the captives were spies.

From the relief you turn to the living scene before you; the angry Chief Inspector, a modern Mahu, sitting in judgment at the end of the tomb, while before him stands the trembling ghaffir, trying to answer the volley of questions. Nearby, like a scribe, the Assistant Inspector makes notes. The faces of the three men could be duplicated in the tomb reliefs. The situation is as old as Egypt. Only the dress and the language have changed.

It is now late afternoon and you are tired, but you have still one more tomb to see; that of Ay, chief favourite of Akhnaten, who later succeeded Tutankhamun as king. Originally his tomb was intended to have twenty-four columns supporting its principal hall, but of these only fifteen were cut. The wall reliefs, beside the usual scenes of honouring, take you into the inner chambers of the royal palace to which Ay, as Akhnaten's friend, must have been frequently admitted. You see the harem, divided into many rooms. In one of these chambers a group of women are dancing to the harp and lute. In another a girl is adjusting her friend's hair, while outside in the corridors the bored eunuchs lounge at their posts.

The main scene shows Akhnaten on the balcony of the palace, showering gifts upon the delighted Ay, who stands with his friends in the courtyard below. The Queen is there, of course, caressing her daughter, while from above the arms of the Aten stretch protectingly down to support the King and Queen. Surely no woman, queen or commoner, has ever been offered sweeter homage than that given to Nefretiti in this tomb.

> The heiress, great in favour, lady of grace, sweet of love, Mistress of the South and North, fair of face, gay with the two plumes, beloved of the living Aten, the Chief Wife of the King, whom he loves, lady of the Two Lands, great of love, Nefretiti, living for ever and ever . . .

Outside the courtyard Ay shows his gifts of gold to his rejoicing friends, who dance and leap in amazement. Even one of the bored sentries is moved to inquire:

> "For whom is this rejoicing being made?"

To which his companion replies:

> "The rejoicing is being made for Ay, the father of the God, with Tiyi" (his wife, not the Queen). "They are being made people of gold!"
> "You will see," rejoins the sentry, "these are the beauties of the age."

Ay himself, in the familiar strain of the Egyptian courtier, makes no concealment of his qualities. "I was eminent," he tells us, "possessing character, successful in opportunities, contented of disposition, kindly . . . following his majesty, according as he commanded. The end thereof was an old age in peace . . ."

The long-dead voices whisper to you faintly from the dim walls of the tomb: idealist and schemer, loyalist and traitor, boaster and true man; all now are equally pitiful. Outside the sunset beckons, the sunset which these ghosts loved as much as you do. The ghaffirs grow restless. The Assistant Inspector, a devout Moslem, paces absently around the chamber, murmuring to himself, "Al-lah . . . Al-lah . . ." Soon you will have to go, and leave Ay and his friends to the silence and darkness. The Chief Inspector beckons you to the door, where the setting sun shines gloriously on the sensuous reliefs of Ay and his wife in their clinging white garments and thick curled wigs. On their delicate, decadent faces there is a faint, melancholy smile as they look toward

the doorway through which they prayed to be allowed to
pass each day.

> Let me inhale the North Wind
> Which is fragrant with the incense of my god . . .

The Inspector points to the hieroglyphs beneath the reliefs
of the King and Queen. "That is the Great Hymn," he says.
And quietly, slowly, he translates for you the concluding
lines:

> The world is in thy hand . . .
> When thou risest they live;
> When thou settest they die
> For thou thyself art length of days
> By thee men live . . .
> Thou has raised them up for thy son
> Who came forth from thy limbs,
> The King of Upper and Lower Egypt,
> Nefer-kheperu-Re, Wa-en-Re;
> Son of Re, who lives in Truth,
> Lord of Diadems, Akhnaten, whose life is long;
> And for the great Royal Wife, his beloved,
> The Mistress of the Two Lands,
> Nefer-Neferu-Aten, Nefretiti,
> Living and flourishing for ever and ever! [1]

CHAPTER XV

THE FUTURE OF EGYPTOLOGY

As they begin this last chapter (assuming that they get so
far) we can hear our Egyptologist friends muttering, 'Is that
all? But why no mention of such-and-such a discovery?
What about Mariette and the Serapeum? What about
Legrain's discoveries at Karnak? And to come to modern
times, why no account of Montet's finds at Tanis or Emery's
at Sakkara?'

The answer is that this book does not attempt to cover the

[1] Breasted's original translation.

whole of Egyptian history or to describe every important discovery. To do so would take several books of this size, and we have already reached the limit of space allowed us by our publishers. Perhaps in a subsequent volume we may be able to cover some of the ground which, unfortunately, we have had to by-pass. Our object has been simply to describe some of the great discoveries which have interested us, to explain their significance and encourage readers to explore for themselves this fascinating world which the Egyptologists have opened up. For, make no mistake, without the labour and devotion of these men and women there would be very little to tell. Read the memoirs of the 18th and early 19th century explorers and you will find little but expressions of wonder and long-winded, unscientific speculation. But the past hundred years have seen an amazing advance in our knowledge of Ancient Egypt and in the technique of excavation. So great has the improvement been that the modern excavator shudders when he reads the accounts of some of his predecessors' work and realises how much information was lost through unscientific methods.

The chief aim of modern archaeologists is information and knowledge, not merely the acquisition of valuable objects. How effective their methods have been can be judged by the story we have tried to tell in the past two chapters. The story of the Amarna Age did not come down to us in fully documented form. It was assembled piece by piece from many sources over a long period; one fragment of information came from a philologist in his study, poring over some inscribed scrap of potsherd; another was dug up by the spade of an excavator on the site; yet another came from a newly-discovered inscription, on a site hundreds of miles from Amarna, which gave a third scholar a vital chronological clue. That is how the modern Egyptologist works. The earlier chapters in this book, on the Pyramids, on Karnak and Thebes, described monuments which would be impressive in themselves even if little were known about them. Amarna, which has little to show but crumbling walls and damaged tombs has yielded one of the most significant chapters in Egyptian history.

Yet consider how the discoveries were made. In 1887 an Arab woman was digging at Amarna for *sebakh*, a nitrous earth which is used as a fertiliser. She came upon piles of small baked-clay tablets. They had no artistic value, and in appearance resembled nothing so much as stale dog-biscuits. Still, she thought, they might be worth a few piastres to the Luxor dealers. When they reached Luxor after being carried in sacks, half the tablets had been ground to powder by rough handling. Specimens submitted to a noted French *savant* in Paris were pronounced forgeries. Grébaut, head of the Antiquities Service, ignored them. It was not until only 350 were left that it was realised that the tablets were genuine. The peasant woman had stumbled on the archives of the Egyptian Foreign Office and the letters dated from one of the most momentous epochs of Egyptian history. Among them were those of Ribbadi and the other vassal-princes quoted in the preceding chapters.

This great discovery, far more important historically than the finding of the tomb of Tutankhamun, led a succession of Egyptologists to the site. Petrie was first on the scene and began to dig there in 1891, uncovering among other things a magnificent painted fresco, part of which is now in the Ashmolean Museum at Oxford. Then from 1907 to 1914 a German expedition continued the work. It was the Germans who discovered the wonderful painted limestone head of Nefretiti which has become world-famous, with those of Akhnaten and other members of the Royal Family. Besides the limestone head of the Queen there is one in brown sandstone which, in the writer's opinion, is even more lovely. After the First World War the Egypt Exploration Society, which has done so much for Egyptology, sent an expedition under Professors Peet and Woolley and later Professors Griffith, Newton, Whiltemore and Frankfort followed. In more recent years the late J. D. S. Pendlebury took over where his predecessors had left off.

The tomb reliefs, previously drawn by Wilkinson and Lepsius, were subjected to the most minute scrutiny by Norman de Garis Davies; thanks to him and other workers the valuable inscriptions and sculptured scenes are no longer entirely at the mercy of vandals and robbers.

Even if they perish, like the chariot-scene from the tomb of Mahu, their reproductions will always be available for study in Davies' volumes.

If Signor Belzoni had dug at Amarna in 1817 he would have found little worth his trouble, except perhaps a few 'heads' to be sold as curiosities to collectors. Yet Petrie and his successors dug from a rubbish heap materials for one of the most vital and exciting chapters in the history of civilisation; a chapter which is still incomplete. Even they were building on foundations laid by their predecessors; Champollion and Young, who discovered the key to the hieroglyphs, Grotefend and his followers, who deciphered the cuneiform script, and other pioneers whose names survive in dusty tomes on library shelves.

Among these pioneers is a succession of British names, for in this truly international science Britain has contributed an impressive quota of brilliant scholars and excavators. Yet when we look around for their successors of to-day— the men who might become the Petries, Carters and Carnarvons of tomorrow—we find the ranks are very thin. There is a crisis in Egyptology as in practically everything else.

The days when rich patrons like Davies and Carnarvon could finance excavation are over, perhaps for ever. There are private societies, such as the Egypt Exploration Society, supported by voluntary contributions both of private individuals and museums. But their funds are depleted and the cost of excavation is much higher than before the war. It seems certain that any future large-scale excavation in the Nile Valley, undertaken by British archaeologists, will have to be financed in part by Government grants; and with so many other urgent demands it will not be easy to convince the Treasury of the importance of such work.

Although the French Government are still subsidising the work of their scholars in Egypt, excavation by Englishmen has virtually stopped, apart from the recent 'dig' at Amarah West in the Sudan, financed by the Egypt Exploration Society with the aid of a Government grant. This means that if and when funds permit digging to be resumed in Egypt, there will be no trained English excavators, nor skilled native workers, and in the meantime few of the young men now being trained in our universities can hope to find permanent employment in Egyptological research. Only those with private means could afford to devote their lives to such work and how many have private means to-day?

It might be argued that the Egyptian Government has its own Antiquities Department with a staff of trained Egyptologists. While recognising the valuable work which Egyptian scholars and excavators are doing, it must be recognised that the foundation of Egyptological study was Occidental and that the great body of knowledge of Ancient Egypt has been contributed by Europeans and Americans. It is only in comparatively recent years that Egyptians have been trained in archaeology. Egyptology is an international science, and if the seeds of research sown by previous generations of scholars are allowed to germinate they will bring forth a rich harvest of knowledge. But the gathering of such a harvest calls for the combined archaeological brains of Egypt, Europe and America.

Part of the present difficulty is due to the nationalism and xenophobia which afflict Egyptian politics.

There is a tendency, common among nations which have newly won their freedom, to extol everything Egyptian and to denigrate everything foreign, even to the extent of resenting the presence of foreign scholars on Egyptian soil. This attitude is rare among Egyptian archaeologists, most of whom received their training from Europeans, but it is common among politicians. Nor are the Europeans without blame. The history of the last 150 years in Egypt is not only a record of scholarship and research but of plunder. It is not surprising, in view of the thousands of treasures which have been shipped to Europe and America in the past century, that the Egyptians should be determined to keep such objects as remain within their own borders. This prohibition has, however, made things more difficult for some of the archaeological societies which are partly supported by museums. Naturally they expect a proportion of any objects found in a 'dig' to go to them. That is why the most recent 'dig' sponsored by the Egypt Exploration Society was carried out in the Sudan and not in Egypt.

Somehow these difficulties must and will be overcome, but there must be a measure of goodwill and forbearance on both sides. In the meantime, what can be done now? H. W. Fairman, one of the younger British Egyptologists and Professor of Egyptology at the University of Liverpool, has put forward the following suggestions in a letter to the author.

On the wider aspects of the present crisis [he writes] I consider there must be international and co-ordinated action, hence the need for support for the new International Association of Egyptologists. I think we need also to work out a list of priorities and concentrate on essentials. I am opposed to the stopping of all excavation but I think that for the next ten years or so emphasis should be laid on the copying and recording of the standing monuments and that excavations should be made only at sites that are in immediate danger, *i.e.* the Delta *must* be dug, particularly all the sites immediately threatened by a rise in the water level, and *every excavation made must be published in full*.

This question of the excavation of Delta sites is a sore point with some European and American archaeologists. Although much excavation has been carried out in Middle and Upper Egypt during the past century, comparatively little has been done in the Nile Delta, where, according to one group of scholars, Egyptian civilisation may have begun.

"In 1945," Fairman told me, "I spent some time touring the eastern Delta. I visited eleven sites and only one of them was adequately guarded and safe. Most Delta sites that I have seen can still be excavated, though much is now hopeless owing to the rise in the water level. But I think that in about ten years the continuous rise of the water and the unchecked activities of robbers will mean the almost total loss of practically every Delta site."

Of these sites the only one which is reasonably safe at present is Tanis, the 'Zoan' of the Old Testament and possible residence of Joseph. Here, in 1940, Professor Montet of Strasbourg University excavated the splendid tomb of the Twenty-first Dynasty King Psusennes, in which the body was enclosed within a sarcophagus of solid silver, richly engraved, the most beautiful object discovered in Egypt since the tomb of Tutankhamun. The 'Tanite' kings of the Twenty-first and Twenty-second Dynasties (1090–745 BC) were buried in stone-built tombs under the temple enclosure.

Besides Psusennes, Montet discovered Amenemopet and a 'new' king, Shoshenk-Hekakheperre of the Twenty-second Dynasty, also in a solid silver sarcophagus. The entry of Italy into the war interrupted the excavations, but they have since been resumed.

Of Sais, another Delta town, we have it on the authority of Herodotus that "the Saites buried all the kings who belonged to their canton inside this temple [*i.e.* that of Sais]: and thus it even contains the tomb of Amasis as well as that of Apries and of his family . . ." Yet the temple of Sais has not yet been excavated.

Fairman goes on:

Among the sites I have seen are Bubastis; worked by Naville, but only scratched; it is intensely important, an enormous site, large parts are being swept away and it is full of antiquities. Then there is Horbeit. Most of the ancient town has been swept away in recent times but the temple appears to be intact and its roofing blocks are the floors or just under the floors of the modern village. I've trodden it all. Mendes I think is pretty well lost for good. But Tell-el-Birkeh and a large district for a mile or more around is untouched and potentially profitable. Qantir is almost lost, but work under the fields would still yield results. Baqlia, the ancient Hermopolis Parva, centre of Thoth worship in the Delta, has never been worked, was badly robbed but the mount is still several feet high, Tell-el-Balamoun has never been excavated . . . then there are such places as Xois, Athribis, Pithom, Tell-el-Bahudieh, Nebesheh and others dug by Naville and Petrie which are all worth re-digging; and most of these are in the Suez Canal area.

We have quoted Fairman's letter at some length not only to show what needs to be done urgently in Egypt, but because it reveals both the enthusiasm and the frustration of young British and European Egyptologists, just itching to get their hands on these important sites and to extract all the information they can yield, before Nature and native pillagers destroy them for ever. "Even ancient Heliopolis itself has never been excavated properly," Fairman continues, "Memphis has only been scratched, and so one could go on and on . . ."

Why are these sites neglected? This is not an easy question to answer, but we will attempt to give one, believing that this may be a case where the amateur can rush in where the archaeological angels fear to tread.

The Egyptian Government's Antiquities Service and its Egyptian staff are now responsible for most present-day excavation in Egypt. They are doing some excellent work, and during our last visit, when we enjoyed the hospitality of the Department, we were shown some of the results of their activities in the pyramid-fields at Dashur and Sakkara, at Karnak, and in the Theban Necropolis. They have also carried out some excavations in the Delta, notably at Bubastis and Elephantine, under the direction of Labib Habashi Effendi, Chief Inspector of Antiquities, and an enthusiast for the Delta. In the main, however, their energies have been concentrated on the pyramids and on sites in Middle and Upper Egypt. For instance their Department of Pyramid Studies has embarked on the monumental task of surveying, measuring and if possible identifying the builder of every pyramid surviving in Egypt. All this is work which will eventually have to be done but which could safely be delayed. No harm will come to the pyramids in the next twenty years or more, whereas the Delta sites, if not tackled soon, will be lost for ever, with all the information they could provide.

Could it be that this interest in the pyramids is due to their comparative proximity to Cairo and its amenities, whereas young scholars working on remote Delta sites would be in danger of being overlooked by the university and museum authorities to whom they must look for advancement? The Department's rest-house at Sakkara is delightfully situated on the pyramid plain, and it is pleasant to sit on the roof in the cool evening, with the great Causeway of Unas at one's back, and the green Valley of the Nile stretched at one's feet. This is Egyptology *de luxe*, whereas Egyptology in the Delta could be tough, uncomfortable, but archaeologically rewarding.

It all depends on one's point of view. Is Egyptian archaeology a pleasant sideline, to be followed in comfort and at leisure? Or is it a serious study, a hard, unremitting pursuit of knowledge? Those who take the latter view suggest that the Service des Antiquités might devote more attention to the fast-vanishing records in the Delta, and, wherever possible, grant concessions to any competent European or American archaeologists able and willing to excavate there.

That, at any rate, is how it appears to a layman.

Summing up, an archaeologist friend suggests "at the present time, when financial stringency here and in Egypt limits expensive excavation, I think the main attention at present should be directed to the rescue and recording of the standing monuments of Egypt; which would mean a combined archaeological and epigraphic survey. There are hundreds of rock inscriptions, several complete temples, tens upon tens, if not hundreds of towns, open and exposed, practically all deteriorating and suffering, and all these should be surveyed, copied and published in accurate, convenient and not too expensive form. What is the use of excavating half a dozen solid pyramids, when the Temple of Philae is under water, falling to pieces and not properly published? Or when Esna is being attacked by salt, hornets, and water, with hardly one of its inscriptions published? And when one thinks of what is happening to the tombs . . ."

That is a matter that must be settled between the Egyptological world and the Government of Egypt. The layman can do little to assist except in so far as an informed public opinion can help individuals fighting the battle against inertia, prejudice and ignorance. But there is a way in which Egyptologists could do much to help their own cause, and that is by emerging from their studies now and then, and talking to or writing for the general public in a language which it can understand. There is (and some scholars can confirm this) a considerable and growing interest in Ancient Egypt among the lay public, but Egyptology and support for Egyptology mean little to laymen, for the simple reason that most scholars do not write for them but only for their fellow-specialists. This is not true of certain branches of science, which have had such able publicists as Sir James Jeans, Sir Oliver Lodge, and others. It is not even true of our older generation of Egyptologists, when one considers all that Petrie did to popularise the subject without vulgarising it. Surely the writing of an accurate and readable book on a highly-specialised subject can be as difficult (and therefore as worth-while) as the writing of a technical work?

Of course, the present crisis in Egyptology is only a minor facet of the general crisis facing mankind. Unless stable conditions return to the world the study of Ancient Egypt, like other branches of learning, must inevitably suffer. It is pathetic to watch the perplexity of some of the older scholars, brought up in a more liberal world, whose work is hindered by a tangle of international regulations. After the war, one distinguished Egyptologist whose works are in every great library in the world, had to make a special journey to Brussels to copy extracts from a book published in Egypt during the war, but which he could not buy direct from Egypt because, at that time, he was not permitted to send even a small sum of money out of the country. Travel being so much more expensive, they can no longer meet and consult with each other as often as before the war. Few have private means, and University grants do not go as far as they did. Again, the publication of learned works is hindered by increased costs. Yet gradually the international web of learning, broken by the war, has been woven again, and erudite ladies and gentlemen in Oxford, Paris, Leipzig and Chicago publish their findings, advance their theories or fire learned broadsides into those of their opponents.

At the other end of the scale boys in their early teens are borrowing Petrie and Breasted from the libraries and writing long earnest letters to distinguished scholars asking, please can they become Egyptologists? The lure of Ancient Egypt is perennial, and those who succumb to it usually do so early in life; Petrie himself began to study it when he was thirteen. Sir Alan Gardiner contracted the malady at the age of eleven, as did Howard Carter. We can only hope that there will be opportunities for the Petries, Newberrys and Carters of the future to develop their talents in a world in which Egyptology is no longer the private pursuit of the wealthy but part of the cultural heritage of all.

In the future, only Governments, supported by their peoples, can provide the means through which Egyptological research can be carried on, and it will not be easy in this increasingly utilitarian age to persuade them of its importance.

For the study of Ancient Egypt has no practical value. It will not earn foreign currency or make us stronger or wealthier. But it can give us profound aesthetic pleasure. It can feed our precious sense of wonder. Above all it can help us to understand ourselves, by lighting up the ancient civilisation of the Nile Valley from which so much of our western culture is derived. Perhaps, by showing us the long road along which we have travelled, it may even help us to find our way into the future.

THE REIGN OF AKHNATEN

READERS who have already learned something of Akhnaten and the Amarna Period, particularly if they have read only the older works on the subject, may be puzzled by some of the facts given in Chapters XIII and XIV. This Appendix is intended for those who are particularly interested in this period and who would like to examine the archaeological evidence on which my story is based.

So great was the interest in Akhnaten when Petrie's excavations brought his name into prominence, that this king has been more exhaustively 'written-up' than any other Pharaoh. Unfortunately for the earlier writers, who based their works on the facts available to them at the time, so much has been discovered about the Heresy Period during the past twenty years that much of the earliest published material on Akhnaten is now quite out of date. The most accurate accounts published within comparatively recent times and available to the general public are Pendlebury's book on *Tell El Amarna* (published by Lovat Dickson in the 'Great Cities' series), an article by Professor Peet in Mrs. Winifred Brunton's *Kings and Queens of Ancient Egypt*, and an article by Professor Glanville in the same author's *Great Ones of Ancient Egypt*. Even these, however, are partly out of date now, and I am again indebted to Professor Fairman, who has carried out the most recent researches into this period, for supplementary information.

Here then are the chief points which may have aroused comment.

(1) *Age of the King*. The earlier books on Akhnaten such as those of Arthur Weigall and James Baikie assume that Akhnaten came to the throne in his early teens, carried through a religious revolution before

he was twenty, and died about the age of thirty. Weigall, for example, states that Akhnaten was only twelve or thirteen years old on the death of his father, Amenophis III. It is now known that Akhnaten was twenty-five or twenty-six on his accession, and that he became co-regent on the thirtieth anniversary of the accession of his father who died about the ninth year of the co-regency.

(2) *Akhnaten's body*. There is no foundation for the belief expressed in early works on Akhnaten, that the body found in the so-called Tomb of Queen Tiyi in the Royal Valley at Thebes was that of Akhnaten. This was questioned as far back as the 'twenties by Professor Sethe, and from both inscriptional evidence (Daressy and Engelbach) and physiological evidence (Dr. Derry) it has been established that this body, which is that of a man of not more than thirty, *cannot* be that of Akhnaten. From certain facial similarities to Tutankhamun it seems likely that it is the body of Smenkhkare.

(3) *Possible political origin of Atenism*. Although, personally, I am reluctant to ascribe a purely political origin to the Aten-faith, it must be admitted that the 'political' school have a strong case. For example, under Amenophis III, Akhnaten's father, the King had temples erected to himself. Never before in the history of Egypt was a temple erected for the worship of a king *in his own lifetime*. Yet there are two places in Egypt where one may see Amenophis III represented as a god, with his son Akhnaten offering to him. As it would have been impolitic to introduce this cult immediately in the capital, it was first tried out at Soleb, in the remote Sudan, and at Sedeinga. When he realised that Amun was too well entrenched in Thebes, Akhnaten decided to move to Amarna.

(4) *Nefretiti's disgrace*. Excavations have shown that after Year Fourteen of Akhnaten's reign, the King lived in one part of the town with Smenkhkare and Meritaten, eldest daughter of Akhnaten, while, on a series of monuments, Nefretiti's name has been erased and replaced by that of Meritaten. As it is known that Nefretiti was still alive after the death of Akhnaten, disgrace is the most likely explanation. Objects bearing her name and that of Tutankhamun, dated *after* Year Fourteen, have been found in a building north of the Northern Palace.

(5) *The King's marriage to his daughter*. Our knowledge of this comes from an inscription discovered at Hermopolis in 1938. It states: "The King's daughter, whom he loves, Ankhsenpaaton the younger, born of the King's daughter Ankhsenpaaton." Amenophis III also married his daughter Sit-Amun before Akhnaten moved to Amarna. It is possible, though unproven, that Smenkhkare and Tutankhaten were the sons of Amenophis by this wife.

(6) *Death of Akhnaten and the aftermath*. Evidence for the belief that Akhnaten may have agreed to an attempt to compromise with Amunism is that:

(a) After marrying Akhnaten's eldest daughter Meritaten, Smenkh-kare went as ruler to Thebes and reigned as co-regent.

(b) In the third year of his reign Smenkhkare was restoring some form of Amun-worship at Thebes (proved by hieratic *graffito* in the tomb of Per-e at Thebes).

Yet at this same time Tutankhaten must have been an Atenist, since he was an Atenist at his succession. Even at his death, after he had changed his name to Tutankhamun, objects found in his tomb reveal his interest in the Aten religion. As he was still a child at Amarna and living under Nefretiti's protection the most reasonable conclusion is that she was also an Atenist, and that this was the cause of her breach with the King. It must have been a fundamental issue to have parted two people whose affection for each other was so frequently emphasised in the earlier tomb reliefs.

Fairman sees the end of the Eighteenth Dynasty as an ugly struggle between powerful courtiers who used the royal children as pawns in their game of power. When Tutankhamun died in the ninth year of his reign, Ay, who had been Akhnaten's principal minister and friend, married the heiress Ankhsenpaaton, already twice widowed, and so succeeded to the throne at the age of sixty. Tutankhamun was little more than a boy. In his tomb was found a box with a sling, some pebbles and one or two simple mechanical toys. Neither he nor Ankhes-namun (whose last desperate gamble was described in Chapter XIV) could have been allowed to live normal lives. Ay and Horemhab (another of Akhnaten's erstwhile followers) were fighting for power.

I have given these facts so that readers may judge for themselves the validity of the latest theories put forward in connection with the Heresy Period. I think they are a useful corrective to the grossly sentimental viewpoint of some early writers on Akhnaten, but I would hesitate to accept them as final and definite. Human motives are usually mixed, and even if Akhnaten's revolution did have a political origin, and in the end went down in a welter of sordid intrigue, it *may* have had its moments of spiritual greatness. Personally I believe it did. Whatever weaknesses Akhnaten possessed, one glance at his features reveals that he was no ordinary man; and he looks far more like a poet than a politician.

Finally, as a dreadful warning to any other amateur Egyptologist who is tempted to sail these perilous seas, here are some of the scholastic cross-currents he will have to encounter.

Of Queen Tiyi :

"Tiyi was an able woman. Kings wrote to her on important matters. She knew well what was happening in the Empire."—*Pendlebury.*

"Ty is one of those characters to whom history had probably done more than justice. For the 'powerful influence' she is said to have exerted over her husband there is no evidence . . . save the fact that she inserted her name after his on royal instructions."—*Peet.*

Of Akhnaten:

"Akhnaten . . . was the first individual in history."—*Breasted.*

"He is not, as has been claimed, the first individual in history."—*Pendlebury.*

Of the 'Amarna Period':

"Akhnaten gave to Egypt the most interesting period of her long history—almost the one period of it in which one can feel the throbbing of real life, and he gave to her in himself one of the most remarkable figures of that or any other time—the king who made his faith the centre of his life."—*Baikie.*

"To-day the impression that the art and civilisation of Amarna gives us is that of an ephemeral butterfly age with that total lack of moral standards usually associated with happy morons."—*Pendlebury.*

Of the Aten :

". . . Here is no subtle or complicated theology but simply an adoration of the physical sun. There is not a word of a power in or behind the sun."—*Peet.*

". . . it was not the actual planet which was being worshipped, but the being who manifests himself therein."—*Erman.*

Of Akhnaten as a moralist :

"In an age of superstition and in a land where the grossest polytheism reigned absolutely supreme, Akhnaten evolved a monotheistic religion second only to Christianity."—*Weigall.*

". . . . So much has been written about Akhnaten in the character of Christ before his time that it must be pointed out that Atenism was in no sense a way of life but merely an exercise in theology."—*Pendlebury.*

BOOKS CONSULTED

Amelineau, E.: *Nouveaux Fouilles d'Abydos* (1899–1904).

Baikie, James: *Egyptian Antiquities in the Nile Valley* (Methuen, 1932).

Baikie, James: *The Amarna Age* (A. & C. Black).

Belzoni, G.: *Narrative of the Operations, etc.* (1821).

Bevan, Edwyn: *The Land of the Two Rivers* (Edward Arnold, 1917).

Breasted, Charles: *Pioneer to the Past.*

Breasted, J. H.: *History of Egypt*, 1946 edn. (Hodder & Stoughton).

Breasted, J. H.: *Ancient Records* (University of Chicago Press).

Budge, Sir Wallis: *The Nile* (Thomas Cook & Sons).

Budge, Sir Wallis: *The Literature of the Ancient Egyptians* (Methuen).

Budge, Sir Wallis: *The Gods of the Egyptians* (Methuen).

Budge, Sir Wallis: *The Rosetta Stone* (British Museum).

Capart and Werbrouch: *Thebes* (Allen & Unwin).

Carter, Howard: *The Tomb of Tutankhamun* (Cassell).

de Garis Davies, N.: *The Rock Tombs of El Amarna* (O.U.P.).

de Morgan, J.: *Recherches sur les Origines de l'Egypte* (1896).

Drioton, Etienne and Lauer, J. P.: *Sakkarah: the Monuments of Zoser* (Institut Français de l'Archéologie Orientale, 1939).

Edel, E.: Neue Keilschriftliche Umschreibungen Aegyptischer Namen aus den Bogazkoytexten (*Journal of Near Eastern Studies*, Vol. VII).

Edwards, I. E. S.: *The Pyramids of Egypt* (Penguin, 1947).

Evans, Sir Arthur: *The Palace of Minos*, Vols. I–IV (Macmillan).

Frankfort, H.: *City of Akhnaten* (O.U.P.).

Gardiner, Sir Alan: *Treaty of Alliance between Hathusil and Ramesses II* (1920).

Gardiner, Sir Alan: *Topographical Catalogue of the Private Tombs of Thebes* (Quaritch).

Glanville, S. R. K.: *Introduction to Egypt* (B.O.A.C., 1945).

Glanville, S. R. K.: article in *Great Ones of Ancient Egypt*, ed. Winifred Brunton (Hodder & Stoughton).

Maspero, Sir Gaston: *The Dawn of Civilisation* (S.P.C.K.).

Maspero, Sir Gaston: *Les Momies Royales de Deir-el-Bahari* (1889).

Newberry, P. E.: Presidential Address to the British Association (Anthropological Section), "Egypt as a Field for Anthropological Research." (*Annual Report*, 1923.) (Anthropological Section.)

Peet, T. Eric: *The Great Tomb-robberies of the Twentieth Egyptian Dynasty* (Clarendon Press, 1943).

Peet, T. Eric: essay on Akhnaten in *Kings and Queens of Ancient Egypt*, ed. Winifred Brunton (Hodder & Stoughton).

Pendlebury, J. D. S.: *Tell el Amarna* (Lovat Dickson, 1935).

Petrie, Sir Flinders: *A History of Egypt* (Methuen, 1924).

Petrie, Sir Flinders: *Naquada and Ballas* (Brit. School of Archaeology, 1896).

Petrie, Sir Flinders: *Royal Tombs of the First and Second Dynasties* (Egypt Exploration Fund, 1901–2).

Petrie, Sir Flinders: *Pyramids and Temples of Gizeh* (1883).

Petrie, Sir Flinders: *Discobolus Parva* (Egypt Exploration Fund).

Reade, Winwood: *The Martyrdom of Man* (1872).

Reisner, Dr.: "The Tomb of Hetepheres," articles in *Museum of Fine Arts Bulletin*, 1925–28.

Shorter, Alan W.: *Everyday Life in Ancient Egypt* (Sampson Low, 1932).

Woolley, Sir Leonard: *Digging up the Past* (Penguin, 1940).

Leonard Cottrell
The Bull of Minos 65p

The thrilling story of the great archaeological discoveries in Crete and Greece made by Heinrich Schliemann and Sir Arthur Evans.

The Enemy of Rome 65p

In May 218 BC Hannibal of Carthage set out from Spain with over 100,000 troops – his aim, the destruction of the great Roman Empire. His immortal campaign, through France, Italy and Africa, lasted sixteen fierce and bloody years and revealed Hannibal as an inspired military genius.

The Great Invasion 65p

This evocative reconstruction of the Roman invasion of Britain brings vividly to life the armies and their bitter forty-year campaign. The soldiers, the battles fought and won – all provide fascinating parallels with modern methods of warfare.

Lost Cities 70p

'Accurate . . . entertaining. Cottrell communicates his own enthusiasm.' TIME AND TIDE

J. H. B. Peel
Along the Roman Roads of Britain 95p

'Watling Street takes him from Dover to Wroxeter; Sarn Helen East conducts him into Welsh mountains; Dere Street from York to the Wall and over the Border; Peddars Way into East Anglia; and a final journey along the Foss Way into the West Country. With his strong sense of history, easy flow of narrative, and wide knowledge of what will repay a digression en route, he is a rewarding companion on each of these excursions' TIMES LITERARY SUPPLEMENT

Eric Newby
A Short Walk in the Hindu Kush 60p

A truly diverting and wonderfully evocative account of a journey from Mayfair to the wilds of Nuristan.

'Eric Newby's depiction of their travels and travails is a total success' NEW YORKER

'A notable addition to the literature of unorthodox travel . . . tough, extrovert, humorous and immensely literate'
TIMES LITERARY SUPPLEMENT

'A pleasurable story of exotic and eccentric adventure.'
NEW YORK TIMES

C. R. Crosher
Along the Cotswold Ways £1.25

Takes the modern traveller in the footsteps of the Iron Age, Roman and Saxon settlers, the medieval monks and traders, salt-carriers, wool merchants and Welsh drovers – who travelled the ancient Ways for more than fifty centuries. 'From Chipping Campden to Dryham, from Burford to Cheltenham, scarcely a village is missed . . . soundly informative about history, landscape and architecture . . .

Richard Gillard
Pepys £1.50

From the Civil War to the Glorious Revolution – The Fire of
London to the Black Death, Pepys lived through the most eventful
five decades of English history and recorded them in the most
famous diary ever written.

The complete man of his time, friend of Newton, Dryden and Wren,
Pepys loved books and music, wenches and wine . . .

'Magnificent . . . a joy to read' THE YORKSHIRE POST

Robert K. Massie
Nicholas and Alexandra £1.25

'Robert Massie makes the whole world-shaking drama all too
humanly understandable – the long wait for an heir to the throne;
the discovery of his haemophilia; the dreadful suffering the parents
had to watch in their child; the ensuing royal dependence on the
miracle-working, sex-ridden Rasputin . . .' HARPER'S

'Contains every imaginable ingredient for a runaway literary
success . . . grandeur and misery; romantic love; a glittering court;
absolute power over one hundred and thirty million people;
Byzantine intrigues; mysterious illnesses and evil influences; an
intimate view of great power politics; war and revolution; the
violent and horrib e death of almost everyone concerned.'
SPECTATOR

Henri and Barbara Van der Zee
William and Mary £1.95

Charles II gave his blessing to the union of the soldier-prince
William of Orange and the sensitive, romantic Princess Mary Stuart,
daughter of James II. A political expedient became a dynastic
marriage of rare significance when William and Mary succeeded to
the throne of England.

'The consequences in the long term were incalculable: an irrever-
sible revolution in England's relation with Europe' THE TIMES

Selected bestsellers

- [ ] **The Eagle Has Landed** Jack Higgins 80p
- [ ] **The Moneychangers** Arthur Hailey 95p
- [ ] **Marathon Man** William Goldman 70p
- [ ] **Nightwork** Irwin Shaw 75p
- [ ] **Tropic of Ruislip** Leslie Thomas 75p
- [ ] **One Flew Over The Cuckoo's Nest** Ken Kesey 75p
- [ ] **Collision** Spencer Dunmore 70p
- [ ] **Perdita's Prince** Jean Plaidy 70p
- [ ] **The Eye of the Tiger** Wilbur Smith 80p
- [ ] **The Shootist** Glendon Swarthout 60p
- [ ] **Of Human Bondage** Somerset Maugham 95p
- [ ] **Rebecca** Daphne du Maurier 80p
- [ ] **Slay Ride** Dick Francis 60p
- [ ] **Jaws** Peter Benchley 70p
- [ ] **Let Sleeping Vets Lie** James Herriot 60p
- [ ] **If Only They Could Talk** James Herriot 60p
- [ ] **It Shouldn't Happen to a Vet** James Herriot 60p
- [ ] **Vet In Harness** James Herriot 60p
- [ ] **Tinker Tailor Soldier Spy** John le Carré 75p
- [ ] **Gone with the Wind** Margaret Mitchell £1.75
- [ ] **Cashelmara** Susan Howatch £1.25
- [ ] **The Nonesuch** Georgette Heyer 60p
- [ ] **The Grapes of Wrath** John Steinbeck 95p
- [ ] **Drum** Kyle Onstott 60p

All these books are available at your bookshop or newsagent
or can be obtained direct from the publisher

Pan Books, Sales Office, Cavaye Place, London SW10 9PG

Just tick the titles you want and fill in the form below

Prices quoted are applicable in UK

Send purchase price plus 20p for the first book and 10p for each
additional book, to allow for postage and packing

Name _____
(block letters please)

Address _____

_____

While every effort is made to keep prices low, it is sometimes
necessary to increase prices at short notice. Pan Books reserve the
right to show on covers new retail prices which may differ from
those advertised in the text or elsewhere